BOETHIUS

GREAT MEDIEVAL THINKERS

Series Editor
Brian Davies
Blackfriars College, University of Oxford,
and Fordham University

DUNS SCOTUS
Richard Cross

BERNARD OF CLAIRVAUX
Gillian R. Evans

JOHN SCOTUS ERIUGENA
Deirdre Carabine

ROBERT GROSSETESTE
James McEvoy

BOETHIUS
John Marenbon

BOETHIUS

John Marenbon

OXFORD
UNIVERSITY PRESS

2003

OXFORD
UNIVERSITY PRESS

Oxford New York
Auckland Bangkok Buenos Aires Cape Town Chennai
Dar es Salaam Delhi Hong Kong Istanbul Karachi Kolkata
Kuala Lumpur Madrid Melbourne Mexico City Mumbai Nairobi
São Paulo Shanghai Taipei Tokyo Toronto

Published by Oxford University Press, Inc.
198 Madison Avenue, New York, New York, 10016

www.oup.com

Library of Congress Cataloging-in-Publication Data
Marenbon, John.
Boethius / John Marenbon.
p. cm.—(Great medieval thinkers)
Includes bibliographical references and index.
ISBN 0-19-513406-0; 0-19-513407-9 (pbk.)
1. Boethius, d. 524. I. Title. II. Series.
B659 .Z7 M346 2002
189—dc21 2002074896

1 3 5 7 9 8 6 4 2

Printed in the United States of America
on acid-free paper

TO SHEILA AND MAXIMUS

ACKNOWLEDGMENTS

I have had the chance to read papers on Boethius to a Boethius conference in Paris, organized by Alain Galonnier; at the Pontifical Institute of Mediaeval Studies, Toronto, at the invitation of John Magee; and at a conference on happiness and rationality in ancient and early medieval philosophy at Buffalo, organized by Jorge Gracia; as well as in Cambridge, at the Philosophy of Religion, and History of Philosophy seminars. I am grateful both for these invitations and for the valuable and stimulating discussion I had from those who attended. More recently, I have received useful criticism in response to papers based on drafts of this book given to the Oxford University Medieval Society and at King's College, London. I am particularly grateful for the comments, on these occasions or at other times, I have received from Brad Inwood, Scott MacDonald, Chris Martin, Thomas Pink, Peter Sarris, and Martin Stone. Anthony Speca kindly sent me, and allowed me to use, a copy of his important book on Boethius and hypothetical syllogisms while it was still in press. Jonathan Evans read my chapter on the problem of prescience with enormous care and perspicacity and sent me a list of criticisms that led me to change my analysis. Peter Dronke read through the whole manuscript and gave me valuable criticisms and suggestions. I have a very special debt indeed to John Magee, who read through each chapter as I wrote it and gave me advice, corrections, and (not least) encouragement. Finally, I would thank Brian Davies, the editor of the series, for asking me to write on Boethius for his series and thus setting me to a task that has proved far more difficult—and far, far more interesting—than I had anticipated.

SERIES FOREWORD

Many people would be surprised to be told that there *were* any great medieval thinkers. If a *great* thinker is one from whom we can learn today, and if 'medieval' serves as an adjective for describing anything that existed from (roughly) the years 600 to 1500 AD, then, so it is often supposed, medieval thinkers cannot be called 'great'.

Why not? One answer often given appeals to ways in which medieval authors with a taste for argument and speculation tend to invoke 'authorities', especially religious ones. Such invocation of authority is not the stuff of which great thought is made—so it is often said today. It is also frequently said that greatness is not to be found in the thinking of those who lived before the rise of modern science, not to mention that of modern philosophy and theology. Students of science are nowadays hardly ever referred to literature earlier than the seventeenth century. Students of philosophy in the twentieth century have often been taught nothing about the history of ideas between Aristotle (384–322 BC) and Descartes (1596–1650). Modern students of theology have often been frequently encouraged to believe that significant theological thinking is a product of the nineteenth century.

Yet the origins of modern science lie in the conviction that the world is open to rational investigation and is orderly rather than chaotic—a conviction that came fully to birth, and was systematically explored and developed, during the middle ages. And it is in medieval thinking that we find some of the most sophisticated and rigorous discussions in the areas of philosophy and theology ever offered for human consumption—not surprisingly, perhaps, if we note that medieval philosophers and theologians, like their contemporary counterparts, were mostly university teachers who participated in an ongoing worldwide debate and were not (like many seventeenth-, eighteenth-, and even nineteenth-century philosophers and theologians) people working in relative isolation from a large community of teachers and students with whom they were regularly involved. As for the question of appeal to authority: it is certainly true that many medieval thinkers believed in authority (especially religious authority) as a serious court of appeal; and it is true that most people today would say that they cannot do this. But as many contemporary philosophers are increasingly reminding us, authority is as much an ingredient in our thinking as it was for medieval thinkers (albeit that, because of differences between thinkers, one might reasonably say that there is no such thing as 'medieval thought'). For most of what we take ourselves to know derives from the trust we have reposed in our various teachers, colleagues, friends, and general contacts. When it comes to reliance on authority, the main difference between us and medieval thinkers lies in the fact that their reliance on authority (insofar as they had it) was often more focused and explicitly acknowledged than it is for us. It does not lie in the fact that it was uncritical and naive in a way that our reliance on authority is not.

In recent years, such truths have come to be increasingly recognized at what we might call the 'academic' level. No longer disposed to think of the middle ages as 'dark' (meaning "lacking in intellectual richness"), many university departments (and many publishers of books and journals) now devote a lot of their energy to the study of medieval thinking. And they do so not simply on the assumption that it is historically significant but also in the light of the increasingly developing insight that it is full of things with which to dialogue and from which to learn. Following a long period in which medieval thinking was thought to be of only antiquarian interest, we are now witnessing its revival as a contemporary voice—one to converse with, one from which we might learn.

The *Great Medieval Thinkers* series reflects and is part of this exciting revival. Written by a distinguished team of experts, it aims to provide substantial introductions to a range of medieval authors. And it does so on the assumption that they are as worth reading today as they were when they wrote. Students of medieval 'literature' (e.g., the writings of Chaucer) are currently well supplied (if not oversupplied) with secondary works to aid them when reading the objects of their concern. But those with an interest in medieval philosophy and theology are by no means so fortunate when it comes to reliable and accessible volumes to help them. The *Great Medieval Thinkers* series therefore aspires to remedy that deficiency by concentrating on medieval philosophers and theologians, and by offering solid overviews of their lives and thought coupled with contemporary reflection on what they had to say. Taken individually, volumes in the series will provide valuable treatments of single thinkers many of whom are not currently covered by any comparable volumes. Taken together, they will constitute a rich and distinguished history and discussion of medieval philosophy and theology considered as a whole. With an eye on college and university students, and with an eye on the general reader, authors of volumes in the series strive to write in a clear and accessible manner so that each of the thinkers they write on can be learned about by those who have no previous knowledge about them. But each contributor to the series also intends to inform, engage, and generally entertain, even those with specialist knowledge in the area of medieval thinking. So, as well as surveying and introducing, volumes in the series seek to advance the state of medieval studies both at the historical and the speculative level.

Anicius Manlius Severinus Boethius (commonly known simply as Boethius) is not really a medieval thinker if we go strictly by his dates and if we understand the word 'medieval' in a somewhat limiting way. He was born ca. 475–477. He died by execution ca. 524–526. So he could be said to belong to the world of late antiquity rather than to that of authors such as Anselm, Aquinas, Scotus, or Ockham. But, like that of St. Augustine of Hippo (354–430), his impact on medieval thinking was profound. And, though some have viewed Boethius as a mere conduit through which ideas of those who preceded him came to medieval writers, he was an original thinker in his own right. Nobody seriously concerned with medieval philosophy and theology, whether from the historical or evaluative perspective, can afford to ignore him. If you lack an understanding of Boethius, you will not appreciate what many medieval writers were about. If you have no views on the value of Boethius's arguments, then you have no views on much that mattered to a number of medieval thinkers. If, however, you want to learn what Boethius had to say, and if you want to be nudged into thinking about its intellectual worth, then the present volume is just what you are looking for.

Boethius is probably, and rightly, best known today for his *Consolation of Philosophy*. In the present book John Marenbon offers a careful account of what Boethius is saying in this text. And he comments on the cogency of its reasoning. But he also deals with other writings of Boethius, especially the so-called *Opuscula Sacra*. In doing so he aims to stress the originality of Boethius as a thinker and to set him contextually with an eye on both his predecessors and those who came after him. Those familiar with Dr. Marenbon's previous writings on medieval philosophy will find in what follows yet another example of the scholarship and intellectual acumen that those working in the field of medieval thinking have come to expect of him. Those who are yet unfamiliar with Dr. Marenbon's work have a new and delightful treat in store for them.

Brian Davies

CONTENTS

ABBREVIATIONS OF BOETHIUS'S WORKS

Ar	*Principles of Arithmetic* (*De institutione arithmetica*). Ed. J. Y. Guillaumin (1995). Trans. M. Masi (1983). Guillaumin's edition has a facing translation into French.
———	*Principles of Music* (*De institutione musica*). Ed. L. Friedlein (1867). Trans. C. M. Bower and C. V. Palisca (1989).
———	Glosses on *Prior Analytics*. *Aristoteles Latinus* (1961–), III, 1–4, pp. 295–372.
———	Translations of Aristotle and Porphyry. Aristoteles Latinus, (1961–), II–III, V–VI.
C	*Consolation of Philosophy* (*De consolatione Philosophiae*). Ed. C. Moreschini (2000); and see note 1 below.
D	*On Division* (*De divisione*). Ed. J. Magee (1998), with facing translation.
InCat	Commentary on *Categories*. Migne (1847), 159–294.
ISC	*Introduction to Categorical Syllogisms* (*Introductio ad syllogismos categoricos*). Migne (1847), 761–794.

OS	Theological Treatises (*Opuscula sacra*). Ed. C. Moreschini (2000); and see note 1 below. Trans. Stewart, Rand, and Tester (1973) with facing Latin text.
SC	*On the Categorical Syllogism* (*De syllogismo categorico*). Migne (1847), 793–832.
SH	*On Hypothetical Syllogisms* (*De hypotheticis syllogismis*). Ed. L. Obertello (1969), with facing translation into Italian.
TC	Commentary on Cicero's *Topics*. Cicero (1833), and see note 2 below. Trans. Stump (1988).
TD	*On Topical* Differentiae (*De topicis differentiis*). Ed. D. Z. Nikitas (1990), 1–92. Trans. Stump (1978).
1InDI, *2InDI*	Commentaries on *On Interpretation*, 1 and 2. Ed. C. Meiser (1877), (1880). Trans. Ammonius and Boethius (1998): the section of *2InDI* on chapter 9.
1InIsag., *2InIsag.*	Commentaries on *Isagoge*, 1 and 2. Brandt (1906). The discussion of universals in *2InIsag.* is translated in Spade (1994), 20–25.

1. Stewart, Rand and Tester's texts of the *Consolation* and *Theological Treatises*, although less good than Moreschini's, are usable, and this edition has the advantage of a parallel English translation. I have given line references to it as well as to Moreschini, because it is so commonly available. Fortescue (1925) remains valuable as an edition because of its annotations and appendices. There are many translations of the *Consolation* available: e.g. Watts (1999), Walsh (1999) [with notes and bibliography]; that of Bk. IV.5–V.6 in Sharples, 1991 (with parallel Latin text) is particularly good.

2. References are also given to Migne (1847), which is more commonly available.

BOETHIUS

I

INTRODUCTION

Boethius may seem an unlikely subject for a book in a series on *Great Medieval Thinkers*, since many would object that he was neither medieval nor a great thinker. The first of these objections seems formidable. Although Boethius did not die until well into the sixth century, his education and milieu attach him to the classical world of late antiquity rather than the early Middle Ages. He thought of himself as a Roman, spoke Latin as a native language, was fluent in Greek and had access (unlike any Latin thinker after him) to a living tradition of Greek philosophy based on the study of Plato, Aristotle, and their commentators. But the objection can be answered in two ways, one practical, one more speculative. The practical reason is that medievalists, far more than classicists, are interested in Boethius. Classicists, their attention fixed on the mainstream Greek schools, have little time for a Latin writer such as Boethius, except when he can be mined for information about lost Greek sources. By contrast, Boethius was one of the shaping figures of medieval Latin culture, and so it is within the context of medieval Western thought that, if anywhere, he will receive the careful attention he deserves. The more speculative, and controversial, reason for including Boethius in the same series as, for example, Eriugena, Robert Grosseteste, and Duns Scotus, concerns periodization. Arguably, it is misleading to regard the Middle Ages—in the usual sense of the time from ca. 600 to ca. 1500—as a distinct period in the history of philosophy preceded by late ancient philosophy, and followed by Renaissance philosophy. A periodization more sensitive to the subject would envisage a 'long Middle Ages,' stretching from the Neoplatonic schools, which grew up in the fourth century, until the end of the seventeenth century. Boethius not only fits into such a long Middle Ages: his work is also a very important link in the chain of philosophical continuity that this periodization supposes.

The second objection—that Boethius is not a great thinker—demands a more direct answer than the first. Indeed, rejecting it is a central aim of my book. Boethius, say most historians of philosophy, is far too unoriginal to be a great thinker. They would agree that for medieval readers, who took the ideas and arguments he proposes to be largely his own, he seemed great. But, they would argue, modern scholarship has shown that he is, to a large extent, merely a transmitter of others' ideas—a writer of vast importance in the story of the transmission of culture but of little account for his own intellectual achievement. The attitude is evident in the very title and conception of one of the most learned studies of Boethius, Pierre Courcelle's *La Consolation de Philosophie dans la tradition littéraire*.[1] Courcelle examines the various sections of the *Consolation*, Boethius's most famous work, first with respect to their sources and then with regard to their influence: it is rather as if Boethius himself is a mere conduit through which images, ideas, and doctrines passed from the ancient to the medieval world. A more moderate version of the same view will be found in almost all modern treatments of Boethius, except for some on his views about prescience and contingency, and some of the more literary examinations of the *Consolation*.

I shall argue that, in his theological treatises (*Opuscula sacra*) and in the *Consolation*, Boethius is an original and important thinker—one who fully deserves to have been treated by medieval readers as a great author. His individual arguments are often far more careful, sophisticated, and, in their own terms, successful than has usually been recognized, although it is certainly true that Boethius often bases himself on ideas taken from others. But Boethius's especial distinction as a thinker lies in how he uses, combines, and comments on philosophical arguments. The *Opuscula* are innovative in their very approach to theology. The *Consolation* is, as its complex literary structure should immediately suggest, a work not just *of* but *about* philosophy: a subtle text which can be understood on various levels. The remaining writings—treatises on music and arithmetic, logical translations, commentaries—that make up Boethius's oeuvre are not usually innovative, but they are at the least very competent examples of genres where originality was not sought. The logical monographs offer an insight into two branches of logic, hypothetical syllogistic and the theory of topical inferences, about which there are no other extensive treatises from late antiquity. The logical commentaries are remarkable for the way they continue the project of the first great Neoplatonic logician, Porphyry, rather than follow the more usual approach of Boethius's contemporaries.

As these remarks will have made evident, Boethius was a modestly prolific writer, and he composed texts of various types in a number of fields. To treat them all in detail is impossible in a medium-length book; in choosing where to place my emphases I have been guided especially by the ideas set out in the preceding paragraphs. I decided not to look closely at his books on arithmetic and music, influential though they were, because of the barrier their technicality raises to readers and to myself.[2] The logical commentaries contain great riches of material—metaphysical and psychological discussions, as well as logical ones—selected and arranged, although rarely invented, by Boethius himself. To have looked in detail at this area of his work would have left little room to investigate properly the works where Boethius has more of a chance to think for himself. I have, therefore, restricted my discussion of these commentaries to a single chapter, where I try to give an idea of Boethius's grand project of translating and commenting on Aristotle and Plato (a project which, in fact, did not go beyond logical writings): what did Boethius's work as a logical commentator involve, and how does it fit into the Greek commentary tradition? I also look there in a little more detail at a few themes and passages in the commentaries, including the famous discussion of universals, but my treatment is anything but comprehensive. The consideration of the logical textbooks in chapter 4 is rather fuller. Although here too Boethius is probably relying to a great extent on the thinking of others, his discussions of hypothetical syllogisms and topical argument are of special importance because, as I have mentioned, they are the only extensive surviving sources for these areas of logic in late antiquity.

Since, however, this book is about Boethius as a great thinker, not just as a competent and influential one, the largest part of it is given to discussing the *Opuscula* (chapter 5) and the *Consolation*, despite the far, far greater bulk of the logical works. The *Consolation* raises so many difficult issues that I have divided my treatment of it into three chapters. In chapter 6, I examine the arguments of the *Consolation*, except for the intricate treatment of divine prescience and contingency at the end of the work, which calls for special analysis in a chapter of its own (chapter 7). Then, in chapter 8, I look at the problems of interpretation raised by the literary form of the *Consolation*, the way its arguments fit, or fail to fit, together and its lack of any explicit reference to the Christian faith of its author.

In all these chapters, my aim will be to understand what Boethius was trying to do, both as the selector and arranger of others' views in his commentaries and textbooks, and as a more original thinker in the *Opuscula* and the *Consolation*. The general introduction to Boethius's times, life, and cultural background provided in chapter 2 is designed to help this investigation into his intentions. But there is a different question that Boethius's texts raise to an audience of medievalists: how were these various books read and used in the Middle Ages? It is a distinct question, and answering it properly would be the task of another, distinct book. The final chapter gives just the lines of an answer, indicating the various ways in which the logical works, the *Opuscula*, and the *Consolation* influenced thinkers and writers throughout the Middle Ages.[3]

2

LIFE, INTELLECTUAL MILIEU, AND WORKS

Nothing about Boethius's life is so well known as the way in which it was ended. But Boethius's imprisonment and execution by the Gothic king Theoderic casts a shadow over attempts to understand his times. It is all too easy to think of Boethius as a last remnant of classical civilization, struggling to preserve and transmit the heritage of ancient philosophy in a barbarian world to which, finally, he succumbed. The impression is strengthened by the facts that no Latin philosopher after him had his direct contact with the Greek philosophical schools, and that his translations and works made available in the early Middle Ages ancient learning that would otherwise have been lost. Yet the circumstances of Boethius's life were not in any simple sense those of encroaching barabarism, and most of his work—both finished and projected—should be seen more as a confident and ambitious plan to surpass previous Latin philosophers than as a desperate attempt to preserve a vanishing culture for future generations.

Boethius's Life

Boethius was born ca. 475–477 into the old aristocracy of Rome. His full name (Anicius Manlius Severinus Boethius) indicates that he belonged to the Anicii, one of the grandest families.[1] When his own father, who had been a consul, died in Boethius's childhood, he was adopted into an even grander family, that of Symmachus. He would marry Symmachus's daughter Rusticiana (ca. 495), and Symmachus himself would be both a role model and friend for the rest of his life, and a near companion in the time and manner of his death.

Boethius's birth coincides roughly with the deposition of the last Western Emperor of Rome, Romulus Augustulus, in August 476 by the army commander Odoacer. The deposition was not, however, of much more than symbolic importance. For decades, the Western Emperors had depended on an army made up of, and led by, barbarians. Spurred by the emperor's refusal to give his soldiers land, Odoacer had merely made transparent where power already lay. His action did not mean, as it might appear, that Romans such as Boethius and his family were now, formally, under barbarian rule. From 395 there had been two Roman emperors, one for the East and one for the West. Odoacer did not set himself up as a new emperor. He was king of the barbarian soldiers but not of the native Romans, who remained, in theory, subject to the authority of Zeno, the Eastern emperor. None the less, Zeno decided that he would not accept Odoacer's position, perhaps because this gave him the chance to send Theoderic and his Ostrogothic soldiers, who were a nuisance in the East, to invade Italy and hold it for him. Theoderic was sent in 489 and, four years later, he had defeated (and murdered) Odoacer. He modelled his constitutional arrangements on those his predecessor had put in place. Theoderic was king of the Ostrogoths, not of the Romans—although some comments by Romans in the West do seem to envisage him rather as if he were a Western emperor, independent of the East.[2] Theoderic and the Goths were Arian Christians (Arians did not accept the full divinity of Jesus), but there was no attempt to make the Romans, who were Catholic Christians, become Arians. The army remained the preserve of Goths, but Theoderic, who had been educated in Constantinople, looked to the cultivated Romans for his senior officials. In many respects, the independence and freedom of the Roman upper classes, to whom Boethius belonged, were as well or better served by these arrangements than they had been for centuries. There were, however, tensions. Relations between Theoderic and the Eastern emperors were as delicate as might be expected in a situation where the location of authority was so unclear. For much of the time that Theoderic ruled them, the Catholics of Italy were divided from those of the East by the 'Acacian Schism' (see below). Once the schism was resolved in 519, Theoderic could not ignore the possibility that the Eastern emperor might decide to remove him (as he had done Odoacer) and would count on the support of fellow Catholics. Indeed, so it would turn out, when Justinian invaded Italy, beginning the Gothic Wars.

By Boethius's time, the imperial capital had been established in Ravenna, a town in northeastern Italy, over two hundred miles away from Rome. Rome had its public life and offices, which followed their centuries-old pattern, although there was little of the substance of power behind the ceremonial, except so far as the city of Rome itself and its inhabitants were concerned. Power lay in the court at Ravenna. A man of Boethius's class and abilities could choose to make Rome the centre of his life, and so lead an essentially private life, or to enter actively into politics at Ravenna. Through his youth and middle age, Boethius chose Rome and learned leisure.[3] Such a career had its public honours; Boethius was consul in 510 and, in 522, his two sons were jointly consuls—an almost unprecedented distinction. Possibly he, along with Symmachus, was prefect of Rome after his period as consul.[4] Boethius was occasionally given small official tasks by Theoderic—to construct a water clock and a sundial, to inspect a case of apparent financial malpractice,[5] and (see below) he played a part in the religious controversies of the time. But he devoted most of his time to writing and translating—ranging from treatises on the mathematical arts of the quadrivium, Aristotelian and post-Aristotelian logic, to theological and more broadly philosophical topics. I shall discuss these works individually later on in the chapter.

In 522, the year of his two sons' consulship, Boethius changed his pattern of life by accepting appointment as 'Master of Offices' at Ravenna. As such, he became one of Theoderic's most important functionaries, the intermediary between the Gothic ruler and the other officials at his court. Shortly afterwards came his downfall.[6] Boethius himself, very plausibly, attributes it in part (CI.4) to the enmities brought about by his upright conduct, defence of the oppressed, and hostility to corruption while master of offices. The immediate occasion of Boethius's troubles was, however, an accusation made by Cyprian against a senator, Albinus. Albinus was accused of treasonable correspondence with those in Constantinople close to the Emperor Justin. Boethius—who may have been, as master of offices, one of those required to judge Albinus—defended him. He was then himself accused of having written letters in which he expressed an aspiration for 'Roman liberty', of suppressing the evidence of Albinus's treachery, and of engaging in magic. All the accusations were, by his own account, false—and they do, indeed, have the air of fabrications, concocted by Cyprian, who stood to be condemned himself if his accusation against Albinus was rejected. Boethius is particularly brisk in dismissing the charge of magic. In the whole affair of Albinus, Boethius saw himself as the spokesman and defender of the Senate. But the Senate did not come to his defence. Asked to judge his case by Theoderic, it (says Boethius: CI.4.23 [80–81])) condemned him. His goods were confiscated and he was sentenced to exile and death. The exact date of his execution—probably 526 but possibly 524 or 525—is uncertain, but his imprisonment was long enough to allow him to write the work by which he is especially known, the *Consolation of Philosophy*. Shortly afterwards, Symmachus, who had apparently not sufficiently distanced himself from his son-in-law, was also executed.

Boethius's sudden fall took place against the backdrop of Theoderic's worsening position. The new Eastern emperor, Justin, had not only resolved differences with the Western Catholics but began to show intolerance towards the Arian Christians in his lands. Pope Hormisdas, a close ally, died in August 523, to be replaced by the more pro-Byzantine Pope John.[7] Shortly before Eutharic, Theoderic's son-in-law and, probably, his intended heir, had also died, leaving the succession unclear. It is tempting, therefore, to see Boethius as the leader of a pro-imperial, pro-Byzantine group, victimized by an increasingly insecure king and his Gothic and pro-Gothic advisers; or, in religious terms, as a Catholic put to death by Arians—medieval lives, indeed, made of him a Christian martyr. The evidence can be read in this way, but it need not. Boethius may well have been the victim of lower-level rivalries, ambitions, and intrigues—disliked, as he himself says, because of his idealistic stand against corruption; unable for the compromises of politics; and unwilling to acknowledge the real powerlessness of the traditional Roman institutions, such as the Senate, with which much of his public life had been identified.[8]

Boethius's Intellectual Milieu and Backgrounds

Boethius's intellectual milieu was one in which veneration for the traditions of Rome, knowledgeable interest in Greek culture, and Christian belief were unproblematically combined. Its best representative, besides Boethius himself, was his father-in-law, Symmachus.[9] Among Symmachus's ancestors was the fourth-century senator who, in the time of Augustine, had led the aristocratic pagan resistance to the imposition of Christianity. The pagan Symmachus was still admired by his descendants, but, unlike him, they saw no incompatibility between being faithful Christians, whose support was eagerly sought by rival Church factions, and preservers of the pagan Roman past. Boethius's father-in-law Symmachus himself collaborated in revising a manuscript of the commentary on Cicero's *Dream of Scipio* by Macrobius, an early fifth-century pagan man of letters; he also wrote a History of Rome, now almost entirely lost. To Cassiodorus, another eminent Roman of the time, though more closely linked to Ravenna and Theoderic, Symmachus reincarnated the virtues of Cato but in a superior, Christian form.[10] The dedication to him of a treatise by Priscian, the great Latin grammarian who worked in Constantinople, shows both Symmachus's importance as a patron of literature and his links with Greek culture. In Symmachus's household, Boethius received a thorough education in the Latin classics and also learned Greek, probably from a native speaker as a second mother tongue, in the way usual among aristocratic Roman families.[11]

Through his education and milieu, Boethius was able to draw on four main traditions of thought and writing: Greek Neoplatonism, Latin philosophical writing, Greek Christian literature, and the Latin church fathers. Of these, Greek Neoplatonism was by far the most important for him.

The founder of Neoplatonism was the third-century philosopher Plotinus. According to Plotinus, everything has its origin from what he calls 'the One' or 'the Good'—even ultimately, it seems, matter. But matter (which Plotinus held to be evil, in so far as it is unformed) is merely a by-product of the lowest 'hypostasis'—level of intelligible reality—Soul. Soul is responsible for the movement and ordering of the physical universe, but it takes its model from a higher hypostasis, Intellect. Intellect consists both of Plato's World of Ideas and of that which contemplates them. Since it is not absolutely simple and unitary, Intellect has to be explained by another, higher hypostasis, that is to say, the One or the Good, a hypostasis that can be described only in negative terms because of its ineffability. Although Plotinus usually speaks in terms of the whole level of being that is Soul, Plotinus's scheme of the intelligible world also sets out the process of ascent for the human individual, which he envisages as a soul entrapped within a body. The first stage is for a person to remove himself entirely from the distractions produced by the body and concern for anything bodily: to remember what he really is—a soul. The level of soul is characterized by rational, discursive thought, which takes place in time. But the sage may ascend further, to the level of Intellect, where knowledge is grasped immediately without ratiocination, and even finally to union with the One.

Plotinus did not propose his ideas as a new philosophy but merely as the correct interpretation of Plato. The allegiance to Plato is indeed unmistakable. But in his treatment of Soul as an immanent, pervasive force, Plotinus is influenced by the Stoic theories popular in his time, although he reacts strongly against the Stoics' materialism. And Plotinus's understanding of Intellect draws not just on Plato's World of Ideas but also on the Intellect (*nous*), wrapped in contemplation of itself, which is the supreme principle of Aristotle's universe.[12]

Plotinus's thought was published and popularized by his pupil Porphyry (ca. 232–305). Porphyry's approach to philosophy differed from his teacher's in two ways that would have an important effect on the development of Neoplatonism. Plotinus was suspicious of Aristotle's logic, because its distinctions seemed to be based on the world of sensible appearances; his *Enneads* (especially VI.1) contain a critique of the Aristotelian doctrine of Categories. By contrast, Porphyry gave Aristotelian logic a place in the scheme of Neoplatonic studies, and he himself wrote commentaries on Aristotle's logical works and an introduction ('*Isagoge*') to Aristotle's *Categories*, which became part of the curriculum. Aristotle's logic, he believed, was valuable to Neoplatonists so long as they realized that its concern was the world of sense-appearances, not the world of intelligible realities which, in their higher studies, they would investigate. This distinction had the effect of promoting within the Neoplatonic schools an approach to logic which, in most respects, was surprisingly faithful to Aristotelian ways of thought and unaffected by the Neoplatonists' characteristic metaphysical preoccupations.[13] Porphyry also differed from his master in his interest in pagan religious ceremonies and his belief that they might have some role in the search for intelligible realities. The link between pagan religion and Neoplatonic philosophy became even stronger in Porphyry's main successors, Iamblichus (d. ca. 326) and Proclus (ca. 411–485), master of the Athenian school. Porphyry, author of a work *Against the Christians*, Iamblichus—one of the main influences on Julian the Apostate—and Proclus were all strongly identified with the pagan resistance to Christianity; indeed, as a result of its obstinate paganism, Justinian would close down the Platonic school at Athens in 529. There was another, flourishing Platonic school in Boethius's time, at Alexandria where Ammonius, a pagan, was master. Some historians have seen the Alexandrian school as generally more accommodating to Christianity. Certainly, Damascius, a pagan contemporary, accuses Ammonius of coming to an agreement with the Christian bishop. But the complaint seems to be not about Ammonius's philosophical position but about his willingness to advance his career by cooperating with the Christians in persecuting his fellow pagan philosophers. The evidence suggests that Ammonius and his pupils continued to cover the range of pagan Neoplatonic philosophy and to teach doctrines that would be unacceptable to Christians.[14]

Boethius was familiar with a whole range of Neoplatonic material, much of which has not survived, at least not in the form he knew it. As well as knowing works by Plotinus, Porphyry, and Proclus, he was familiar with the developments of Greek Neoplatonism in his own times. A comment by Cassiodorus suggests that he was most influenced by the Athenian school, though 'from a distance'; he did not actually study there.[15] It has been maintained that he did, however, spend time at the Neoplatonic school in Alexandria, but the basis for this argument is weak. Although Boethius's father probably spent time in Alexandria, his son was too young at the time to have been studying philosophy. Boethius certainly shares some important ideas with Ammonius. But he could easily have read them or may well have had them from another source, which Ammonius himself used.[16]

Compared to the richness of the Greek tradition, Latin philosophy had less to offer Boethius directly in the way of ideas and arguments. Yet the handful of Latin philosophical writers were important to Boethius because of the precedent they set for his career as author and translator. Boethius was very conscious of Cicero's example as someone who combined high public office with writing Greek-based philosophy in Latin, and in his work on topical argument he regarded him as a serious authority. The fifth-century Martianus Capella's *On the Marriage of Mercury and Philology* influenced the literary form of the *Consolation*.[17] Boethius also looked back to Marius Victorinus, though without the respect he evidently felt for Cicero. He regarded Victorinus less as a trailblazer than as an unworthy rival, even beyond the grave. Marius Victorinus was the pagan Orator of Rome who, in about 355, converted to Christianity. His philosophical interests had been wide, as is evident both from the theological works he wrote after his conversion and the translations of Plotinus, now lost, which he is thought to have made. He was also interested in logic, translating Porphyry's *Isagoge*, commenting on Cicero's *Topics*, a work on the borderline between logic and rhetoric, and producing two textbooks related to this commentary, one on hypothetical syllogisms and one on definition.[18] Boethius is scornful of Victorinus's philosophical abilities, but—as will become clear—his own programme of work partly coincided with, though it went beyond, his predecessor's.[19]

By Boethius's time, there existed a large library of Latin theological literature. Whether he read widely in it is uncertain, but he knew well the work of the most philosophically gifted of the Latin Fathers, Augustine, as his short theological treatises make clear both implicitly and explicitly.[20] By contrast, Boethius seems to have owed very little to the great exponents of Greek Christian (and often deeply Platonic) thought, such as Origen, Gregory of Nyssa, and Gregory of Nazianzus.[21]

Boethius's Works and the Quadrivium

Boethius's works fall into four main groups. There are (1) his textbooks on the mathematical subjects of what he called the 'quadrivium'; (2) his translations, commentaries, and textbooks on logic and areas of rhetoric closely related to logic; (3) his five short theological works; and (4) the *Consolation of Philosophy*. Groups 2 to 4 will be examined in detail in the rest of this book: 2 in chapters 3–4; 3 in chapter 5; and 4 in chapters 6–8. I shall consider the first group very briefly here.

In his letter dedicating the *Arithmetic* to Symmachus (Pref. §4), Boethius writes as if he was planning to compose treatises on music, geometry, and astronomy, as well as music, and a letter written by Cassiodorus suggests that he fulfilled this plan.[22] Arithmetic, geometry, astronomy, and music had long been linked together. They were all seen as mathematical subjects. Arithmetic studied multitude (discrete units of quantity) in itself; music studied relative multitude, since its concern was with the arithmetical ratios of harmonics. Geometry studied magnitude (continuous quantity) at rest, and astronomy, in charting the movements of the stars, studied magnitude in motion.[23] Boethius invented the word 'quadrivium' ('four-fold path'; *Ar* I, 1 §7) to capture the relation between the four mathematical subjects—they were to be regarded as 'paths' because, in Boethius's words, they lead 'from the senses . . . to the more certain things of the intelligence'; they were steps on the way to the Neoplatonic philosopher's grasp of the intelligible world. Of his works on the quadrivium, only the *Arithmetic* and, incompletely,

Principles of Music survive. Cassiodorus's *Institutions*, written well after Boethius's death, very clearly mentions a work by Boethius about geometry based on Euclid, and so it is almost certain that it once existed.[24] But no copy of it is known. There are some medieval fragments of Euclid in Latin that some consider to be derived from this work of Boethius's, but this origin is by no means certain.[25]

The *Arithmetic* is a free translation—abbreviating here, expanding there, always in the interests of ease of understanding—of the *Art of Arithmetic* by the second-century neo-Pythagorean Nicomachus of Gerasa.[26] Although Nicomachus's *Art* is more down to earth than another of his works, the *Theologoumena*, it has little to do with arithmetic as a tool for practical calculations—what the Greeks called 'logistic'. Rather, Nicomachus considers the properties of numbers—how, for instance, various numbers are built up from one another, how numbers relate to geometrical forms, and how they can be placed in ratio to one another.

The abstraction of Boethius's Pythagorean approach to arithmetic may not seem altogether strange to a modern reader: what could be more abstract than modern pure mathematics? The distance between his *Principles of Music* and actual music-making is more disconcerting today.[27] Near to the beginning of *Principles of Music*, Boethius distinguishes three types of music: instrumental, human, and cosmic. In each case, what is to be studied are harmonic ratios. According to the Pythagoreans, and also to Plato's *Timaeus*, the universe is constructed according to harmonic ratios. Human music is the harmonic relation between body and soul; human capacities, virtues and behaviour are seen to be linked to particular intervals.[28] In instrumental music is included that for strings, pipes, and voice. But to Boethius—and to most though not all ancient musicologists—the performance of music was of no concern. *Principles of Music* sets out to treat all three types of music. Although the final parts of the treatise, dealing with human and cosmic music, were lost before the Middle Ages, even the section that survives, dealing with instrumental music, is a single-mindedly theoretical account of the mathematics of harmonic proportions. The opening sections of *Principles of Music*, however, give a vivid impression of the elevated and by no means purely cerebral attitude to music that underlies the more rigorously technical parts of the treatise. Boethius considers that harmonious music naturally delights human beings, and he links this observation to Plato's view that the world soul is structured according to musical intervals. Plato is also cited as an authority for the power of music to affect people's mood and behaviour;

the various modes are each considered to have different psychological effects, some soothing, some exciting.

Principles of Music, though derivative, probably diverges more from its main sources than the *Principles of Arithmetic*. The first four books were probably based on Nicomachus of Gerasa's now lost *Introduction to Music*, the fifth and (lost) following books on Ptolemy's *Harmonics*. But there is good evidence that Boethius adapted his material, especially Ptolemy, in accord with his overall Pythagorean approach.[29]

3

BOETHIUS'S PROJECT

The Logical Translations and Commentaries

Boethius's Project

Boethius devoted much of his intellectual energy for most of his working life to a grand project of philosophical translation and commentary.[1] The project began, perhaps unplanned, as one concerned with logic, and things so turned out that it remained limited to logic—although Boethius had, meanwhile, conceived a far more ambitious plan which he would have had difficulty in completing even had he lived to a ripe old age.

Perhaps as early as 500, Boethius produced a commentary in dialogue form on Porphyry's *Isagoge*, the standard introduction to logic in the Neoplatonic schools (see below).[2] He used the existing Latin translation by Marius Victorinus, but he had a Greek text too, and he found the translation he was using unsatisfactory. In future, he would make his own translations of the Greek texts on which he commented. Before 510, he decided to write a commentary on the *Categories*. He proceeded, it seems, by translating the text at the same time as writing the commentary on it (relying very heavily on Greek sources: see below).[3] He learned, that is to say, as he went along. Only after he had finished, or written a large part of, the commentary did Boethius conceive the idea of writing a second commentary to the *Categories*, in which he would deal with the more demanding problems that he had left out of his present work, intended for beginners. Whether he ever wrote the second commentary is unknown.[4]

No later than 516, Boethius announced (*2InDI* 79:9–80:9) his plan to translate into Latin all the works of Aristotle he could find, and all Plato's dialogues, to comment them, and then write a work to show that Plato and Aristotle agree on the most important philosophical points.[5] Between writing the *Categories* commentary and this time, he had already made his own translation of the *Isagoge* and, using it, produced another commentary to the work, and he had translated Aristotle's *On Interpretation* and provided it with a short, elementary commentary. The announcement of his project is made in the course of a second, much longer and more advanced commentary on *On Interpretation*.

What Boethius finally accomplished was much less, but in certain ways also more, than this very ambitious plan. Boethius almost certainly translated all Aristotle's logical works (though the translation of the *Posterior Analytics* did not survive into the Middle Ages) and Porphyry's *Isagoge*. He did not, however, translate any other Aristotle or any works by Plato.

As a translator, Boethius was extremely literal, sacrificing Latin style, of which the *Consolation* shows his mastery, to precision. So far as possible, he follows the word order of the Greek and tries to render each word, even the particles. The result, though grammatical, is often awkward and heavy, but it is accurate—although there are some cases where his choice of word and phrasing does betray his own, particular interpretation of the text.[6] He seems to have revised each of his translations, and there is evidence of two forms for all of them except the *Sophistical Refutations*.[7]

As a commentator, again Boethius concentrated on logic, although he did apparently write some sort of glosses or commentary to Aristotle's *Physics*.[8] His work as an exegete stretched less widely over Aristotelian logic than his translations: he provided, as already mentioned, two commentaries each for the *Isagoge* and *On Interpretation*, one (or perhaps two) for the *Categories*, a commentary on Cicero's *Topics*,[9] very probably a commentary on (Aristotle's) *Topics* and some glosses, at least, for the *Prior Analytics*.[10] He also wrote a set of logical monographs, mainly on different sorts of argument (see chapter 4). Since Boethius's working life was unexpectedly and violently curtailed, his failure to complete his original plan cannot be taken as proof that he did not propose it in earnest. Still, he seems to have given logic the priority and was willing in this area to go beyond the project he had set out, writing double commentaries and logical monographs, rather than hurrying on to Aristotle's nonlogical works and to Plato.

Boethius and the Neoplatonic Commentary Tradition

Apart from the need to translate the texts by Plato and Aristotle into Latin, the broad outlines of Boethius's project, as he announced it, were completely in line with the aims and practices of the Greek Neoplatonic schools. From the time of Porphyry, if not earlier, the teaching of philosophy had been based on commenting the great texts of the past, mainly those of Plato and Aristotle, and it was Porphyry, especially, who had established an important place for Aristotle, especially Aristotle's logic, in the Neoplatonic curriculum. Of his logical works there survive just his *Isagoge* (see below) and a question-and-answer commentary on the *Categories*; but Porphyry also wrote (at least) a longer *Categories* commentary and a lengthy commentary on *On Interpretation*. Among the works of his great follower Iamblichus was a commentary (now lost) on the *Categories*. Lectures are preserved by Ammonius (435/45–517/26) on Porphyry's *Isagoge* and on Aristotle's *Categories* and *On Interpretation*, and on a whole range of Aristotle's other logical, scientific, and philosophical works. In the sixth century, Simplicius would comment on the *Categories*. Similarly, Boethius's intention of showing the concord between Plato and Aristotle was widely shared; Porphyry probably wrote a work on the subject, and Simplicius would even go so far as to make it one of the commentator's explicit duties to show this harmony. In outcome, however, Boethius's project differed sharply from the Neoplatonic school tradition by what turned out to be its exclusive concentration on logic (even if logic in a wider sense than the modern term suggests). This emphasis, not planned by Boethius, although partly the result of his fascination with logical questions, would have an enormous influence on the development of philosophy in the Middle Ages.

Only a few of the surviving Neoplatonic commentaries are works of much originality. Certainly, great philosophical inventiveness was needed, at some stage, to devise the far from obvious ways of interpreting Plato and Aristotle and to arrive at the arguments and positions expounded in these works. But most writers of commentaries from the late fifth century onwards were concerned to carry on a school tradition, repeating what they had learned from their masters and from the older commentators. The way in which material was transmitted down the generations is illustrated rather strikingly by Ammonius's commentaries. All except one are transcripts of his lectures, written out by his students. Three are published under his own name, but eight under the names of the students of his who wrote them down, Asclepius and Philoponus. The one commentary written out by Ammonius himself, on Aristotle's *On Interpretation*, seems in its turn to be largely based on the oral teaching of Ammonius's own master, Proclus, though with some additions.[11] There is no reason to think that Boethius was any *more* original than his Greek contemporaries although, except under the improbable hypothesis that he studied in Athens or Alexandria, he had to rely on written material rather than oral teaching.

There has been some debate about the nature of this written material, and one scholar, James Shiel, has championed a hypothesis that turns Boethius into an even less original thinker than the Greek commentators of the time—indeed, into an entirely slavish imitator. Noticing that Boethius's commentaries do not each seem to derive from a single earlier Greek commentary, Shiel argued that Boethius simply translated the marginalia (themselves derived from a mixture of Greek sources) he found in manuscripts of the Greek text. But why accept Shiel's view? Evidence of such extensively annotated Greek manuscripts from Boethius's time is lacking, and Boethius's commentary on Cicero's *Topics* (see below), where he cannot have been following a Greek original, shows him perfectly capable of discussing a text, using many borrowed ideas but choosing his own words and deciding himself how to proceed. Most probably, then, Boethius's method was to base himself mainly on an existing commentary, turning also to other commentaries, exercising considerable personal judgement about how to proceed, though little originality in logical thought.[12] It does, however, remain a fair possibility that Boethius came by *some* of his material through the marginalia of Greek manuscripts and used it, with thought and discrimination.[13]

The *Categories* Commentary

Despite the wide scope of his intended project, Boethius ended by producing substantial commentaries on just three works in the Aristotelian corpus: the *Categories*; Porphyry's *Isagoge* (the standard introduction to the *Categories*), and *On Interpretation*. Each provided a different set of problems and opportunities for the Neoplatonic commentary tradition, and so for Boethius himself.

Porphyry's attitude to Aristotle's *Categories* was one of the boldest elements of his thinking. There is, on the face of it, every reason why a Neoplatonist should find this text hard to accept. On one, obvious reading, it is a piece not of logic but metaphysics—and distinctly anti-Platonic metaphysics. The *Categories* makes a fourfold division of all existing things into universal substances, particular substances, universal accidents and particular accidents, and then discerns nine sorts of (particular and universal) accident—quantity, qualification, relatives, having, where, when, being-in-a-position (i.e., posture), doing, being affected (1b26–27)—which, along with substance, make up the ten categories. In his discussion of substance, Aristotle makes it clear that universals are ontologically posterior to particulars. 'If the primary substances did not exist, it would be impossible for any of the other things to exist' (2a5–6)—apparently the very opposite of the Platonic position.

Yet Porphyry, in striking contrast to his teacher Plotinus, welcomed the *Categories* into the Neoplatonic curriculum and gave the treatise special prominence by providing it with an introduction, the *Isagoge*, which itself became a standard text.[14] Porphyry was able to accept the *Categories* because he considered, not without some textual support, that it classifies into ten categories not things but 'significant expressions'—words regarded not according to their grammatical type (as in *On Interpretation*) but according to their reference.[15] Words, Porphyry believes, refer primarily to the things humans know and perceive, particular sensible objects, even though by nature the intelligible things of Neoplatonic metaphysics are primary. When species and genera are discussed in the *Categories*, therefore, what Aristotle has in mind are universals conceived by abstraction from sensible particulars, and of such universals it is indeed true, he argues, that if every individual of a given species were to disappear, so would the species.[16]

Porphyry wrote two commentaries on the *Categories*: a fairly short commentary in question-and-answer format, which survives in part, and a long commentary dedicated to Gedaleion, which has been lost. The later Platonic tradition of commentary on the *Categories* was heavily dependent on a commentary by Iamblichus, which does not survive but from which ideas have been preserved in the *Categories* commentaries of Dexippus (4th century, a pupil of Iamblichus), Ammonius, and Simplicius.[17] In many parts of his commentary, Iamblichus apparently followed Porphyry's long commentary closely. But on certain, important points, Iamblichus apparently disagreed with Porphyry and advanced a more directly Platonic reading of Aristotle's text, in which the ten categories are applied to the Platonic Ideas and the intelligible objects of Neoplatonic metaphysics.

In commenting the *Categories*, Boethius mostly (where the comparison can be made) follows Porphyry's question-and-answer commentary rather closely. But he also had some further source of information. After a careful weighing up of the evidence, Monika Asztalos has concluded that it was a commentary written by a follower of Iamblichus, dependent on Iamblichus's commentary (and therefore, indirectly, on Porphyry's long commentary) in most places, but with some criticisms of Iamblichus.[18] Boethius gives special emphasis to Porphyry's view of the *Categories* as a work about significant expressions by tying it to a story about the origins of human language, which he places right at the beginning of his commentary (*InCat* 159A–C). Only human beings are able to give names to things. So, for instance, a human impositor called this sort of body 'man', that 'horse', that 'branch', that 'colour'. When someone procreated a child, the impositor called him 'father' and he gave words to measurements, such as 'two-foot long'. After this initial process of giving names to things (first imposition), the impositor went on to give names to names (second imposition), distinguishing between, for example, nouns and verbs. This discussion enables Boethius to make clear Aristotle's intention in the *Categories*: to treat 'words that signify things with regard to their signifying' (*InCat* 160A): words are its subject matter, but words as linked to things by their first imposition.

Boethius borrows from Porphyry his solution to the problem about the priority of particulars (*InCat* 183C–184B). Language is the subject of the *Categories*, and words refer primarily to particular sensible things. The objects of Neoplatonic metaphysics—Boethius mentions God and the soul—are not, then, germane, and the second substances that are ontologically posterior are mental concepts. But Boethius links to this account his story about the origins of human language. The person who first said 'man'—the impositor—had in mind a given, particular man, not 'the one who is made up from [many] single men'—not, that is to say, the species man, regarded as a mental concept. Although Boethius himself wishes to pass quickly from the discussion, these remarks of his raise, though they do not tackle, a whole area of problems that Porphyry's commentary leaves undisturbed. If species words and genus words first named a particular individual, how did they acquire their power to refer to each and every individual of a given sort?

Boethius's discussion of matters such as this is intentionally brief, because he is very much aware that he is writing a commentary for the use of beginners. In a passage that appears near the beginning of the work (*InCat* 160A–B) but was probably written when Boethius was some way through the commentary (and has probably been inserted at not quite the right place),[19] he makes this aim clear, and he mentions his decision to compose another commentary on the categories 'for the more learned', where he will teach 'Pythagorean learning' and discuss the intention, order, and utility of the text, setting out and adjudicating the different views about its intention. The mention of 'Pythagorean learning' suggests that Boethius is thinking—along with other late ancient commentators, such as Ammonius[20]—that the doctrine of the categories was invented before Aristotle by the Pythagorean Archytas. This idea, fostered by the existence of a treatise on the *Categories* falsely claiming to be by Archytas, helped to justify Iamblichus's un-Aristotelian reading of the text.[21] Possibly, then, Boethius planned a heavily Iamblichean second commentary on the *Categories*, or wrote one that has not survived.[22] A few paragraphs later (*InCat* 162A–B), however, Boethius mentions the work by Archytas and remarks that whilst it led Iamblichus to conclude that Aristotle had not invented the Categories, Themistius did not accept that the treatise was written by the ancient Pythagorean Archytas. It would not, then, have been so straightforward for Boethius to have accepted the Iamblichean approach to the *Categories*, and the existing commentary shows him to have rather clearly decided about the work's intention, on Porphyry's Aristotelian lines. It is tempting to think that Boethius remained sufficiently suspicious of the 'Pythagorean learning' needed to interpret the *Categories* for the more learned to have postponed the undertaking indefinitely.[23]

Commenting the *Isagoge*

Porphyry believed that, even before they read the *Categories* using his simpler, question-and-answer commentary, beginners required an introduction to the terms and concepts used in these works. His *Eisagoge* ('Introduction'—latinized as *Isagoge*) filled this need.[24] Whereas the *Categories* considers ten different ways in which a thing can be characterized, and so ten different sorts of term that can be used as a predicate in a sentence, the *Isagoge* discusses and compares five 'predicables'—more general types of predicate:

genus (as in 'Man is an animal'); species (as in 'Socrates is a man'); *differentia* (as in 'Man is rational'); *proprium* (as in 'Man is capable of laughter'; plural—*propria*); and accident (as in 'Socrates is white'). The treatment of genus, species, and *differentia* helps to bring out the idea of a hierarchy in the category of substance, touched on but not fully developed by Aristotle (and so appropriately known as 'Porphyry's tree'). The most famous passage of the *Isagoge* occurs near the beginning,[25] where Porphyry raises three questions about the nature of genera and species, which he refuses to answer in a work intended for beginners: (1) Do they exist or do they consist only in bare concepts? (2) If they exist, are they bodies or are they incorporeal? (3) If they are incorporeal, are they separated from sensible things, or do they exist in, and in connection with, them?

As has emerged from looking at the *Categories* commentary, and will be borne out in the commentaries on *On Interpretation*, Boethius looked back to Porphyry, rather than any later writer, both for much of the material in his logical commentaries and for his overall approach to Aristotelian logic. Commenting on the *Isagoge* presented, therefore, a special problem: because this text is by Porphyry himself, there is no commentary on it by Porphyry. Modern scholars have an additional problem. No sample of the Greek commentary tradition on the *Isagoge* from before the time of Boethius survives. The fullest surviving Greek commentary is by Ammonius (it is also the earliest, fragments apart)—that is to say, roughly contemporary with Boethius. The others, which seem to belong to the same tradition as Ammonius's, are later than Boethius.[26] Although there are some passages in both of his *Isagoge* commentaries where Boethius is close to Ammonius, there are many differences. It appears that Boethius either had access only to part of the material that Ammonius (and to some extent the later writers in the tradition) used or that he chose to disregard a large part of it. For example, in his treatment of accidents, Ammonius goes into three problems: how an inseparable accident (such as a crow's blackness) can be regarded as an accident at all; the incorporeality of accidents; and the status of accidents, such as extreme cold, that destroy the subjects in which they inhere. In his two commentaries, Boethius discusses just the first of these problems.[27]

Boethius's two commentaries are each much the same length as Ammonius's. They do not provide a simpler and a more complex exposition (in the manner of Boethius's two commentaries on *On Interpretation*) but rather a first attempt at exposition and a second, sometimes more sophisticated, one which goes over a good deal of the same ground. In neither of the commentaries are there the wide-ranging discussions, recounting and criticizing the views of various ancient philosophers, which Boethius took from Porphyry in, especially, his long *On Interpretation* commentary (see below). The emphasis is, rather, on elementary exposition, through explanatory paraphrase, of what the text of the *Isagoge* itself says (with help, in the second commentary, from what Boethius had learned from carefully studying the *Categories* and Porphyry's simpler exposition). Given Boethius's leaning toward Porphyry and his approach to logic, perhaps this strategy towards an introductory text by Porphyry himself is not at all surprising.

Boethius's most dramatic—and historically by far his most important—difference from the tradition best represented by Ammonius's commentary comes when he discusses Porphyry's three unanswered questions about universals. In Ammonius and the tradition, there is a distinctive way of tackling this passage.[28] Porphyry's questions do not admit of a straightforward reply, it is said, because there are three sorts of genera and species. What they are, and how they are related, is explained using an analogy. Consider a signet ring that has a picture of Achilles on it: many pieces of wax are stamped with it and bear the picture of Achilles impressed on them; and, if someone looks at them, then he will have in his mind the picture of Achilles. Similarly, there are the archetypes (*paradeigmata*) of all things, according to which the demiurge makes all things: forms 'before the many', which are separate from matter. There are the forms in particular things, such as the form of human being in each human: forms 'in the many', which are not separated from matter. Finally, there are the forms collected by the mind: forms 'after the many' separate from matter, because they are in the soul, but not unqualifiedly separate like one of the archetypal forms. This distinctive and popular theory about three states of the universal is not to be found in either of Boethius's commentaries on the *Isagoge*. Alain de Libera, who has drawn attention to the importance of this absence, makes the obvious inference that he did not know the theory.[29] Probably his conclusion is correct, although there remains the possibility that he knew the theory and rejected it. He would certainly have had reason not to adopt it, since the theory would not have fitted well into his line of thinking, which closely followed Porphyry's approach to logic.

In the first *Isagoge* commentary (*1InIsag*. 24:3–31:10), Boethius deals with Porphyry's questions, which he takes to be about all five of the predicables, in a matter-of-fact way. Of course they are not mere thoughts, like imaginary animals, because they are in everything that exists, cemented and somehow conjoined to them; in any case, Porphyry would not have gone on to ask if they were corporeal or incorporeal, if they did not really exist. This next question receives a double answer. There are species, *differentiae*, *propria*, and accidents that are corporeal (for example, human being, four-footed, ability-to-laugh, curly-hairedness) and those that are incorporeal (for example, God, rational, ability-to-add-up, knowledge); genera, because they may have corporeal and incorporeal species, are neither corporeal nor incorporeal, on this view. If, however, genus is considered in that it is genus (in that it has species beneath it), species in that it is species (in that it is below genus), and *differentia* and *proprium* are regarded similarly, then they will all be seen to be incorporeal; accidents, though, 'are clearly like the things of which they are accidents'. Boethius answers the final question by saying that the genera, species, *differentiae*, *propria*, and accidents of corporeal things, although incorporeal (in the sense he has explained), cannot be separated from bodies, whereas those of incorporeal things are never linked to bodies.

By the time he wrote the second commentary, Boethius had become acquainted with, or now decided to make use of, an approach to the problem which he says (*2InIsag.* 164:4) is that of Alexander of Aphrodisias, the great third century (AD) reviver of Aristotelianism.[30] Recently, Alain de Libera has examined the argument here and its sources, especially in the thought of Alexander, in the finest and most illuminating detail.[31] De Libera shows that Boethius must have had access to material transmitting some of Alexander's central ideas on universals (perhaps in marginalia to his Greek manuscripts[32]) and that, in addition, Porphyry—Boethius's logical authority par excellence—was himself, in logic, a follower of Alexander's. Discerning the exact relation of the position proposed by Boethius and Alexander's views is, however, a delicate matter, both because Alexander's stance is open to conflicting readings, and Boethius's argument here is notoriously difficult to interpret. I shall suggest, tentatively, that Boethius is a little less of a follower of Alexander than according to De Libera, or indeed to Boethius.

Boethius begins by presenting a metaphysical argument against universals (hereafter MAU; *2InIsag.* 161:14—164:2), which leads to a conclusion that would make the rest of Porphyry's treatise—and indeed Aristotle's *Categories*—wasted effort. MAU (which is ostensibly about just genera and species but is said to apply to all five predicables[33]) begins with a disjunctive syllogism. Either (A) genera and species really exist (*sunt atque subsistunt*) or

(B) they are formed by the intellect, in thought alone. Boethius then argues (*2InIsag.* 161:16—162:3):

1. Every thing that really exists is one in number.
2. Nothing that is common to many at the same time can be one in number.
3. Genera and species are common to many at the same time.
4. Genera and species do not really exist, i.e., (A) is false.

This is a powerful argument, because (1) is a fundamental principle accepted by Boethius and many other philosophers, (2) and (3) are arguably analytic truths, and (4) clearly follows from (1), (2), and (3). This central argument is backed up by two further points: one of them (*2InIsag.* 162:15–163:3) reinforces (1) and (2) by showing that if genera and species were one in number they would not be able to be common to many in the way they need to be. The other (*2InIsag.* 162:3–15) considers the possibility that genera and species are multiplex—that is to say, are collections (not themselves one in number) of things that are one in number; (1) is not supposed to rule out the existence of such collections. But, Boethius points out, using a version of the classic 'third man' argument, if a genus is multiplex, then the members of the collection that make it up will themselves have a genus; and so on, to infinity.[34]

(A), then, is false. From the disjunctive syllogism, Boethius therefore concludes:

5. Genera and species are formed by the intellect, in thought alone, i.e., (B).

But what sorts of thoughts are they? Thoughts, Boethius says, are of two types. They all have an object (*subiectum*)—something of which they are the thoughts. But some thoughts derive from their object in the way it is—that is to say, they correspond to how it is in reality (I shall call them 'corresponding thoughts') and some do not. Now, argues Boethius

6. If the thoughts that are genera and species are corresponding thoughts, then genera and species would not be merely thoughts; they would also exist in reality.
7. Genera and species do not exist in reality (i.e., not (A), as established above).
8. Genera and species are non-corresponding thoughts.
9. Non-corresponding thoughts are false or empty ('false' in the sense

> that they misrepresent how things are and would give rise to sentences that are false in the stricter sense).

Therefore, since genera and species neither exist nor, when they are understood, is the thought of them a true thought, all enquiry into them (Boethius in fact says into the five predicables) should be abandoned.

In order to understand the reply Boethius now gives to MAU, it is useful to consider a line of argument that I shall call the 'abstractionist reply'. According to the abstractionist reply, every particular belonging to a natural kind has a nature—John Marenbon, for instance, has the nature of man, and Fido has the nature of dog. When, pointing at Marenbon, we ask 'What is it?' and we give in answer a definition, 'A mortal, rational animal', the definition refers to this nature. We can grasp these natures in thought by a process of abstraction, in which we disregard all of, for instance, Marenbon's accidental features and are left just with his nature of man. The process of abstraction here is similar to that in mathematics where, for example, we consider a line, disregarding the body of which it is part. If I, John Marenbon, were the only man, I would still have the nature of man. But since there are many men, my nature (like anyone else's) has the accidental feature of being common—that is to say, it is exactly like many, many other natures. The concept we form of this nature of man is a universal, in that it applies, not just to one or some, but to every man. This universal concept of man does not, then, correspond directly to any one thing, because there exists no universal man, only individual men, each with a human nature; but it is not empty or false, because it is a way of thinking, by abstraction, about particular men and their natures. And so the abstraction involved is a *constructivist* abstractionism, in that it constructs thought-contents, rather than discovering really existing objects to be grasped by thought.

This reply clearly makes use of the idea of abstraction in order to challenge, not any of the steps by which, from (1) to (8), MAU is elaborated, but rather (9). The abstractionist reply accepts the conclusion of (1) to (4), that universals are not things, and the conclusion of (5) to (8), that they are non-corresponding thoughts. But it denies that non-corresponding thoughts, when based on abstraction, are empty and false. The abstractionist reply, whether judged successful or not, is a good strategy for answering MAU, which it tackles at its weakest point. MAU may well be an argument that goes back to Alexander (certainly, it makes use of Alexandrian ideas).[35] The abstractionist reply is, in a crude form, one possible interpretation of Alexander's own position,[36] and it may well be roughly the position contained by the Alexandrian material transmitted to Boethius. It stands in an interesting relationship to the response Boethius gives: to a considerable extent, Boethius seems to be following it, but he gives it his own peculiar twist.

Boethius's reply to MAU divides into three parts: first (Part α; *2InIsag.* 164:3–166:8) he sets out and discusses a theory of abstraction; then (Part β; *2InIsag.* 166:8–23) he uses the theory of abstraction in order to tackle MAU; and then (Part γ; *2InIsag.* 166:23–167:7), he adds an extra idea, which helps to clarify his point of view. After replying to MAU, he goes on to answer Porphyry's three questions. I shall describe the line of his reasoning and then try to clarify it, by reference to the abstractionist reply.

Part α introduces the notion of abstraction. Boethius starts with the example of a line. A line can never be separated from a body: it owes its existence to the body to which it belongs. Yet when we consider a line in our understanding, we consider it in separation from any body. The soul 'distinguishes, so that it may gaze at and see the incorporeal nature in itself (*per se*), without the bodies in which it is fixed (*concreta*)' (*2InIsag.* 165:5–6). Boethius goes on to discuss genera and species in the same light, and here there are close parallels with his first *Isagoge* commentary. The genera and species of corporeal things, like lines, are bound up with bodies, although they are themselves incorporeal. In their case too, he argues (*2InIsag.* 165:9–166:8), the soul 'takes the nature of the incorporeal thing from the bodies and gazes at that pure nature alone, as the form is in itself.'

In Part β, Boethius introduces inductive, as opposed to mathematical, abstraction. What happens, he says, when genera and species are thought of is that

> [β 1] from the singular things in which they [the species and genera] are, the likeness between the things (*eorum similitudo*) is collected—for instance, a likeness of humanity from singular men, unlike one another; and this likeness, thought of in the mind and truly inspected, becomes a species. Again, when the likeness of diverse species—a likeness which cannot be except in the species themselves or the individuals belonging to them—is considered, it produces a genus. (*2InIsag.* 166:9–14).

Boethius can therefore say that

> [β 2] . . . a species should be considered as nothing other than a thought (*cogitatio*) collected from the substantial likeness (*similitudo*) of many individuals which differ by number, whilst a genus is a thought collected from the likeness of species (*2InIsag.* 166:16–18).[37]

Yet he goes on to make a remark that complicates the relationship between these likenesses and genera and species:

> [β 3] . . . this likeness becomes sensible when it is in singulars and in universals it becomes intelligible, and in the same way when it is sensible it remains in singulars, when it is grasped by the intellect (*intellegitur*), it becomes universal. (*2InIsag.* 166:19–21)

Part γ adds a new idea, which reinforces this line of thought. Just as a concave and a convex line are always found in one and the same object, so singularity and universality belong to the same object. An object is both singular and universal: 'universal when it is considered in thought, single when it is perceived sensibly in those things in which it has its being.' Boethius considers, after this, that the question has been resolved and, turning to Porphyry's three questions, he says that

> genera and species subsist in one way, they are grasped by the intellect in another way, and they are incorporeal, but they are joined to sensible things and subsist in sensible things. But they are grasped by the intellect as subsisting in themselves and not having their being in anything else. (*2InIsag.* 167:8–12)

Boethius's argument is like the abstractionist reply in that it begins by using the idea of mathematical abstraction to reject (9). Moreover, although they are introduced by calling on inductive abstraction, which plays no part in the abstractionist reply, what Boethius calls 'likenesses' seem to be the same as what the abstractionists call 'natures'. And when Boethius says in (β 2) that species and genera are thoughts based on the likenesses of individuals and species, he seems fully to be following the abstractionist reply. But there are important differences.

It becomes clear in α that Boethius does not regard the thoughts obtained by abstraction as merely not false or empty. It is they, rather than the thoughts corresponding straightforwardly to things, which grasp the incorporeal nature of lines, genera, and species: they alone (*2InIsag.* 166:4–5) 'can find that which is true in its distinctive form (*in proprietate*).' Boethius seems to be using abstraction, not in a constructivist way as in the abstractionist reply but in a realist way. He seems to be suggesting that incorporeal lines and universals do really exist, but that lines are, as a matter of fact, always tied to bodies and universals to particulars, so that it is only by abstraction, which sets them apart from these accompaniments, that they are properly grasped. This realist version of abstractionism gives rise to a perfectly plausible view of mathematical objects, and it is a good way to consider the *natures* of substances. Boethius clearly wishes to use it as one of the elements in his answer to Porphyry's questions. But realist abstractionism has one striking disadvantage for his purposes. When applied to universals, it does not at all answer MAU, since it posits that there really are universals (though attached to particulars) which, apparently, will be one and many in the way that MAU shows to be impossible. It may be for this reason that, in the second part of α, when Boethius applies the analogy of abstracting a line to genera and species, he applies it, not to their universality—which is the point put at issue by MAU—but to their incorporeality.

In β, as observed, Boethius appears for a moment to be following constructivist abstractionism, but soon he devises an idea that seems intended to shore up his different, realist abstractionism. Boethius claims (β3, reinforced by γ) that the very same things are both particular and universal: as sensed in particular things they are particular, but as grasped in thought they are universal. It would seem—but Boethius never spells it out explicitly—that these things are what are called 'likenesses' when they are considered as particulars, and species or genera when they are considered as universals. If accepted, this claim would allow Boethius, as the phrasing of his replies to Porphyry's questions indicates, to make genera and species the objects of realist abstraction (they really do exist, though they are always attached to particulars).

The position, though, is far from clear. Perhaps, as De Libera has suggested, a clue to Boethius's thinking here may be provided by a passage from the *Consolation*.[38] There Philosophy cites what I shall call the 'Modes of Cognition Principle' (for a detailed discussion of the Principle and this passage, see chapter 7). The Modes of Cognition Principle relativizes knowledge to different modes of cognition and it assumes a hierarchical ranking of modes of cognition: human reason, which knows universally, is lower than divine intelligence but higher than the senses, which cognize things as particulars. This Principle would suggest that Boethius's abstractionism, though not simply constructivist, is not simply realist either. Genera and species *are* constructs, but they are more than a convenient mental tool: by constructing them, we understand reality more fully than if we were limited to the particulars cognized by our senses.

In treating Porphyry's questions, then, Boethius showed himself for the most part Porphyry's loyal disciple, by considering the problems raised in Aristotelian logic in Aristotelian terms. At the end of his account (*2InIsag.*

167:17–20), indeed, Boethius explicitly claims that he has been following an Aristotelian line—and the absence of Platonic Ideas from his discussion of species and genera indicates his good faith. Yet it is not fanciful to see a principle at work here in the *Isagoge* commentary that will reappear in the Platonic ambience of the *Consolation*'s discussion of divine eternity, and to suggest that Boethius's discussion, though muddled, has an original thrust, to be found neither in his Platonic contemporaries nor in Alexander and Porphyry. The value of Boethius's treatment for medieval discussions was not *just* that it was badly enough argued to be able to support almost any interpretation.[39]

On Interpretation: The Commentary Tradition

Aristotle's *On Interpretation* is a much more obviously logical work than the *Categories*. The *Prior Analytics*—the core of Aristotle's formal logic—is a study of syllogisms (see chapter 4). Syllogisms consist of sentences,[40] and *On Interpretation* prepares students for learning about them by introducing the elements of sentences (words, of which nouns and verbs are specially important), distinguishing between straightforward affirmations and negations and modal sentences (involving possibility or necessity). It considers the notions of truth and falsehood and, using them, some of the basic logical relations, such as contrariety and contradiction, which hold between assertoric sentences. Despite its preparatory character, the treatise was regarded as especially difficult and received detailed, wide-ranging and philosophically important commentary in later antiquity. Unfortunately, less of this commentary tradition survives than for the *Categories*.

Porphyry wrote a detailed commentary, which has been lost. Boethius's commentaries—especially his second, longer one—provide the best idea of Porphyry's views: Boethius says explicitly (*2InDI* 7:5–9) that he has taken his exposition mostly from Porphyry's, which he judged the most penetrating and best ordered. The other important surviving commentary from late antiquity is by Ammonius. As mentioned above, this work is Ammonius's revised and supplemented record of the lectures on *On Interpretation* given by his teacher, Proclus.[41] Proclus would have probably used Porphyry's commentary to an extent but modified it very considerably. Although, then, there are parallels between Boethius's commentary and Ammonius's, they probably reflect Porphyry's commentary as a common, ultimate source. But there are very many differences, and no evidence at all that Boethius knew Ammonius's commentary; Boethius's post-Porphyrean material seems to have come from elsewhere.[42]

Although the contents of *On Interpretation* did not present the same sort of problem for Neoplatonic interpreters as those of the *Categories*, there seems to have been a similar difference here between Porphyry's strategy of, mainly, reading the treatise within its own Aristotelian terms and the more blatant Neoplatonizing of some later commentators in the tradition. So, at least, it appears from contrasting Boethius, probably a more or less faithful follower of Porphyry's approach, with Ammonius, reflecting the teaching of Proclus (and Iamblichus, although Iamblichus may not have actually commented on this text). To take just two, striking examples. In his discussion near the beginning of *On Interpretation*, Aristotle very clearly considers that words are purely conventional signs: there is no reason in the nature of things why 'horse' or '*equus*' should be the sign for that sort of animal. Plato's *Cratylus*, however, suggests the idea that words are not merely conventional. Ammonius takes great trouble to find a way of reading Aristotle so that he supports a version of the doctrine of the *Cratylus* (some names, of universal and eternal things, are imposed so as to be consonant with the things).[43] This whole discussion is entirely absent from Boethius (and presumably Porphyry). Much later on, discussing future contingents, Ammonius turns to an Iamblichean theory about God's way of being and knowing in order finally to solve the problem. In his *Consolation*, Boethius would use this theory, although in a different way, to tackle the same problem; here, however, there is no such discussion and the solution is much closer to the terms of the Aristotelian problem.[44]

As these comparisons will already have indicated, the preparatory character of *On Interpretation* did not prevent it from becoming the object, in the commentary tradition, of elaborate discussions, in areas far beyond formal logic. They ranged over semantics, psychology, metaphysics, ethics, and theology. Since Boethius's second commentary cites, usually from Porphyry (and with Porphyry's criticisms), the views of various earlier commentators, it is a precious source for this, mainly lost, tradition. Here, however, I shall concentrate on the positions Boethius chooses as correct and, to give some idea of the commentary, look at two important areas of debate: first, the discussion of semantics linked to the opening of *On Interpretation*; second, the famous problem about future contingents and free will linked to

Aristotle's treatment of future tense truths in chapter 9. For convenience, I shall refer to the views and arguments proposed as Boethius's, although in most cases (some exceptions are discussed) he is probably following Porphyry.

On Interpretation: Semantic Theory

Aristotle begins *On Interpretation* with some remarks on the relationship between written letters, spoken words, mental contents, and things in the world. Both the text itself and how it should be construed have been subject to controversy from the time of the early commentators. Boethius's choice of translation already shows the decisions about interpretation that he elaborates in the commentary.[45] According to Boethius, the second to fourth sentences of *On Interpretation* run as follows:

> Therefore those things that are said (*ea quae sunt in voce*) are the signs (*notae*) of those affections (*passiones*) that are in the soul, and those things that are written of those that are said. And just as there are not the same written letters (*litterae*) for all, so there are not the same spoken words (*voces*). But what they are signs of primarily,[46] the affections of the soul, are the same for all, and those of which these are likenesses (*similitudines*)—things—are also the same.

On Boethius's reading, Aristotle is here presenting in compact form a semantic theory. As the commentary brings out, the theory has two important, and related, aspects.

First, spoken words are linked to things in the world not directly, but only indirectly, by means of what are called, in this passage, 'affections of the soul' and 'likenesses', but are also described by Boethius, more frequently, as 'thoughts' (*intellectus*). As Boethius puts it (*2inDI* 20:17–20): 'The thing is conceived by the thought, and the word signifies the conceptions of the mind and thoughts, and the thoughts themselves both conceive the things which are their subjects and are signified by the words.' The result is that words in the first place (*principaliter*) designate thoughts, and things only in the second place (*2InDI* 24:12–13). Boethius (referring explicitly to Porphyry) presents this theory (*2InDI* 26:21–27:25) as Aristotle's answer to a debate among the ancient philosophers, some of whom held that words stand directly for things; some (most importantly Plato), that words stand for 'certain incorporeal natures'—that is to say, the Platonic Ideas; some that they signify sense-impressions, and some that they signify mental images.

The second aspect of the semantic theory is the sharp distinction between written letters and spoken words, on the one hand, which are conventional and so differ between different peoples, and, on the other hand, things themselves and the thoughts that signify them, which are 'the same for all'. But what does it mean to say that thoughts are the same for all? When, to take the example Boethius gives (*2InDI* 21:18–24), a Roman, a Greek, and a barbarian all look together at a horse, the thing—that is, the horse—is, of course, the same for all, though the words used by the observers (*equus*, *hippos*, horse) are different. But the observers cannot think numerically the same thought in the way that they observe numerically the same horse. Although Boethius does not explicitly bring out this problem, a distinctive answer to it emerges from his exegetical discussion.

Consider first an obvious answer, which Boethius does *not* give: I shall call it 'the language-token theory.' The language-token theory is suggested by the case of the differing words. Suppose that the observers were not people who spoke different languages but rather three Romans. In that case, they would all say the same word, *equus*. But they would not say the same word numerically. They would utter different tokens of the same type-word. Indeed, the very idea of a language, employed by many different people, requires that users are able to identify numerically different language tokens as being of the same type. Might not each person's thoughts be tokens in a mental language? The Roman, Greek, and barbarian, seeing the horse, would all have the same type-thought, in the same way as the three Romans would all utter the same type-word.

Boethius, however, considers that numerically different non-complex thoughts are the same, not because they are tokens of the same type but because of their origin: they are caused by the same thing. Boethius adopts, then, what might be called a 'causal theory'. When, therefore, the Roman, Greek, and barbarian name a horse using their different languages, the thought is the same for each of them because the same horse causes it by a process that Boethius considers to be much the same for every human.[47] Metaphysically, this account is underpinned by Aristotle's theory that the immanent form of a thing informs the intellect of the person thinking of the thing.[48] But the metaphysics is left very much in the background. Boethius is interested, rather, in giving a causal, psychological account. He describes (*2InDI* 28:18–29:23) the process of arriving at a simple thought—one that is not true or false until combined with other thoughts. First of all, it is necessary to sense something and to have an image of it in the imagination.

Boethius does not say anything here about the different functions of the senses and imagination.[49] The important point for him is that, from some original sensory contact with a thing, the perceiver has a preconceptual mental image of it. The intellect then works on this image, so that it can be said to conceive the thing or have a thought of it. Boethius describes the intellect's way of working in two ways (*2InDI* 29:2–6, 8–10). According to the first, an image is like a line drawing, and the work of the intellect is compared to adding the colours, through which it becomes the picture of a particular person's face. According to the second, the intellect separates and clarifies what was confused in the imagination. The two descriptions fit together, because both suggest that it is through its transformation by the intellect into thought that the image properly expresses the thing it images.

The example Boethius considers, involving the horse and the three speakers of different languages, is limited in its direct application, since it concerns a situation where numerically the same, particular bodily thing is the cause of the common thought. But the causal theory can presumably be extended, so that when we think of a horse, we can be said to have the same thought, so long as the origin of the thoughts was, in both cases, a horse, even though not the same horse. Boethius is strongly committed to the position that there are passions of the mind not just of bodily things, but also of (for instance) the good and the just (*2InDI* 41:16–42:6). He does not explore the origin of such thoughts, but he argues that someone who judges what is good to be bad does not really have a thought of what is good (*2InDI* 41:25–27). This position makes best sense on a causal theory, since it requires a distinction between the presumed identity of a thought, according to its thinker, and its real identity. The causal theory identifies thoughts according to their origins, so that a thought will not be of the good or a good thing—whatever the thinker believes—unless it really originates from what is good.

Boethius is usually taken to have been an important exponent of the idea of a language of thought.[50] On such a semantic theory, there is a mental language, common to all human beings, many of the terms of which refer to things in the world. The various spoken and written languages, such as Latin and Greek, refer to this common mental language, and only indirectly, through it, to things in the world. This theory was, in various different and often sophisticated versions, common in the Middle Ages and often linked to reading *On Interpretation*, sometimes with the aid of Boethius's commentary. The fact that Boethius identifies thoughts causally, and not as tokens of types in a mental language, does not mean that he completely eschews the notion of a language of thought. Indeed, some of his remarks very literally endorse this position—as when (29:17–21) he says that the Peripatetics 'very rightly' held there to be three sorts of discourse (*orationes*): that written with letters, that spoken by the voice, and the other put together in thought (*cogitatio*).[51] He certainly believes that simple thoughts can be combined into complex thoughts, bearers of truth and falsehood, in the same way as words are combined into sentences, and he is willing to talk about mental, as well as written and spoken, verbs and nouns (*2InDI* 30:7–10).

Nonetheless, as the causal theory of the identity of thoughts suggests, Boethius is far from having a fully developed notion of a mental language (by contrast with, for instance, Augustine). Other passages bear out this impression. Consider, for instance, his rather tortuous account (*2InDI* 34:2–13) of how the processes of thinking and speaking are linked. Speaker A has an image of object *x* and his intellect grasps its characteristics: that is, he has a thought or passion of the mind with regard to *x*. Then he has the wish to indicate this thought of *x* to B. How does he do so? Boethius offers a first explanation: there is a further act of the intellect, which is 'explained and poured out' in speech—speech which is based on the original passion of the mind (the thought of *x*). There follows what Boethius considers a better, second account. Unfortunately, the text itself and the meaning are rather obscure, but the burden seems to be that the process of thinking and speaking are simultaneous.[52] Certainly, Boethius envisages no well-worked-out language of thought, which needs merely to be translated into Greek or Latin. Rather, as becomes clear during Boethius's detailed discussion of nouns and verbs, thought is seen to take on a linguistic form, insofar as it does, in the process of expressing something in a given spoken language.[53]

On Interpretation: Future Contingents and Divine Prescience

One of the main concerns of *On Interpretation* is truth and falsehood. A defining characteristic of the assertoric sentences discussed in the work is that they are true or false (17a1–4): that is to say, that they all have just one truth value, True or False (the Principle of Bivalence). But there is a problem with regard to future-tense sentences about events that we consider to be contingent—the sea battle that may or may not take place tomorrow (as opposed to tomorrow's sunrise, which will in the Aristotelian scheme of things necessarily occur). If the assertoric sentence, 'There will be a sea battle tomorrow' obeys the principle of bivalence, then it must be true or false: but if it is true, then there *will* be a sea battle tomorrow, and if it is false, then there *will not* be a sea battle tomorrow. And so it is not, apparently, open whether or not there will be a sea-battle tomorrow: it is a matter of necessity.

Aristotle raises this difficulty in chapter 9 of *On Interpretation* (18a28–19a4). He clearly believes that it is absurd to accept that everything happens of necessity, but it is less easy to be sure what solution he favours. One interpretation, still popular among Aristotelian scholars, is that Aristotle is willing to abandon bivalence in the case of future contingent sentences. This reading was adopted by the Stoics (as Boethius says: *2InDI*, 208:1–2), although they themselves thought that Aristotle should have retained bivalence and accepted that all things happen of necessity. Boethius does not, however, agree with this interpretation:

> For Aristotle does not say this—that both ['There will be a sea battle tomorrow' and 'There will not be a sea battle tomorrow'] are neither true nor false—but indeed that each one is either true or false, but not definitely in the way that happens with past-tense sentences, nor in the way that happens with present-tense sentences. But [Aristotle says] that in a certain way the nature of statement-making utterances is twofold. Some of them are such that not just are true and false found in them, but in them one [of a pair of contradictory sentences] is definitely true, the other definitely false. But in others, one is indeed true and the other false, but indefinitely and changeably—and this is as a result of their nature, not our ignorance or knowledge. (*2InDI* 208:7–18)

Boethius's own interpretation, then, makes Aristotle retain bivalence but seek also to preserve contingency by saying that future contingent sentences are only indefinitely, not definitely, true or false.

What, exactly, does Boethius's position amount to? What is meant by saying that 'There will be a sea battle tomorrow' is true or false indefinitely? It is not easy to find a satisfactory answer. If 'indefinitely' is taken in a weak sense, according to which an indefinitely true sentence is really true or false although with some qualification, how does the position answer the original problem, that the future will be determined if sentences about it are true or false? If 'indefinitely' is taken in a strong sense, so that indefinitely true or false sentences are not really true or false, how can it preserve bivalence? Recently, Norman Kretzmann proposed an interpretation of Boethius's position which, he believes, makes it give a coherent and sensible solution to the problem.[54] When Boethius says that sentences about future contingents are true or false, but not definitely, he means that, until the occurrence or non-occurrence of the event, such sentences are either-true-or-false; after the event, they acquire retrospectively a truth value for the time before the event (and they acquire the truth value False for the time after the event, because it is not the case that a past event *will* take place). For instance, 'There will be a sea battle on May 31, 1916' was either-true-or-false until the sea battle took place on that day. Thereafter it retrospectively gained the truth value (definitely) True for all times up to the event; for all times after the event it is (definitely) false.

Although some of Boethius's phrasing points in the direction of this interpretation—especially the comment that future contingent sentences are true or false 'changeably' (*commutabiliter*)—the working out of the theory in terms of truth-at-a-time and truth-for-a-time is Kretzmann's. At best, what Kretzmann has done is to show how Boethius's position might be rescued, not what Boethius actually argued. And it may be questioned even whether Kretzmann's solution works. It avoids determinism, but does it preserve bivalence? Kretzmann claims it does, so long as bivalence is considered in a sufficiently broad way, because every assertoric sentence *eventually* has the value True or False. But Aristotle, at least, seems to have had a narrower view of bivalence, since in his comments on it he does not suggest that an assertoric sentence can be anything other than true or false *at any time.*

One long part of Boethius's discussion (*2InDI* 209:20–216:24) seems, rather, to bear out a different way of understanding indefinite truth and falsity. Here Boethius insists that someone who says 'A sea battle will take place tomorrow' is speaking falsely, even if turns out that there is a sea battle the day after he said it. The falsehood results from his having made the claim that it *will* take place—which Boethius understands as amounting to the claim that it will take place of necessity. What the speaker should have said, Boethius claims (*2InDI* 212:4–15), is 'Tomorrow a sea battle will take place contingently' which he glosses as 'it happens, if it happens, in such a way as it will have been able not to have happened.' This apparently extreme claim is more plausible against the background of Boethius's view of modality, which has no place for the notion of alternative synchronic possibilities.[55] Modern philosophers would deny that if 'Socrates is now running' is true now, then necessarily Socrates is running now. They would insist (whether or not they wished to put their view in the language of different possible worlds) that, although Socrates is indeed now running, it is possible that he is not running. Boethius disagrees: 'if it is true to say, that something is, it is necessary that it is' (*2InDI* 210:18–19). The same reasoning, he immediately adds, applies to what is said about the future: 'if it is true to say that it will be, without doubt it is necessary that it will be.'

Although this position seems to put a stark choice between sacrificing bivalence or accepting determinism, Boethius finds in it the way out of the problem. Determinism is threatened only if it is true to say of future contingent events that do in fact happen that they will happen (or of those that do not happen, that they will not). But such sentences are never true, precisely because they entail the denial that the event is contingent, and that denial is false. Let *e* be an event of any sort: Boethius holds that

(1) '*e* will take place' is true implies that *e* will take place necessarily.

Suppose *e* is a contingent event: '*e* will take place' is true implies a contradiction—that an event is both contingent (*ex hypothesi*) and necessary (from (1)). Therefore it is false that '*e* will take place' is true. All that speakers can do is either to make false unqualified statements about future contingents ('*e* will happen') or qualified statements about them ('*e* will happen contingently') that are sometimes true.

Nonetheless, Boethius insists (215:16–19) on the grave error of those who hold that both of each pair of contradictories about future contingents are false. Although at first sight a blatant contradiction of what he has just said,[56] Boethius need be guilty of no more than slightly sloppy presentation. His point is that if interpreters read Aristotle as talking only about definite truth and falsity, then they either hold that each pair of contradictory future contingents are one true and the other false, and so deny their contingency, or else that both members of each pair are false, which entails the self-contradiction that the same event necessarily will and will not happen. But if they recognize that future contingent statements are true or false indefinitely, then they are able (in principle) correctly to assert the truth or falsity of statements such as 'this event will take place contingently', 'that event will not take place contingently'.

This interpretation is borne out by what Boethius goes on to say (225:9–226:25) about the problem, not mentioned by Aristotle himself but present in the commentary tradition[57] of divine prescience. Must we not either deny that God knows all that will happen in the future, or else accept that everything happens of necessity? Boethius's answer is completely in line with his solution to the problem of the truth of future contingents. God does not know that future contingents will happen necessarily: indeed, since contingent events do not occur necessarily, it is a falsehood, not an item of knowledge, to believe that they do. What God knows is that future things will take place contingently, in such a way that they could happen otherwise than they do.

Boethius himself came later to find this solution to the problem of prescience inadequate, and it is questionable whether his approach really solves even the easier problem of the truth of future contingents. But it is a more coherent and developed strategy than usually recognized. Along with it, Boethius's extensive commentary on chapter 9 includes a wider-ranging treatment of free will and determinism, which not only gives valuable information about the views of the Stoics and other ancient schools but also sets out a subtle view of how events are brought about by the interplay of factors including human free will.[58] Here too, when he returned to think about the issues in the *Consolation*, Boethius would find them harder to resolve.

The Legacy of Boethius's Commentaries

The vast influence exercised by his logical commentaries on Latin philosophy up to, and beyond, the twelfth century may seem to be the result more of historical circumstances than of anything to do with Boethius as an individual thinker, with particular views and preferences.[59] He was one of the last Latin writers to whom the Greek commentary tradition was, at least in part, available and comprehensible and, by transferring some of it into Latin, he provided early medieval thinkers with intellectual riches which, otherwise, would have remained hidden from them. Yet there are two factors, touched on above, which—especially when taken together—make Boethius something other than a neutral intermediary. First, there is the exclusive concentration of his commentaries on Aristotelian logic. Second, there is Boethius's adoption of Porphyry's approach to interpreting Aristotelian logic, as opposed to that followed by the later Greek Platonists: he does not try to find Platonic doctrines in the logical texts but considers that Aristotle does not contradict Plato because his subject matter is different. Both these factors may, to some extent, have been produced by outside circumstances: Boethius's unnatural death and his possibly rather limited access to Greek material. Both seem also, however, to reflect his own intellectual preferences, and together they set the sober, Aristotelian tone for much that is most remarkable in early medieval philosophy.[60]

4

THE LOGICAL TEXTBOOKS AND TOPICAL REASONING

Types of Argument

As well as logical commentaries, Boethius wrote a series of logical textbooks. Five survive. One is about the various ways of dividing things and links most closely with the subject matter of the *Isagoge*. In the other four, the emphasis falls on the theory of different types of argument. Two of them (partly covering the same ground) introduce Aristotelian syllogistic; one is about 'hypothetical syllogisms'. And one is concerned with topical argument—an area Boethius also considered in his commentary on Cicero's *Topics*, which shares its subject matter). Boethius wrote at least one further logical textbook, which does not survive: it was called *On the Order of the Peripatetic Disciplines* and it explained in what order students should study logic.[1] The textbooks date from relatively late in Boethius's career: the earliest was probably written ca. 513 and the latest only a year or two before the *Consolation*.

Of these texts, the most interesting are those on hypothetical syllogisms and topical reasoning, because they are almost the only surviving late ancient treatments of these fields in Latin or Greek. The works on categorical syllogisms, by contrast, mostly cover ground familiar from Aristotle himself and other textbooks. But since categorical syllogisms are the basis of Boethius's study of arguments (and Aristotelian syllogistic is now unfamiliar except to experts), it is valuable to look at these two treatises before looking at the others. First, however, I shall consider *On Division*—the one treatise that does not consider a type of argument, although—as I shall explain at the end of the chapter—it, like the others, fits closely to the lines of Boethius's whole logical project.

On Division

Not all of Boethius's textbooks were concerned with the theory of argument. The surviving and widely read *On Division* (D) (probably 515–520[2]) is about the different types of divisions made by philosophers and logicians. Like so much of Boethius's logical writing, D is most probably based on now lost work of Porphyry—on prolegomena to a commentary by him on Plato's *Sophist*; Porphyry, in his turn, was using, so Boethius tells his readers (D 876D), a treatise by Andronicus.[3] Although prefacing Plato, Porphyry's prolegomena seem to have developed ideas to do with Aristotelian logic and linked to Porphyry's *Isagoge* and to Aristotle's *Categories*.

There are two main types of division: intrinsic (per se) and accidental (*per accidens*). An accident, as Porphyry explains in the *Isagoge*, chapter 5, is a feature that can affect and leave its subject without the subject being destroyed—the whiteness of a wall, for example, or its coldness. Accidental division (D 878AB) can be of a subject into accidents (of all men, some are black, some white, some medium-coloured), of an accident into subjects (of things that are sought, some are in the soul, some in bodies), and of an accident into accidents (of all white things some are hard, some are soft). Boethius's main interest, however, is in intrinsic divisions, and he criticizes the earlier Peripatetics for mixing accidental divisions with intrinsic ones (D 892A).

Intrinsic division is of a genus into its species, a whole into parts, and a word into its different meanings. The division of wholes (which may be conceptual rather than actually possible) varies according to whether they are discrete or continuous (D 887D–888D). Words may be divided either into the different meanings they have, individually or in phrases, in cases of ambiguity ('bank' is an excellent English example), or into different 'modes' ('infinite' can mean infinite in quantity, infinite in time, and so on), or into different determinations (as when a word or phrase is used vaguely—for instance, 'man' or 'give me'—and then made precise by the addition of a determination—'every man', 'that man there'; give me the pen, give me the book) (D 888D–890D). Boethius spends about half of the whole treatise (D 880A–887D), however, considering how a genus is divided into species; the subject matter is close to that of the *Isagoge*. The skill in this sort of dividing lies in finding intrinsic *differentiae* that divide a genus in two, and in ordering the division, so that each genus is divided by its own *differentiae*, not those of genera beneath it. For instance (D 884D–885A), it would be wrong to divide substances into animate and inanimate; rather, the division must be of substances into corporeal and incorporeal, and then of corporeal substances—bodies—into animate and inanimate.

Boethius distinguishes carefully between the division of a genus into species and that of a whole into parts (D 879B–880A). Division into species is in respect of quality, whereas that into parts is in respect of quantity. Every genus, he says, is 'naturally prior' to its species, whereas a whole is posterior to its parts. Boethius goes on to explain this comment in a way that need not imply any position on the questions discussed in the *Isagoge* commentaries about the reality of genera and species. If, he says, the genus is destroyed, its species will perish: this point is certainly right, because were there no animals, for instance, then there could be no men. He adds that if the species is destroyed, the genus remains undestroyed in its nature. This point is uncontentious if just one or some species are destroyed; it is unclear whether Boethius would insist that it holds even if *all* the species of a genus no longer exist. By contrast, parts can exist without the wholes to which they belong, but if any part perishes, then the whole to which it belonged will no longer be a whole.

As this summary indicates, in D Boethius limits himself to a rather bald and unargued statement of positions that might well prove rich in problems and paradoxes. There is one passage that is especially interesting in the way it relates to Boethius's positions elsewhere, although it too poses and suggests problems rather than investigating them. In the *Isagoge*, and in Boethius's commentaries, there are discussions about separable and inseparable accidents.[4] D introduces its own distinction (D 881BC). Rather than accidents and *differentiae*, as in the *Isagoge*, the distinction here is between *differentiae per se*, which are what should be used in dividing a genus into its species, and *differentiae per accidens*. *Differentiae per accidens* divide into those that 'regularly leave' their subjects—ordinary, separable accidents, such as sleeping and sitting—and those that 'follow on their subject' (*consequentes*). Some such accidents can be separated from their subject only by reason, such as the greyness of my eyes: I cannot cease to be grey-eyed, but were I not grey-eyed, I would still be a man. Some cannot even be separated from their subjects by reason. Boethius gives counting and learning geometry as his examples: if the possibility of doing these things were removed from man then he would no longer be man. But they are not *differentiae per se*, because man is not man because he can count or learn geometry but because he is rational and mortal.[5]

Categorical Syllogisms

Boethius wrote two textbooks on categorical syllogisms. One, usually known as *On the Categorical Syllogism* (SC), goes through the preliminaries for understanding syllogisms (explained by Aristotle in his *On Interpretation*) in a first book, and in its second book gives a fairly elementary guide to Aristotelian syllogistic itself.[6] The other, known as *Introduction to Categorical Syllogisms* (ISC) (and sometimes called *Antepraedicamenta* in the manuscripts), has only one book which covers the ground, but in greater detail, of Book I of *On the Categorical Syllogism*. In ISC Boethius apparently tries to rewrite and expand his earlier textbook: he may have left it unfinished, or a second book may have been written and lost in transmission. Both may have been composed ca. 513–514, when Boethius was engaged on commenting *On Interpretation*.[7] Among his sources, Boethius mentions (SC 813C, 829D) Aristotle, Porphyry, Eudemus and Theophrastus.

Aristotle's syllogistic[8] presupposes a theory of sentences like that he develops in *On Interpretation*, and Boethius devotes Book I of *On the Categorical Syllogism* and most of the *Introduction to Categorical Syllogisms* to expounding it. In a declarative (*enuntiativa*) sentence, there are two main parts: a subject and a predicate, a general term which is predicated of the subject. So, for example, 'Plato is a philosopher' predicates 'philosopher' of 'Plato'.[9] The declarative sentences from which Aristotelian syllogisms are made have as their subjects general terms that have a quantity: they are either particular ('some man') or universal ('every man'). Moreover, the sentences have a 'quality': they are either affirmative or negative. They divide, therefore, into four groups: universal affirmative ('Every man is mortal'—or, using letters, as Aristotle and Boethius did, to stand for any general term: 'Every *A* is *B*'); universal negative ('No *A* is *B*'); particular affirmative ('Some *A* is *B*'); particular negative ('Some *A* is not-*B*'). In his theory of syllogisms,[10] expounded by Boethius in Book II of SC, Aristotle studied the combinations of two such sentences, in which they have one term (the 'middle term') in common. What Aristotle noticed was that from some combinations of two such sentences there follows a third sentence, which has as its subject and predicate the two terms (the 'extremes') which the first two sentences do not share. For example, from 'Every *B* is *A*' and 'Every *C* is *B*,' it follows that 'Every *C* is *A*.' As the use of letters brings out—and Boethius recognizes (SC 810CD)—the validity of this argument depends just on the way in which the terms are arranged, not on what *A*, *B* or *C* stand for. A combination of two quantified and qualified sentences as premisses from which a third such sentence follows as a conclusion is called a syllogism. (In the *Prior Analytics*, Aristotle in fact writes syllogisms out as 'If . . . then . . .' statements, with the conjunction of the two premisses as their antecedent and the conclusion as the consequent. But scholars now believe that Aristotle probably envisaged syllogisms as deductions; Boethius's way of writing them out—premise; premise; therefore, conclusion—does not distort Aristotle's intentions[11]).

One function of the theory of the syllogism is to classify which combinations of premisses produce which conclusions. It arranges syllogisms into three classes ('figures') by the position of the middle term: the subject of one premise and predicate of the other (Figure 1), the predicate of both (Figure 2), the subject of both (Figure 3). Aristotle considered that there were four types of syllogism in figures 1 and 2, and six in Figure 3. For instance, in Figure 1, as well as the example given above, the three following combinations are valid: (2) 'No *B* is *A*, Every *C* is *B*, therefore no *C* is *A*'; (3) 'Every *B* is *A*, Some *C* is *B*, therefore some *C* is *A*'; (4) 'No *B* is *A*, Some *C* is *B*, therefore some *C* is not *A*.' Boethius (SC 813C; 814C–816C) follows a tradition that goes back, he says, to Theophrastus and Eudemus, of adding to Figure 1 five supplementary, 'reflected' syllogisms, which passages in the *Prior Analytics* make clear Aristotle would have regarded as valid arguments, although he does not list them under any of the figures.[12] Boethius also mentions, but rejects as without authority in Aristotle, an extra, variant form of a third figure syllogism.[13]

Aristotle was not content just to classify: he wanted to show that the combinations he excluded were invalid and to prove that the combinations he chose were valid. Boethius completely ignores the first of these tasks, which Aristotle had accomplished through an economical process of finding counterexamples (e.g., *Prior Analytics* 26a5–9), but he devotes considerable space to the second. Aristotle had called the first figure syllogisms 'complete' (Boethius translates *perfectus*), because nothing needs to be added for their validity to be evident (24b23–24). He thought of second- and third-figure syllogisms, it seems, as incomplete but as able to be turned into complete deductions by the rules that converted them into first-figure syllogisms. But this question of completeness was much debated in antiquity, opinions ranging from the view that second- and third-figure syllogisms are not only incomplete but invalid to the position that syllogisms in all the figures are perfect. Boethius does not have a detailed discussion of the problem, but he calls the first-figure syllogisms (excluding the five added ones) 'indemonstrable' because they are 'not proven through others' and 'complete' because they are 'proven through themselves' (SC 823A). Syllogisms in Figures 2 and 3 he describes as 'incomplete' (*imperfecti*), but only in the sense that they need something (application of a conversion rule) for their completeness to be made evident (SC 817B, 812CD).[14]

Aristotle puts forward (*Prior Analytics* 25a7–26) three rules of conversion: in the case of universal negatives and particular affirmatives, subject and predicate can be swapped around without change of truth value (If no *A* is *B*, then no *B* is *A*, and if some *A* is *B*, some *B* is *A*), and from a universal affirmative (Every *A* is *B*) there follows a particular affirmative with subject and predicate exchanged (Some *B* is *A*). Boethius states and proves these rules (and more—see below) at some length in Book I of SC (804C–807A) and in ISC (785C–787C). When he sets out the syllogisms in Book II of SC, Boethius uses these principles to show how the 'incomplete' syllogisms follow from the complete first-figure ones. For example, the second-figure syllogism 'No *B* is *A*, some *C* is *A*, therefore some *C* is not *B*' becomes a type (4) first-figure syllogism by converting the first premise, a universal negative, to 'No *A* is *B*'.

Boethius has been accused of obscuring the theory of the syllogism by helping to make it unclear *why* first-figure syllogisms are evidently valid. In the *Prior Analytics*, Aristotle did not set out syllogisms as I have done above, using ordinary sentences such as 'Every man is an animal' of the sort he had discussed in *On Interpretation*. Rather, he adopts the rather awkward form: 'Animal belongs to (or sometimes, 'is said of') every man.' The great advantage of this form is seen when a first-figure syllogism is put in it: the validity of '*A* belongs to every *B*, *B* belongs to every *C*, therefore *A* belongs to every *C*' is transparent. This transparency can be kept even with the more normal 'Every man is an animal' type of formulation by reversing Aristotle's order of premisses: 'Every *C* is *B*, every *B* is *A*, therefore every *C* is *A*.' Günther Patzig, who first drew attention to this point about transparency, explains that the Greek commentators regularly changed the order of the premisses of first-figure syllogisms when they formulated them with 'is', and he assigns to Boethius 'the dubious honour' of being the first to combine the Aristotelian ordering of the premisses with the un-Aristotelian formulation with 'is', thus preventing the validity of the first-figure syllogisms from being evident.[15] This charge is not quite fair. In his example syllogisms, Boethius does indeed have the Aristotelian order and the formulation with 'is'. But whenever he is explaining the form of a syllogism or proving it, and using letters for terms, Boethius adopts a Latin equivalent of Aristotle's formulation and says, for instance, not 'Every *A* is *B*' but '*B* is predicated of every *A*.'

Boethius departs most from Aristotle and the earlier Aristotelian tradition in the space he gives to discussing various types of conversion. To Aristotle's three rules, he adds a fourth: that just as a universal affirmative converts with a particular affirmative, so a universal negative converts with a particular negative.[16] And he is particularly interested in another type of conversion altogether: conversion by contraposition, which involves negating the terms themselves, so that 'Every man is an animal' converts to 'Every not-man is a not-animal'. Universal affirmatives (as in this example) and particular negatives convert by contraposition—precisely the two forms which do not convert normally with themselves. One of the main ways ISC goes beyond SC is in its lengthy treatment of this area, which is prepared by a separate examination of sentences with negative (*aoriston*, 'indefinite'; *infinitum* in Latin) terms (780A–785B), and then a comprehensive treatment of contraposition (787B–794A), including a sort of partial contraposition, where the subject alone, or the predicate alone becomes an indefinite term. Boethius goes further than showing just when conversion by contraposition or partial contraposition preserves truth values whatever the terms. He sees that in many cases these sorts of conversion, though not universally truth-preserving, are truth-preserving so long as the terms bear a given relation to each other and to everything else. For instance, suppose '*A*' and '*B*' are such that every *A* is *B* and nothing which is not an *A* is *B* (as when '*A*' is 'man' and '*B*' is 'able to laugh').[17] This interest in the effect of the contents of sentences on their relations leads sharply away from the theory of syllogisms—is it any surprise that ISC stops at this point, without going on to discuss syllogisms themselves at all?—but it links with the general concerns of an area which seems to have fascinated Boethius: topical reasoning. Before looking at Boethius's works on the topics, however, I shall examine his monograph on syllogisms of a sort hardly considered by Aristotle—what Boethius calls 'hypothetical syllogisms'.

Hypothetical Syllogisms and the Question of Ancient Propositional Logic

Boethius's treatise on what he calls 'hypothetical syllogisms' (SH), probably written after the logical commentaries, between 516 and 522,[18] has attracted much more scholarly interest than SC or ISC. Historians of logic used to think that it was a discussion of the logic of sentences and therefore of great historical importance, because Aristotelian syllogistic is a logic of terms; sentence logic in the ancient world is, by and large, the preserve of the Stoics.[19] Recent scholars, however, have rejected this analysis of SH[20]—and quite rightly so, as will become clear from the contents of the treatise and Boethius's approach to them.

Hypothetical syllogisms are those where at least one premise is a hypothetical sentence (*propositio*[21]) not a categorical one. Boethius devotes Book I of SH to discussing the nature of these hypothetical sentences and how they are distinct from categorical sentences. A categorical sentence makes a predication—for instance, it predicates animal of man. A hypothetical sentence involves a condition: it says 'that something is, if something else is,' as in 'if it is day, it is light' (SHI.1.5)[22] Hypothetical sentences, then, will be made up of two or more categorical sentences (SHI.2.5), linked by 'if'[23] or by 'or' (*aut*), which is understood as indicating an exclusive disjunction ('either it is day, or it is night' is true, but not 'either it is white or it is black' because something might well be neither) (SHI.3.1–3). Sentences with 'if'—which occupy almost all of Boethius's attention—are hypotheticals 'by connection' and those with 'or' hypotheticals 'by disjunction'. It might well seem, from what Boethius has said so far, that since hypothetical sentences have categorical sentences as their elements, 'if' and 'or' are here logical operators on sentences (so, 'if it is day, it is light' has the form 'if p, then q', where p and q stand for sentences), and that hypothetical syllogistic will therefore be a sentence logic. Some features of the following discussion strengthen this impression. Boethius considers that there are 'accidental' conditionals—such as the sentence, 'If fire is hot, the heavens are spherical'—which are true because it is always the case that when the antecedent is true, the consequent is true, even though there is no causal relation between what they each assert (SHI.3.6). Since there is no term in common between the antecedent and the consequent in this conditional, it seems as though 'if' must be connecting two sentences. Moreover, Boethius gives as fundamental rules for the logic of hypotheticals two of the Stoic indemonstrables (those which amount to *modus ponens* and *modus tollens*), even using numbers, in the Stoic way, to stand for, it seems, sentences: 'if the first, then it follows that there is the second,' and 'if the second is not, it follows necessarily that the first is not" (SHI.4.6). Nonetheless, the impression that Boethius is propounding a sentence logic is misleading (though it reflects on some of his sources and perhaps on a certain strand in his thinking); his development of the theory of hypothetical syllogisms will show why.

In order to understand how Boethius goes about his task, it is useful to bear in mind what Aristotelian (categorical) syllogistic achieves pragmatically (by contrast with, for instance, modern symbolic logic). Aristotelian syllogistic provides its students with a neat, well-ordered table—which medieval logicians even managed to encapsulate in a mnemonic verse—that shows which inferences are valid and which not. If they wish to formulate a syllogistic argument, they need only follow one of these inference patterns; if they wish to check whether an argument in syllogistic form is valid, they need only see whether it conforms to one of them. Aristotle does, indeed, provide the apparatus to reconstruct his tabulation from first principles, but the table can be learned and used by someone who has no very thorough understanding of the principles on which it is based. Boethius's aim is to construct a similar sort of table for hypothetical syllogisms. He has, therefore, to set out a classification of the different sorts of hypothetical sentence, and the different types of valid hypothetical syllogism that can be formed with them. In doing so, he sticks almost entirely to those constructed with 'if', because his main interest is in hypothetical syllogisms from connection. An initial division of sentences containing 'if' is into four types, according to the different combinations of positive and negative antecedents: Boethius gives the examples 'If it is day, it is light', 'If it is not an animal, it is not a man', 'If it is day, it is not night', 'If it is not day, it is night' (SHI.3.5). Later in Book I, Boethius considers the various types of hypothetical sentences there might be—many more indeed than these four. The four he has considered involve merely two terms, but there might be sentences involving three terms ('If, if it is A, then it is B, it is C' and 'If it is A, then if it is B, it is C') and four terms ('If, if it is A, it is B, then if it is C, it is D') (SHI.5). Boethius goes on to consider other factors that might multiply the number of types of hypothetical sentences: they might be qualified by the modes of necessity or possibility, and each of these modes might be understood in two ways—necessary or possible eternally, or necessary or possible so long as the thing signified by the term in question exists. The resulting number of types of hypothetical sentence begins to reach the absurd (SHI.6.6–8.7). And it might be increased still further, Boethius speculates (SHI.9.2), if the sentences are also quantified—but Boethius rapidly drops this idea, and also gives up thinking about modally qualified hypothetical sentences, on the grounds that, whatever the modality of the individual parts, the connection represented by the conditional itself is always necessary (SHI.9.4–5). Even Boethius's simplified scheme leaves him with a long and tedious enough task in tabulating the valid hypothetical syllogisms.

Books II and III are devoted to this tabulation. Boethius usually talks about sentence types and the syllogisms they make—just as in his classification of the four different two-term hypothetical sentences in Book I—by using letter symbols: for instance: *si est a, non est b*. How should such a formula be translated? One possibility would be as 'If A is, B is not', where 'A' and 'B' would stand for states of affairs and the formula would be very close to 'If *p*, not-*q*'. But Boethius frequently stops to give examples to substitute for the letters, and these examples are always predicates, such as 'man', 'animal', 'ensouled'. It is clear, therefore, that Boethius understands *si est a, non est b* as meaning 'If it is A, it is not B', where 'it' designates a vague subject for the predicates in question. Further evidence that Boethius is thinking about terms and their connections, not about sentences, comes quite soon in his discussion of the simplest sort of hypothetical syllogism, formed from one of the four two-term hypothetical sentences classified in Book I and a categorical sentence: for instance, 'If it is A, then it is B; it is A; so it is B'. Boethius's main concern here is to show, by reference to the two fundamental principles he has discussed in Book I (what we call *modus ponens* and *modus tollens*), that a conclusion follows here from affirming the antecedent, or from denying the consequent, but not from denying the antecedent or affirming the consequent. For three of the four forms of the two-term syllogism, he has no trouble. When he considers 'If it is not A, it is B' (SHII.2.3–4.6), however, he finds a problem. Nothing should follow from affirming that it is B, or from affirming that it is A (that is, denying that it is not A). But, says Boethius, in the nature of things it will always be the case that it is not A *does* follow from affirming that it is B, and that it is not B *does* follow from affirming that it is A. The reason, as Boethius makes clearest much later in his work (SHIII.10.4) is that 'If it is not A, it is B' will be true only if 'A' and 'B' are immediate contraries, that is to say, predicates such that everything is either A or B, and nothing is both A and B (such as 'corporeal' and 'incorporeal'). If 'A'and 'B' are immediate contraries, then it will indeed be the case that if something is not A it is B, and not B it is A. Had Boethius been thinking in terms of sentences, this complication would not have arisen.

Boethius moves on from hypothetical syllogisms involving two terms to those involving three terms. He needs to set out the various possible permutations of three terms in hypothetical sentences and then show what syllogisms can be constructed using these sentences as premisses. Three-term hypothetical sentences are of two types: (I) a complex hypothetical made up of a hypothetical and a categorical subsentence, and (II) a complex hypothetical made up of two hypothetical subsentences. Boethius first considers type I, which divides into two schemes: (Ia) categorical + hypothetical (If it is A, then if it is B, it is C) and (Ib) hypothetical + categorical (If, if it is A, it is B, it is C). (Ia) and (Ib) each contain eight forms, which are determined by the positioning of (one or more instances of) 'not'. For instance:

Ia (1). If it is A, then if it is B, it is C
Ia (2). If it is A, then if it is B, it is not C
Ia (3). If it is A, then if it is not B, it is C
Ia (4). If it is A, then if it is not B, it is not C

(followed by the same four, except with the antecedent 'If it is not A'). Boethius then considers what syllogisms can be formed using these premises. In Ia(1), for example, if (Syll 1) 'it is A' is made the second premise, it follows as a conclusion that if it is B, it is C. When (Syll 2)'if it is B, it is not C' is made the second premise, then according to Boethius it follows as a conclusion that 'it is not A'. This second syllogism seems very strange to those who are thinking of Boethius's hypothetical syllogistic as sentence logic. If we take Ia(1) as being like 'If *p*, then (if *q*, then *r*)', then the second premise needed in order to reach the conclusion 'not *p*' is 'not (if *q*, then *r*)' rather than what Boethius's formulation, read as sentence logic, would be: 'if *q*, then not-*r*'.

Some commentators have read passages such as this, where Boethius talks about the negation of a conditional, as evidence that he was proposing a form of sentence logic in which, unlike what happens in 'standard modern logic', the contradictory negation of 'if *p*, then *q*' is 'if *p*, then not-*q*', and so 'if *p*, then not-*q*' is in effect assimilated to 'not (if *p*, then *q*)'.[24] Christopher Martin has explained incisively why this analysis sets out from the wrong point.[25] Boethius lacked the conceptual apparatus to envisage negation (or other logical operators) operating on sentences. Boethius's own discussion shows him using examples of different predicates (such as 'man', 'ensouled' and 'animal') in order to work out which hypothetical sentences are true. He lists various constraints about the relation between the terms of such sentences which must be fulfilled if they are to be true. (SHII.4.5–7). Some are designed to avoid redundancy. In premisses like that of Syll 2, it must not simply be the case (Constraint 1) that if it is B, it is C (which would make 'If it is A' redundant), nor (Constraint 2) that if it is B it is A (which would make 'If it is B' redundant). But Boethius also adds (Constraint 3) that in premisses of this form A and B must be such that if it is A, it is B. Interestingly, given Constraint 3, it seems possible to formulate an argument in sentence logic that validates a sentence-logic analogue to Syll 2; and similarly for other syllogisms of this type and their constraints.[26] So far from proposing an odd form of sentence logic, what Boethius seems to be doing is to work out, painstakingly, by example, a term logic of hypotheticals that mimicks the results of standard modern sentence logic.[27]

When Boethius comes (SHII.9.1) to classifying three-term hypothetical sentences of type II (those which involve two hypothetical subsentences) he notices that they can be classified into 'figures', on analogy with categorical syllogisms, because like them—although Boethius does not state this explicitly—they have a middle term, which appears in both of the hypothetical subsentences making up the whole hypothetical. And so, where the shared term occurs in the consequent of one, and the antecedent of the other, the hypothetical belongs to the first Figure (for example, 'If it is A, then it is B, and if it is B, then it is C'); where it occurs in the antecedent of both, the hypothetical belongs to the second Figure (for example, 'If it is A then it is B, and if it is not A then it is C'); and where it occurs in the consequent of both, to the third Figure (for example, 'If it is A then it is B and if it is C, then it is not B'). As earlier, Boethius's exposition consists in going through each of the permutations of quality of the various terms and working out what syllogism can be made using the hypothetical as a First premise. His labour is a little less than it might be, because he sees that a second-figure hypothetical can act as a premise for a syllogism only if the quality of the antecedents of the two hypothetical subsentences is different, and that a third-figure hypothetical can be used as a premise only if the quality of the consequents of the two hypothetical sub-sentences is different (SHIII.3.7–4.1; 6.3–6.4). Boethius ends his tabulation by considering four-term hypothetical sentences (SHIII.6.4–9.7):

1. If, if it is A then it is B, then, if it is C then it is D
2. If, if it is A then it is B, then, if it is C then it is not D

And so on until number 16 is reached—

16. If, if it is not A then it is not B, then, if it is not C then it is not D.

The syllogisms constructed with these sentences as premisses present the same problem as those that use the three-term hypothetical sentences of type I. With (1) as first premise, Boethius believes (SHIII. 9.2) that two syllogisms can be made, one (completely unproblematic) which has as second premise, 'If A then B' from which follows 'If C then D', and one which has as its second premise 'If C then not D' from which follows, apparently strangely, 'If A then not B'. As earlier, there are constraints on how the terms involved are related in especial, that if it is A, it must be C, and if it is B it must be D (SHIII.7.1). And again, if the premisses and constraints are translated into term logic, a sentence-logic analogue to Boethius's strange conclusion can indeed be proved.[28] Boethius finishes (SHIII.10.3–11.7) the treatise with a brief look at hypothetical syllogisms 'from disjunction', which he considers can all be translated into ones 'from connection' and so need little separate consideration.

Some recent research by Anthony Speca into the history of hypothetical syllogistic explains the reason behind the strange mixture of elements in SH.[29] Aristotle and the early Peripatetics regarded as hypothetical those syllogisms that either involve a proof 'through impossibility' (an indirect proof) or are based on a shared assumption. Aristotelian hypothetical syllogistic had nothing to do with sentence (as opposed to term) logic. But even by the time of Alexander of Aphrodisias, at the beginning of the third century AD, the doctrine of the hypothetical syllogism was strongly influenced by the sentence logic of the Stoics. By the time of Boethius, the confusion between these two, originally completely different logical theories was complete. Speca points to one particularly clear aspect of it. In the Aristotelian tradition hypotheticals were described, whatever their verbal form, as being 'by connection' if they expressed an entailment, and 'by disjunction' if they expressed an incompatibility; the distinction was, therefore, semantic. In the Stoic tradition, however, the logical form of sentences was distinguished according to their linguistic form—that is, according to whether they contained 'if' or 'or' as their main logical operator. Boethius, although not developing a sentence logic like that of the Stoics, follows the Stoic way of distinguishing between hypotheticals by connection and by disjunction, through whether they use 'if' or 'or'—even though, as the account above shows, he then passes over hypotheticals with 'or' in a few paragraphs. Speca also shows that in TC, Book 5, where Boethius discusses Cicero's list of the Stoic indemonstrables, there is a similar mingling of Stoic and Peripatetic ideas.

Boethius says that SH is a fuller and more systematic treatment of the subject than anything he can find in Greek (SHI.1.3–4). He credits Theophrastus and Eudemus with providing a start, but claims that it will be his own task to fill in the detail and repair their omissions. No doubt Boethius, who knew early Peripatetics such as Theophrastus and Eudemus only through much later sources, never had the chance to see their genuine teaching on hypothetical syllogisms and picked up, instead, a doctrine in which it was already mixed up with Stoic ideas; although he was also sufficiently distant from Stoic logic to fail to see—except sporadically, in Book I—hypothetical syllogistic as sentence logic. Book I is probably highly derivative. But there is no good reason to doubt that the detailed working out of the patterns of hypothetical syllogisms in Books II and III is Boethius's own, just as he claims.[30]

The Topics and Their Place in Logic

In what turned out to be the last years of his life, Boethius turned to a new area of logic—topical argument. He translated (in two versions) Aristotle's *Topics* and probably wrote his now lost commentary on it; he commented on Cicero's *Topics* (TC) and, last of all (ca. 522–523), wrote his textbook *On Topical Differentiae* (TD).[31] Boethius's commentary and textbook are almost the only surviving sources for what the theory of topical argument had become by late antiquity. In neither of these two works does it seem likely that Boethius is closely following or translating an existing text. Marius Victorinus had already written a commentary, now lost, on Cicero's *Topics*, which Boethius knew. But since Boethius justifies his own commentary by the inadequacy of his predecessor's, it is reasonable to assume that he did not greatly rely on it. In this commentary, besides discussing topical argument, Boethius discusses Stoic logic and ventures into a whole variety of philosophical questions—universals, causation, and free will.[32] TC seems, then, to have a special importance as the most original and personal of Boethius's didactic works.[33] The task of the first three books of TD is to compare the different classifications of topical inferences proposed by Cicero and Themistius, so the work explicitly draws its classifications from these authors. But Boethius substitutes for Cicero's by then arcane legal examples (which he explains in detail in his commentary) straightforward philosophical ones, and he himself was presumably responsible for the presentation of the principles of topical reasoning (Book I) and the analysis of how the two classifications coincide. Book IV is devoted to the topics as used in rhetoric, and draws especially from Cicero's *On Invention*.[34]

Boethius's writings on the Topics are among the most bewildering parts of his work for the modern reader, since they seem to have little in common with any part of modern logic (or with any other modern discipline), and, without some explanation, it is not at all clear what they are about, even in the broadest sense. Yet there are four immediate reasons for looking at them carefully. First, in the years immediately before his imprisonment Boethius himself seems to have become interested in this field above all others. He tackled it through four pieces of work (the translation of, and lost commentary to, Aristotle's *Topics*, as well as TC and TD) which, from the cross-references he makes, he clearly regarded as complementing each other. Second, as mentioned, Boethius's works are almost the only available source for the way in which topical reasoning developed in late antiquity. Third, Boethius's theory of topics was extraordinarily influential on medieval logic, although often in ways Boethius himself would not have envisaged.[35] Fourth, it turns out that his discussions of the topics help towards understanding one of the areas of Boethius's logic and its influence that especially interests modern philosophers: his treatment of conditionals and propositional inferences.

At the origin of this branch of ancient logic is Aristotle's *Topics*. The *Topics* is a handbook for the participants, especially the questioners, in argument contests like those made familiar through Plato's earlier dialogues. It provides them with a set of strategies which, using a knowledge of four elements—definition, property, genus and accident—will enable them to find arguments to defeat their opponents. Most of the work is devoted to outlining these strategies one by one, in some cases adding an explanation of the basis of the argument. The individual topics which Boethius found listed by Cicero and Themistius were mostly different from Aristotle's, as was their arrangement; topical reasoning had been developed over the centuries by a process largely impossible now to reconstruct.[36] Moreover, rhetoricians—especially lawyers—had developed their own system of topics (*loci*), more suited to the particular, practical arguments they had to make. (Boethius would devote Book IV of TD to explaining how these topics resemble and differ from the topics used by logicians.) Nonetheless, the two most distinctive features of Aristotle's topics still characterized the discipline Boethius expounded. Study of the topics remained a supposedly practical means of learning how to make arguments, and these are arguments which, unlike those treated in the *Analytics*, are not supposed always to arrive at the truth but merely to reach conclusions that are plausible.

Boethius sets out this understanding of the purpose of the topics at the beginning of TC, when he divides the whole of logic into finding and judging. Whereas the Stoics limited their logic to judging, Aristotle developed both parts of the subject: finding in his *Topics*, judging in the *Analytics* and *Sophistical Refutations*. Boethius also explains that topical arguments are not necessary but 'truth-like'. In TD he introduces a subtler distinction, which makes this position clearer. Arguments, he explains, are either 'readily believable' or 'necessary' or neither or both. Topical arguments must be readily believable, and they may also be necessary or not necessary.

Boethius's understanding of topical argument as readily believable turns out, however, to be different in an important way from Aristotle's. For Aristotle, the difference between the sort of arguments found by the topics and those discussed in the *Analytics* is in the character of their premisses, not in the validity of the arguments. The arguments he examines in the *Analytics*—demonstrative arguments—are ones that have necessary sentences as their premisses ('necessary' in Aristotle's sense of physically necessary). Topical arguments, by contrast, can have premisses that are merely *endoxa*, 'commonly accepted' or 'plausible'. Since the premisses are not necessary, neither are the conclusions. The process of argument itself is, however, of exactly the same, logically valid syllogistic form as that described in the *Prior Analytics*, which ensures that, given the truth of the premisses, the conclusion too will be true. From the way Boethius sets out the parts of logic in TC, it would seem as if he shared this view. For there, when he considers the different parts of logic concerned with judgement, he applies the distinction between necessary, plausible[37] and false to the sentences from which arguments are made, rather than to the way they are put together into an argument, which is the object of a special part of logic, dealt with undivided in the *Prior Analytics* (see Table 1). It would seem reasonable to imagine that, in the logic of discovery too, the distinction between necessary and plausible would apply to the premisses of arguments, rather than to their structure. Yet, as will become clear, many of the arguments found by the topics as

Table 1.

	Finding	Judging
Necessarily true sentences	———	*Posterior Analytics*
Plausible sentences	*Topics*	[Obvious, says Boethius, once we can judge necessarily true, and false sentences—1047C]
False sentences	[presumably not wanted]	*Sophistical Refutations*
Putting-together of sentences	———	*Prior Analytics*

Boethius presents them, though syllogistic in form, are *not* formally valid; they are plausible rather than necessary, not just on account of their premisses but also because of their structure.

Using the Topics to Find Arguments

Arguments are sought in order to answer questions. In Boethius's account of topical reasoning, a question is, strictly speaking, a conjunction of two sentences, in one of which a predicate is attributed to a subject and in the other of which it is denied of the same subject–for instance, 'The heavens are spherical or the heavens are not spherical' (*A* is B or *A* is not *B*) (TC 277:28–278:21 [1049A]). A topical argument is made in order to establish the truth of one side of the conjunction. In practice, Boethius usually presents questions as simple interrogatives ('Is *A B*?') and shows how the topics enable us to answer in the affirmative. For Boethius, this means that someone arguing that *A* is *B* needs to establish that '*B*' is a term either greater than or equal to '*A*'—that whatever '*A*' refers to is also referred to by '*B*'; and someone arguing that *A* is not *B* needs to show that '*B*' is not greater than or equal to '*A*'. Although (as will become clear) topical arguments are not usually genuine syllogisms, because usually they are not valid, Boethius envisages their structure as syllogistic, and so he presents the arguer's task as finding a middle term. (The middle term, as explained above, is the term common to the two premisses of a syllogism, which does not appear in the conclusion.) Suppose, then, I were trying to find an argument that would form a genuine syllogism. If I were starting from a conclusion of the form 'Every *A* is *B*' or 'No *A* is *B*', it would be straightforward to provide the premisses from which it follows, once the middle term had been found, since 'Every *A* is *B*' follows from 'Every *A* is *M*, and every *M* is *B*', and 'No *A* is *B*' follows from 'No *A* is *M*, and every *B* is *M*'. Exactly the same process applies to finding topical arguments, which Boethius envisages as syllogistically structured, although the premisses and conclusion are usually indefinite, not universal, and the range of usable middle terms is far wider, precisely because the arguments need not be valid but merely plausible.

The theory of the topics systematizes the process of looking for middle terms.[38] It does not make it a purely mechanical process, requiring no non-logical knowledge—that would be impossible. Rather, it shows the arguer where to look in the stock of knowledge he has in order to find the middle term he needs. The basis of the theory is the idea that if '*A* is *M*' and '*M* is *B*' are to be true, what '*M*' designates must be related to what '*A*' designates and to what '*B*' designates. The arguer needs, therefore the, systematic method of considering what is related to some given sort of thing or attribute: that is to say, a classification of the different sorts of relations that can obtain. And it is exactly this that the so-called topical *differentiae* provide. Suppose that I want to show that a tree is not an animal. One of the sorts of relation classified by topical theory is being-the-definition-of. Once I light on it, I will quickly see that it gives me the middle term I need, since the definition of animal, I know, is animate substance capable of perceiving, and I know that trees are not animate substances capable of perceiving (TD 1196C).[39]

The way Cicero arrived at his list of topical *differentiae*, Boethius believes, was to start off from those closest to the matter in question and move to those farthest away from it (TC 315:34–39 [1088BC]). Three of the *differentiae*, according to Cicero, 'inhere in the matter at issue': these are 'from a whole', 'from parts' and 'from a sign' and they classify respectively the relations of being-the-definition-of, being-the-integral-parts-of and being-the-meaning-of. Boethius's idea is that, in using these *differentiae* to make an argument, the arguer analyses the thing he is arguing about and finds the middle term. The question about the tree in the last paragraph is one example; there the analysis is by definition. Or, suppose I am asked whether the soul is corporeal: using the *differentia* 'from parts', I reason that the soul is made up of a vegetative, a perceptive, and an intellective part; none of these is corporeal, and so the soul is not corporeal (TD 1196D). There are, however, many more relations that provide middle terms than these three which arise from analysing the matter at issue. The other relations are derived from things related to what is in question—by being its genus, its species, or its specific *differentia*, by being similar or contrary to it, greater or less than or equal to it, associated or incompatible with it, or its cause or effect or antecedent or consequent. For instance, suppose I want to argue that it was right to execute a major traitor such as Catiline. I know that a more minor traitor, Gracchus, was executed, and so, using the *differentia* 'from the lesser', I argue: Gracchus was executed as a traitor, but Catiline was a greater traitor; so it is right for Catiline to be executed (TD 1199BC). All these *differentiae*, according to Cicero's classification, are 'intrinsic'. There is just one extrinsic *differentia*, 'from judgement'—extrinsic because, instead of using skill to make an argument, the arguer rests his case on the fact that most people or those who are skilled in such things hold it to be so (TD 1199CD; TC 386:8–388:20 [1168B–1169D]); as when, for instance, the lawyer simply cites a legal document (309:19–29 [1082AB]).

Perhaps a little embarrassingly for Boethius, he had inherited from Themistius another, different list of the *differentiae*, which classifies them into three main groups (intrinsic, extrinsic, and intermediate). Since Boethius claims that the list of topical *differentiae* is complete, a main aim of TD is to show that the two schemes coincide, although sometimes one divides up a *differentia* the other leaves undivided, and their labels are often different. This coincidence supports the idea that topical theory is not just a haphazard list of some ways to discover arguments but provides an exhaustive and systematic classification (cf. TD 1194B–1196A) of where to look for middle terms.

In addition to the *differentiae*, the student of the topics is also taught a series of 'maximal sentences' (*maximae propositiones*)—and, rather confusingly, both the *differentiae* and the maximal sentences are known as 'topics', or *loci* (which means *places* in Latin). Maximal sentences, Boethius explains, are universal and are so well known that there is nothing more fundamental by which they are demonstrated (TD 1185A); other sentences 'are embraced in them as bodies are in place' (TC 280:22 [1051D])—hence their name. What Boethius has in mind are very general self-evident statements of truth or of high probability. For instance, in the example given above of the *differentia* 'from the lesser', the maximal sentence is: 'What applies to a lesser thing applies to a greater one'. There are many more maximal sentences than there are topical *differentiae*: indeed, the topical *differentiae* give the *differentia*—the characteristic, differentiating feature shared by the maximal sentences grouped under each of them. Boethius lists just one maximal sentence for each of the *differentiae* he distinguishes, but often there are variations in the maximal sentences assigned to the same *differentia* in his different lists (Cicero's in TC, Cicero's in TD, Themistius' in TD). So for the *differentia* 'from an efficient cause', Boethius gives these three maximal sentences for it: 'Those things which have natural efficient causes are themselves also natural' (TD 1189C); 'Where there is the cause, the effect cannot be absent' (TD 1199A); and 'Everything should be considered according to its causes' (TC 306:37 [1079B]). As these comparisons suggest, the maximal sentences which belong to a given *differentia* state the same theme, more or less generally and from different perspectives.[40]

What is the purpose of the maximal sentences?[41] Boethius does not explain, but it seems that a maximal sentence will help to suggest exactly what sort of argument can be made using the *differentia* in question. Take, for instance, the example just given. I want to show that justice is natural. I scan through the list of *differentiae* in my mind and decide that 'from efficient causes' will give me the middle term I need, since the efficient cause of justice is people being gathered together. The maximal sentence (MS1) 'Those things that have natural efficient causes are themselves natural' shows me the exact argument I need to give (TD 1189C):

1. It is natural for people to be gathered together.
2. The gathering together of people is the cause of justice.

So

3. Justice is natural.

As this example illustrates too, for discovering arguments the maximal sentences might be helpful, but they are hardly necessary. Once I had spotted that the efficient cause of justice gave me my middle term, I could have formulated (1)–(3) without bothering to recall a the maximal sentence.

Boethius himself is silent about exactly how arguers are supposed to use maximal sentences to find arguments. Instead, he asserts that maximal sentences give arguments their force (TC 280:24–27 [1051D]; TD 1185B–D). This lends credence to the idea that, whereas the *differentiae* derived from the argumentative strategies set out in Aristotle's *Topics* and so were directly linked to finding arguments, the maximal sentences came from the explanations of the arguments that Aristotle sometimes attached to his instructions.[42] By understanding how the maximal sentences relate to the arguments to which they give force, it may be possible to gather how Boethius imagined that topical arguments work as arguments—a question he tends to gloss over in his practical approach to the subject.

Boethius gives two ways in which maximal sentences can give force to a topical argument: either from within, as one of its premisses, or from outside. In practice, however, Boethius never explicitly illustrates any of the topics with an argument in which a maximal sentence appears, and so it is just the second, external way of giving force which needs to be considered. Boethius gives this example (TC 280:34–40 [1052A]; TD1185CD). I want to show that an envious person is not wise. I do so as follows:

4. An envious person is distressed by the good things of others.
5. A wise person is not distressed by the good things of others.

So

6. An envious person is not wise.

Boethius comments that the maximal sentence, although not included in the setting out of the argument, 'provides it with force. For faith in this syllogism comes from the sentence through which we know that things which are different in definition are also different themselves.'[43] He goes on (TD 1185D–1186A) to explain that maximal sentences contain all other sentences and hold the force of these sentences and of the way in which the conclusion of the argument follows (*ipsius conclusionis consequentiam tenent*). In the light of the example here, and his practice in TC and TD, these rather vague comments seem to mean that the maximal sentence is (a) a general statement of which the conclusion of the argument it supports is a particular exemplification and (b) the principle on the basis of which the premisses of the argument yield the conclusion. So, in the example, the conclusion 'An envious person is not wise' is an instance of the general principle that things which are different in definition are also different themselves, and it is this principle that allows this conclusion to be drawn from the premisses (4) and (5). The same applies, for instance, to the argument about justice exemplifying the *differentia* 'from efficient causes'. Its conclusion, 'Justice is natural', is a particular instance of the principle stated by the maximal sentence (MS1) 'Those things that have natural efficient causes are themselves natural', and it is this principle that allows the conclusion to follow from the premisses (1) and (2). The same pattern is repeated time and again in Boethius's discussion of the individual topics.

So far as the nature of topical arguments is concerned, it is (b) that is of special interest. Many pieces of topical reasoning need to be 'provided with their force' by a statement of the principle on the basis of which the premisses yield their conclusion because, without such a statement, they do not constitute a valid argument. Consider, for instance, (1)–(3): (3) follows from the conjunction of (1), (2) and the maximal sentence (MS1), not from (1) and (2) alone. Similarly, the conjunction of (4) and (5) does not entail (6), given the indefinite quantity of its premisses (they are not '*every* envious person', '*no* wise person'); a valid argument for (6) will need the maximal sentence to be stated explicitly as a premise.[44]

Boethius did not, however, envisage a fully formulated piece of topical reasoning as involving an explicit statement of a maximal sentence, so as to make the argument (as we would say) formally valid. Rather, the maximal sentences provide the arguments with their force from the outside. Topical reasoning does not usually consist in formally valid argument but in argument that people will in general accept as leading to a true conclusion, so long as the premisses are true, because they also accept the truth of the (unstated) maximal sentence. Maximal sentences state certain very general truths about things, in the light of which we can formulate a far wider range of reliable arguments than if we were confined purely to factual premisses and the rules of Aristotelian syllogistic. There is, though, a considerable variation in the reliability of these maximal sentences. Some propose analytic truths: these include, arguably, the two illustrations discussed above and the maximal sentence—'Where the definition is absent, that which is defined is also absent'—given for the argument to show that trees are not animals (TD 1196CD), discussed at the beginning of this section, along with such obvious examples as 'where the material is lacking, that which is made from the material is lacking' (TD 1189D—for the *differentia*: From matter). But there are a number of maximal sentences that are far from being analytic or near-analytic truths. Consider the *differentia* From the lesser (TD 1199BC), discussed above. Even if Boethius's sample argument is made firmer by taking the first premise as 'Gracchus was *rightly* executed as a traitor', the conclusion that it is right for a greater traitor, Catiline, to be executed might well be contested: perhaps, for instance, a great public good could be achieved by showing Catiline mercy, precisely because his treason was so obvious and serious. The maximal sentence giving force to this topical argument, 'What applies in a smaller thing applies in a larger one', is at best a rule of thumb. As for the maximal sentence for the one topic Cicero judged to be extrinsic, From judgement, 'What seems so to all or to many or to learned people should not be contradicted' (TD 1190CD), it is doubtful whether it is even that. One of the tasks facing the medieval logicians who studied Boethius's works on topical reasoning would be to sort out these, from the philosopher's point of view, very different sorts of maximal sentence.

The Aim of the Monographs and Boethius's Project

Is there anything which ties together the various works discussed in this chapter and links them to Boethius's more general aims, other than the interest that they all, except D, evince in forms argument? The monographs all have one feature in common, which has been referred to but not yet explicitly mentioned—their practicality. Boethius aims to enable a student with a good memory and an orderly mind, but without much logical ability or any grasp of fundamental logical principles, to master the use of categorical and hypothetical syllogistic, of logical divisions and of topical argument. TC, a commentary not a monograph, is more discursive and less of a practical guide.

There is also another feature that unifies all these works, including TC, and links them closely to the way Boethius carries out his logical project in his commentaries. As a logical commentator, Boethius is remarkable, by comparison with his Greek contemporaries, for how he follows Porphyry (and sometimes goes behind Porphyry to Aristotelians such as Alexander of Aphrodisias) in taking an Aristotelian approach to Aristotelian logic.[45] The same attitude to choosing sources is found in the monographs. D is based on Porphyry himself. For SC and ISC, the sources given are Porphyry again, along with the very early Aristotelians Eudemus and Theophrastus, whilst Eudemus and Theophrastus are cited also in SH. Although Boethius probably did not know the works of these early Aristotelians directly, nonetheless they are his explicit points of reference; though Boethius was in fact conveying a doctrine heavily influenced by Stoicism, he believed that he was transmitting Aristotelian teaching. For his works on topical argument, the position is slightly different because of the importance of his fellow Roman, Cicero. But Boethius's other main source here is Themistius, a follower of Aristotle although living in the fourth century, when Neoplatonism was dominant.[46] And, had the commentary on Aristotle's *Topics* survived, the Aristotelian bias of this area of Boethius's work would have been even more evident.

5

THE *OPUSCULA SACRA*

Metaphysics, Theology, and Logical Method

At first sight, the five short treatises known as the *opuscula sacra* ('short theological works') do not seem to form a coherent group. OSI, II, and V—each of them logically rigorous discussions of intricate points in Christian doctrine linked to contemporary debates—appear very different both from OSIV, an unargumentative presentation of the central doctrines of Christianity, and OSIII, an elegant philosophical essay, which, like the *Consolation*, contains no explicit mention of any specifically Christian doctrines. On closer scrutiny, the five works fit closely together. If, as seems likely, it was John the Deacon (probably the same John who became Pope in 523) who made and published the collection, he showed by doing so how well he understood the mind of his pupil and friend.[1] Looking at these five works together not only makes their positions clearer; it also helps in understanding the attitudes to philosophy and religion of the man who, not much later, condemned and imprisoned, would write the *Consolation*.

OSIV: The Demands of Christian Doctrine

OSIV—sometimes called *On the Catholic Faith*—is by far the least studied of the *opuscula*, and until recently it was considered by many scholars to be inauthentic.[2] It is a good place to begin looking at the *opuscula*, not only because it may well have been the earliest written[3] but also because implicitly it sets out the range of problems the other treatises will tackle.[4]

OSIV begins by stating that the Christian faith is based on the authority of the Bible and continues with a succinct summary of orthodox teaching on the Trinity and a statement of how catholic doctrine differs from the Arian, Sabellian, and Manichaean heresies. Boethius then traces the course of sacred history from the creation and the fall of the angels, the fall of man (where he pauses to condemn the Pelagian heresy), through the early chapters of Genesis, the story of Moses and the Ten Commandments, and, briefly, the kings and prophets of Israel. The incarnation, virgin birth, life, and crucifixion of Christ are described, and Boethius comments briefly on the different Christological heresies of Eutyches and Nestorius. Finally, Boethius tells how Christianity has spread through the whole world, and how Christians who have lived well can look forward to the resurrection of their bodies after the end of the world. 'And this is the most important point of our religion', he adds (OSIV. 240–243 [254–258])[5], 'that it holds that not only do our souls not perish, but that our very bodies too, which the coming of death had undone, are restored to their pristine state in our future blessedness.' The resurrection of bodies was one of the Christian doctrines that pagan Neoplatonists found most rebarbative. But here, and throughout OSIV, as Henry Chadwick has observed,[6] Boethius emphasizes the aspects of Christianity least amenable to rational explanation from first principles.

Christianity, as Boethius presents it, is a revealed religion, built around a particular sacred history, and with precise doctrines that it is heretical to infringe. What room is there for a philosopher—someone such as Boethius, trained in the Neoplatonic reading of Aristotelian logic, and in metaphysics—to exercise his intelligence in discussing and defending such a faith? It might seem that there is none, and that someone in Boethius's position should have compartmentalized his mental life, accepting the doctrines of Christianity on faith and pursuing his philosophical investigations in isolation from them. Such, indeed, is the approach that some superficial readings of the *Consolation* do attribute to him there. But Boethius's answer to the question, as the *opuscula* indicate, is positive. In OSV—probably the earliest treatise except for OSIV—Boethius shows how Aristotelian logic and physics, carefully applied, can show up heretical Christology as incoherent and how, so long as they are taken to apply to God only up to a certain point, they can help to describe orthodox doctrine. In OSI and OSII, Boethius develops much further the idea that Aristotelian logic can be used to discuss God, but only to a certain extent. There are systematic differences between logically acceptable constructions about created things and those about God, because of the radical difference between God and created things. In OSI, Boethius turns to Neoplatonic metaphysics to explain these differences and, in OSIII, using the same metaphysics, he is able to answer a problem about God that, unlike the doctrines of Christ and the Trinity, concerns non-Christians and Christians alike and can be set out in doctrinally neutral terms.

Against Eutyches and Nestorius: OSV: The Background

The *opuscula* seem not to have been works designed for a wider public but rather for Boethius's close circle of educated friends and teachers.[7] OSI was addressed to his father-in-law, Symmachus; OSII, III, and V were addressed to John the Deacon, and OSIV may derive from his lessons with John. Nonetheless, there is a more public background to the themes of V, especially, and of I and II. The background to V reflects both a wider and narrower historical framework.

The wider framework is the story of the heresies that split the Church in late antiquity and have influenced its regional development ever since. As its title explains, Boethius's treatise is an attack on the two contrasting Christological heresies of Nestorius and Eutyches. Orthodox Christian doctrine, as enunciated at the Council of Constantinople (381), held that the Father and the Son are consubstantial. Nestorius (380–450/1), a priest of Antioch, wished to qualify this position, by emphasizing the distinction between the two natures, human and divine, of the incarnate Christ and positing two distinct hypostases (for the meanings of this word, see below), that of the Word and that of the man, to correspond to them. Eutyches (ca. 370–after 451) proposed his doctrine in opposition to Nestorius, although it was itself declared heretical by the Council of Chalcedon (451). So far from there being two natures of Christ and two hypostases, Eutyches held that not only is Christ one hypostasis but also that in Christ, even when incarnate, there is just a single, divine nature: his position was known, therefore, as 'monophysitism' ('one-nature-ism'). Although both Nestorianism and monophysitism were condemned by the orthodox Church in Constantinople, they had a wide following further East—Nestorianism in Persia and monophysitism (in a moderated form, championed especially by Severus of Antioch) in Syria, Egypt, and Ethiopia.

The narrower historical framework for OSV was provided by the split between the Catholics of Italy and of Byzantium and the attempts to heal it. From the Western point of view, the formula endorsed by the Council of Chalcedon in 451—that Christ was made known *in* two natures, but without division or separation—was a satisfactory solution. In Byzantium, Monophysites were more influential. For them, the idea that Christ continued to exist *in* two natures, human and divine, after the Incarnation seemed to break up the unity of Christ, although they were willing to accept that Christ exists *from* two natures. In his *Henotikon*, Acacius, Patriarch of Constantinople (471–489), though condemning Nestorius as well as Eutyches, did not reaffirm the statement from Chalcedon that there are two natures *in* Christ. It was this deviation from Chalcedonian orthodoxy that had provoked the Acacian schism.

There had already been attempts to find a formula to reconcile the Eastern and Western Churches. Gelasius (Pope from 492–496) had tried in his treatise *On the Two Natures*, which unfortunately misrepresented his opponents' views too seriously to be effective.[8] Boethius may have been incited to apply himself to this theme by a letter, probably dating from about 513, addressed by a group of bishops from the lower Danube region in the Eastern Empire to the Pope.[9] The bishops, who wanted to remain loyal to the doctrine of Chalcedon, found themselves under pressure from the Monophysites, who were at that time being favoured by the Emperor. They were therefore seeking the support of the Pope, and they proposed a compromise Christological formula that they hoped was close enough to Chalcedon for the Western Church to accept as a basis for reconciliation. They proposed to accept the Chalcedonian '*in* two natures', but to add that Christ is also '*from* two natures', thus making a certain concession to Monophysite sensibilities. But the Pope was closed to any compromise and any change from Chalcedon. Although Boethius's treatise gives the appearance of logical detachment, it reaches a conclusion of immediate relevance to the doctrinal controversy of the time, by accepting the formula that Christ is '*in* and *from* two natures.' But the philosophical interest of OSV and its importance from the point of view of theological method are far greater than this rather technical conclusion might suggest.

Against Eutyches and Nestorius: OSV: The Argument

In OSV Boethius is defending what he considers to be the orthodox doctrinal position—that Christ is one person in and from two natures. What is the matter at issue? All the parties to the debate agreed that God, though one, consists of three persons (in OSI, Boethius would examine how this can be so), and that one of these persons, the Son, became incarnate as a man, Jesus Christ. The orthodox doctrine defended by Boethius is a straightforward statement of this position, couched in more technical terms than in OSIV, where (196–197 [207–208]) he is content to say that in the incarnate Son of God 'both the splendour of divine nature shines forth and the taking on of human fragility is apparent.' Christ is one person, with two natures, divine and human: these two natures are not merely what he is 'out of'—what he takes his nature from; he is actually 'in' these two natures—he has them both. The difficulty about the orthodox doctrine is that it seems paradoxical: how can one person have both a divine nature and a human one? In their contrasting ways, Nestorius and Eutyches sought to lessen this paradox. As Boethius puts it (OSV, 5.391–399 [7–16), the errors of each come from supposing that where there are two natures there must be two persons. Nestorius accepted that Christ has two natures and therefore argued that in him there are two persons, one divine, one human. Eutyches took the other alternative and, accepting that there is only one person in Christ, denied that he has two natures.

Boethius begins by defining his two main terms, 'nature' and 'person'. It is characteristic of his method that he opts for definitions in line with the Aristotelian tradition of logic and metaphysics, rather than trying to find ones that would suit his position by making it easy to accommodate a single person's having two natures. For 'nature', he recognizes a variety of definitions (OSV, 1), but the one he will use in his argument is that which he adds almost as if it were an afterthought: 'nature is the specific *differentia* which informs a thing' (OSV, 1.111–112 [57–58]). The context of this definition is the system of genera and species of Aristotle's *Categories*, as put forward by Porphyry in his *Isagoge*. A species is distinguished from the genus to which it belongs by a differentiating feature that is an essential to all its members but does not belong to members of other species of the genus. According to the logical tradition, men are differentiated from other animals by being rational. The tradition, however, envisaged two species of rational animals:

those that are immortal (pagan gods) and those that are mortal (men). The *differentiae* of the species man were thus usually taken as being rationality and mortality.

'Person' (*persona*) was a word which, by Boethius's time, already had a long and complicated history in discussions of Christian doctrine.[10] From the time of Tertullian (end of the second century), the word *persona* had been used to describe each of the Father, Son, and Holy Spirit. In the language of the time *persona*, it seems, denoted a distinct character in a drama, or a distinct grammatical person ('I', 'you', 'he'); and this made the term appropriate, since various passages of the Bible distinguished the Father, Son, and Holy Spirit as speakers. Greek writers used the word *prosōpon*, which had a similar meaning. In the third century, however, they began to use the word *hupostasis* (usually anglicized as 'hypostasis') for each of the three persons, and by the fourth century, in theological discourse *persona* (and also *prosōpon*) had taken on the sense of *hupostasis*. For Aristotle, *hupostasis* means a substance, in the sense of a thing (for example, a particular man or tree) which acts as a substrate for accidents (literally the word means 'something which stands under'). But the Aristotelian meaning was stretched and altered by Plotinus and his followers. They were especially interested in how one and the same hidden form could make itself known in different realizations: these realizations were *hupostaseis*. In particular, according to the Platonists God was made manifest as the One, as Intellect and as Soul, the three *hupostaseis* ('hypostases') of their intelligible world.[11] This way of thinking deeply influenced Christian ways of conceiving the Trinity, both in Greek and Latin theology, and in official pronouncements of dogma, such as the decrees of the Council of Chalcedon (451), around which revolved the Christological controversies of Boethius's time.

Boethius, however, goes out of his way to link his definition of *persona* to an Aristotelian understanding of *hupostasis*. He is helped by a linguistic accident. In order to explain this, it is useful to introduce a new term—one obviously different from any word Boethius himself uses—for things that belong to Aristotle's first category (*ousia*): I shall accordingly speak of 'first-category things/individuals/universals'. The linguistic accident consists in the fact that the usual, Latin translation of *hupostasis* was *substantia*. But *substantia* was also the Latin word used by some, including Boethius himself, as the word for first-category things.[12]

Boethius begins (OSV, 2) his discussion of *persona* by using, as he had done in defining 'nature', Porphyry's version of the Aristotelian system of species and genera. Here it serves as an instrument to set out clearly the ordinary language meaning of *persona*, which Boethius intends to follow. According to Aristotle's and Porphyry's system, things are either first-category things or not, and they are either individuals or universals. What we mean by 'person' (*persona*), says Boethius, is an individual substance; Boethius uses the word *substantia* and clearly means a first-category individual. But, he explains, a person is not just any individual substance: it is—in the definition which became classic in medieval theology—'an individual substance of a nature endowed with reason' (OSV, 3.171–172 [4–5]: *naturae rationabilis individua substantia*).[13] 'Nature' here indicates (in line with the fourth meaning of the word) that 'rational' refers to a specific *differentia*.[14] A person is, then, an individual substance, the species of which has as a *differentia* endowed-with-reason. This *differentia* belongs to species under both of the two main genera of substance: corporeal substance and incorporeal substance. There are rational corporeal substances (men—Boethius does not include pagan gods, who would also fit this description, in his survey), but there are also rational incorporeal substances—God, angels, and souls. All of these are persons.

Boethius's definition has the great advantage of making both individual men and God—Father, Son, and Holy Spirit—persons. But it is an advantage bought at a high price, because the definition implies that the persons of the Trinity, like individual men, are first-category things, and God would therefore be straightforwardly classifiable under the Aristotelian categories—a view Boethius himself would reject in OSI (see below). Boethius therefore goes on to propose a way in which God can be *substantia*—or, rather, three *substantiae* and hence, since they are rational and individual, three persons—without this making him into a first-category thing (or, even worse, an assemblage of first-category things).

Boethius begins by setting up some distinctions that very clearly belong within the framework set by the *Categories* but unscramble part of the confusion created by the fact that Aristotle uses *ousia*, the substantive from the verb 'to be', to refer only to first-category things and that, in his logical writings, Boethius himself refers to first-category things, both individual and universal, as *substantiae*, a word that etymologically has the meaning of a substrate for accidents. In this treatise, Boethius makes the verb 'to be' (*esse*) and its substantive (*essentia* = *ousia*) into the broadest ontological terms, which apply to particulars and universals in (so Boethius's scheme implies) all of the categories. He takes a rare Platonic term, *ousiōsis*—in Latin, *subsistentia*—

and redefines it for his Aristotelian scheme. Existing things are *subsistentiae* if they do not require any accidents in order to exist (OSV, 3.210–211 [45–46]), and they themselves are not accidents (cf. OSV, 3.247 [83]). *Substantia* is explicitly defined in accord with its etymology: things are *substantiae* if they act as the subject for accidents, which they thus enable to exist (OSV, 3.211–213 [46–49]). First-category universals are *subsistentiae*, but not *substantiae*. First-category individuals are both *subsistentiae* and *substantiae*: they do not need accidents in order to exist since they are 'informed by their distinguishing properties and specific *differentiae*' and they allow accidents to exist by being their subjects.[15] It is easy to see, then, that an individual man will, as well as existing—being an *ousia*—also be a *subsistentia* and a *substantia*; and Boethius adds that, being an individual and rational substance, he will also be a person. God, too, is an *ousia* and a *subsistentia* and—Boethius adds, using both the Latin and the Greek terms—he also 'stands under' (OSV, 3.253–254 [89–90]). God, then, is a substance; but at the moment Boethius avoids the noun *substantia*—he just says that God *substat*—and he quickly explains that God is a substance in a different way from created things. For God 'standing under' is not a matter of being a substrate for accidents but rather of so coming before all things 'that he is also under all things as their origin (*quasi principium*), bringing it about for them all that they subsist' (OSV, 3.262–264 [99–101]). God, however, is not one but three substances (this doctrine is simply accepted from revelation); Boethius has, though, to point out that Latin Church usage forbids this way of speaking, although it is standard in Greek, where the Trinity is described as three *hupostaseis*. Latins must talk, rather, of God as three persons; yet this point is merely a matter of usage, since 'person' has been defined as a type of substance.

Boethius's sleight of hand in this discussion is to introduce the term 'person' as if it had been defined as a rational, individual substance-*in-the-sense-used-here*, whereas in its definition 'substance' had meant first-category thing. With regard to the ordinary meaning of 'substance' used here—a substrate for accidents—the switch is slight, since, on Boethius's view, whatever is a substrate for accidents is also a first-category thing. But with regard to the special meaning of 'substance' which applies to God—that which is the origin of being—the change is all-important. There is no reason to believe that a substance in this sense belongs to the categories at all; and that is precisely the result Boethius needed.

The discussion so far has just been a preliminary to Boethius's attempt to show that orthodox Christology is logically coherent, and the positions of

Nestorius and Eutyches are not. In section 4, he sets out his arguments against Nestorius. Then he turns to Eutyches. Eutyches accepted that the natures of man and God had to be united at some time in order to make the single—as he held it to be—nature of Christ. In section 5, Boethius asks when this union could have taken place and finds fault with any of the answers. In section 6, he asks how the two different natures could be united, and he argues that they could not. Section 7 explains the orthodox teaching on Christ's person and two natures, and section 8 discusses a new question, about the humanity assumed by Christ: was it that of Adam before the Fall, or was it the fallen state of humanity, or neither? As this summary suggests, OSV is more disparate than the other *opuscula* and much longer (it is nearly as long as the other four combined). I shall discuss just the arguments that are more interesting in themselves and in illustrating Boethius's method.

Nestorius claims that Christ not only has two natures, which Boethius accepts, but that he is two persons. He is open to the obvious objection that he has not given an account of the incarnation at all. According to Nestorius, all that happens, it seems, is that a person with a divine nature, Christ, remains God, and a separate person with a human nature, a man, remains a man. So far from being a miracle, on the Nestorian account nothing out of the ordinary takes place at the coming of the Saviour, and there is no reason why the birth of Jesus should be linked to our salvation any more than that of any other child (OSV, 4.320–336 [60–78]). The Nestorian defence would need to be (and apparently was[16]) that the two persons—one of divine, one of human nature—were joined together in some specially close way, so that while they remained two, they nonetheless constituted a single thing which combines man and God. Boethius refuses to consider the possibility of such a special form of conjunction. Rather, he insists (OSV, 4.286–289 [24–27]) that the conjunction can only be 'by being placed together'—what happens when two bodies are put side by side without any effect on each other.

The argument against Eutyches is more complicated. Eutyches holds—rightly, according to Boethius—that Christ is one person, but wrongly that he is one nature. Eutyches does not, however, deny that, as well as a divine nature, there was also at some time a human nature that went into the constitution of the incarnate God. Eutyches is willing, then, to allow (OSV, 6. 559–574 [83–99]) that Christ is 'from' (*ex*) two natures but not that he is 'in' (*in*) two natures—not that the two natures remain distinct in him. The most interesting critical argument Boethius develops is that the two natures must be distinct, because there are conclusive conceptual objections to any of the ways in which they could merge. If the two natures do not remain distinct, then either (*i*) the divine nature becomes human, or (*ii*) the human nature becomes divine, or (*iii*) the two natures combine into a single, divine-human nature. Boethius considers that (*i*) gives rise to contradictions—most strikingly that divine nature, which is immutable, would be changed.[17] In order to reject (*ii*) and (*iii*), Boethius describes what happens when one thing is transformed into another or two things are mixed (OSV, 6.497–558 [18–82]). He draws heavily here upon Aristotle's *On Generation and Corruption*.[18] Suppose *a* is to be transformed to *b*: *a* and *b* must both consist of matter (which is the same for each) and of the quality (or qualities)—call them *A* and *B*—which make them each what they are. In the transformation, the matter of *a* and *b* will simply be combined, and *B* will act on *A* so as to destroy *A*. For instance, suppose I throw my glass of wine into the sea: its winey quality is destroyed entirely by the watery quality of the sea. Boethius also explains mixing of *a* with *b* on the same lines. In this case, the matter of each is combined, but *A* and *B* act on each other to produce a new, mixed quality *A-B*. For instance, suppose I throw my glass of wine into a glass of water: what results is winey water (or watery wine). According to Boethius's model, transformation or mixing will be able to take place only when the things in question both share common matter and have qualities that are able to act and/or be acted upon by each other. Boethius thinks that all bodily things share common matter and that incorporeal things lack all matter. It follows that neither can incorporeal things be transformed into or mixed with each other, nor can a corporeal thing be transformed into, or mixed with, an incorporeal thing because in none of these cases will the sharing-of-matter condition be satisfied. In the case where human nature is transformed into, or mixed with, divine nature, an incorporeal thing, the human soul, would have to be transformed into, or mixed with, an incorporeal thing, God; and a corporeal thing, the human body, would have to be transformed into, or mixed with, an incorporeal thing, God. All these transformations or mixings are, on Boethius's account, impossible, and so (*ii*) and (*iii*) can be rejected.

Boethius's argument does not, in fact, seem quite fair. He relies on the point that there is no common matter between the things to be transformed or mixed. But he and Eutyches both accept that Christ is one person. The question is about whether human *nature* can be transformed into, or mixed with, divine *nature*; and these natures correspond to the qualities (*A* and *B*, winey or watery) not to the things (*a* and *b*, wine and water) in Boethius's physical example. Even leaving aside this problem, Eutyches could well object that Boethius is unfair to demand that the way human and divine combine should fit with what Aristotelian physics allows, when—as his explanation of how the persons of the Trinity are substances indicates—he does not make his own theories fit God to the logic and physics of created things entirely but only to a certain extent, by analogy. Nestorius could make the same complaint about Boethius's refusal to countenance a special form of combination. More generally, however, Boethius does win a philosophical victory over both heresies through the way he defines nature. The fault of both heresies is to have imagined that a nature was something individual, like a person, and so that, if Christ is one person, he has just one nature, or if he has two natures, he has two persons. By insisting that a nature is something universal, not individual, Boethius removes the grounds for maintaining this correspondence.[19] He may not, as he hoped, have shown that the Nestorian and Monophysite positions are incoherent, but he has succeeded in removing their main philosophical motivation.

What has been Boethius's method in this treatise? It turns out to have been very different from that of the philosophically educated theologians, such as Augustine and Marius Victorinus, who certainly influenced Boethius in his terminology and positions. In OSV, it is the logical side of Boethius's Neoplatonic training that dominates (as it turned out to dominate in his life's project of translation and commentary). Boethius puts the orthodox position, and tries to expose the failing of heretical views, by using the language and techniques of the *Categories* and the *Isagoge*, with some help from Aristotelian physics. He does not, however, suggest that logical language is directly suitable for expressing Christian doctrine. As his treatment of substance and person shows, he believes, rather, that at a certain point, in dealing with the Godhead, ordinary logical distinctions provide merely an analogy to guide us in our understanding. OSI, II, and III will develop this methodological position.

God, Predication, and the Trinity: OSI, II, and III: The Background

OSI, II, and (at first sight, surprisingly) III form an interlinked group, and it is tempting to see them as all dating from late in Boethius's career, at the beginning of the 520s, just before Boethius's elevation to high administrative office and his dramatic fall from power and prosperity. OSI and II can be linked, like OSV, with the doctrinal controversies of the time, although more loosely.[20] In 519, a group of monks from Scythia, led by John Maxentius, travelled to Rome. Like the Greek bishops who had written to the Pope six or seven years earlier, they were proposing a formula for reconciliation between Eastern and Western Churches—this time with the implicit approval of the Eastern regime, which was looking to end the schism. One of the positions the Scythian monks wanted to be accepted was that 'one of the Trinity suffered in the flesh' (Theopaschism). They thereby directed attention to the question of the Trinity itself: in what sense can its members be counted, so that the phrase 'one of the Trinity' makes sense? Although Boethius does not deal explicitly with Theopaschism, it seems at least that his decision to go back to Augustine's thinking about the meaning of the Trinity, and then to seek a more rigorous logical understanding of the mystery, was provoked by the Scythian monks.

OSII and Augustine's *On the Trinity*

The part of Augustine's work to which, in particular, Boethius turned was Book V of *On the Trinity*. He had, no doubt, already studied it carefully when writing OSV; it is one of the (untypical) passages where Augustine, as Boethius would do, is probing the applicability of Aristotelian logical terminology to God. Augustine is answering an objection (V.3.4) raised by the Arians to the doctrine of Christ's divinity. They drew attention to the usual division between two sorts of predication: (*i*) substantial—as when its genus, species or *differentia* is predicated of something ('Socrates is a man', 'Socrates is rational') and (*ii*) accidental—when an accidental attribute is predicated of something ('Socrates is white', 'Socrates is sitting'). God, both orthodox Christians and Arians would agree, is immutable, and so nothing can be predicated of him accidentally. Therefore, the Arians concluded, every predication about God is substantial. But the Father is ungenerated and the Son is generated, and since these are substantial predications, it follows that the Son and the Father differ in substance.

Augustine replies (V.5.6) by rejecting the dichotomy his Arian critics proposed. With regard to God, a predication can be relative, rather than substantial, and yet still not be accidental. No accidental predications are true of God, because accidental predications concern only attributes that can be lost or diminished. When God is called 'Father' or 'Son', these predications are not accidental, because God never began and never will cease to be a Father and to be a Son. Nor, however, are 'Father' and 'Son' said substantially, because the Father is a Father only from the fact that he has a Son, and the Son a Son only from the fact that he has a Father. Predications about God are, therefore, either substantial or relative. Augustine goes on, beyond answering the Arians' criticism, to explain how predications about God in the other eight categories set out by Aristotle are to be understood (V.8.9). Predications about posture, condition, places, and times (*situs*, *habitus*, *loca*, *tempora*) should be taken metaphorically; those about making or doing can be taken literally—indeed, in a sense they are only ever literally true of God; those about being acted upon are never true of God, 'so far as the substance by which he is God is concerned.' With regard to quantity and quality (V.10.11), predications of such attributes to God ('God is good', 'God is great') are substantial, not accidental. The reason is that, when things other than God are, for instance, great, they are great by participating in greatness: the things are not greatness itself, and it is 'one thing for them to be (i.e., to be a mountain or a house), another thing for them to be great.' But God is greatness itself (and goodness itself, and so on, for any of the qualitative or quantitative attributes true of him). When, therefore, we say 'God is great', we are not saying that he has some extra attribute beyond what he is substantially. Attributes such as unity, divinity (*deitas*), greatness, goodness, eternity, and omnipotence are truly predicated of God the Trinity, because he is in himself all of these things, and also they are predicated of each person of the Trinity, without thereby entailing that there is a plurality of things sharing the attribute. (Augustine's reasoning seems to be that if, for example, Socrates, Plato, and Cicero are all good, by participation, there will be three good things, whereas, when we say that the Father, Son, and Holy Spirit are good, we are referring in each case to one thing which is good by substance, God.) By contrast, 'Father', 'Son', and 'Holy Spirit', because they are predicated relatively, are said only of the person in question, not of the other persons or of the Trinity (cf. V.8.9–V.11.12).

OSII is a summary of one aspect of this Augustinian teaching, which Boethius turns into a rather neat deduction.[21] He starts by observing that the thing referred to by the terms 'Father', 'Son,' and 'Spirit' is a substance. Since it is one simple substance, not consisting of parts, then

(1) Whatever is truly predicable of God's substance, will also be truly predicable of each of the three persons separately.

Boethius gives (OSII.61–64 [65–68]) a list of such substantially predicable attributes, although he makes it clear that there are others too: truth, goodness, omnipotence, substance, immutability, virtue, wisdom (and earlier he has mentioned deity (*deitas*), and justice: OSII.21,37 [22,39]). From (1) it follows by *modus tollens* that

(2) An attribute that is not truly predicable of each of the three persons is not substantially predicable of God.

The attributes that the words 'Father', 'Son', and 'Spirit' predicate are not truly predicable of each of the three persons (for instance, the Father is not the Son), and so by (2) these attributes are not substantially predicable of God; nor, for the same reason, is triunity. Rather, these attributes are predicated *ad aliquid*—relatively. Both OSI and OSIII will explore more deeply this area which Augustine had investigated and OSII considers neatly but quite superficially.

On the Trinity: Boethius's Metaphysical Scheme

OSI is very clearly related to the problem discussed in OSII and to Augustine's speculations: indeed, in his prologue Boethius explicitly links his enterprise to his predecessor's, hoping, as he puts it (OSI, Prol. 30–32 [31–33]) to bring forth the fruits from the seeds of Augustine's arguments. First, Boethius shows that the persons of the Trinity cannot differ in number: difference in number is made by accidents (OSI, 1, 3) but God has no accidents—a view that he justifies by setting out concisely first a division of the branches of knowledge and then a metaphysical scheme (OSI, 2). Boethius then examines (OSI, 4) in some detail how predications in the different categories apply to God, before turning to explain (OSI, 5–6) how in particular relatives (such as 'Father' and 'Son') are to be applied to him.

Boethius's metaphysical scheme uses the distinction brought out by Augustine in *On the Trinity* V between God, who depends on nothing outside himself, and other things, which have their attributes through participation.[22] But he takes into account a complication. On Augustine's scheme, the contrast was between predications of quality and quantity about creatures, all of which are accidental and are to be interpreted in terms of participation, and such predications about God, which are substantial. Where a thing has an attribute by participation, it is possible for the thing to lack that attribute: Socrates might not, for instance, be white. The same is not true of God's substantial attributes. They are, in modern terms, essential: it is impossible for God to exist and not have these attributes (I shall, in what immediately follows, use the term 'essential', rather than Boethius's 'substantial', because it is clearer to the modern reader.) Creatures too, however, have attributes that (at least arguably) are essential. Although Socrates, who is in fact white, might be black, it is impossible that he should not be human and, as human, be mortal and capable of reason. Boethius must explain how the relation Socrates has to his attribute of being human differs from that to his attribute of being white.

To do so, Boethius uses an Aristotelian idea, though within a Platonic setting. Ordinary things (perhaps—see below—all created things) are concrete wholes, made from matter and form. By form, Boethius understands the essential form, by which a thing is the sort of thing it is: for instance, the humanity by which Socrates is a man. It is the form that makes the concrete whole what it is—a man, a horse, a stone. Using the infinitive of the verb 'to be' (which I shall usually leave untranslated because of the varieties of meaning it has), Boethius says that 'All *esse* comes from form' (OSI, 2.83 [21]: *Omne namque esse ex forma est*). Things exist only by being things of a particular sort. In the everyday world, however, forms inform matter. Boethius takes the example of a statue (OSI, 2.83–91 [21–29). The statue can be seen as a series of combinations of form with matter, where in each case it is the form that makes it what it is. Basic, formless matter is made into earth by the forms of dryness and heaviness; earth is made bronze by the form of bronze-ness; and the bronze is made into a statue by taking on the shape of (for instance) a human. Boethius chose this example probably because it illustrates the point in a dramatic, tangible way. His real point is not to do with the forms, in the sense of shapes, of statues, but with the essential forms of particular members of natural kinds, such as individual men.

God, however, is not a concrete whole of matter and form but 'form without matter'. Therefore, in Boethius's phrase, he 'is one and is what he is', whereas with other things

> . . . each thing has its *esse* from the things from which it is, that is from its parts, and it is this and that, that is its parts joined together, but not this or that singly. For example, since earthly man consists of soul and body, he is body and soul, not body or soul separately. Therefore he is not what he is. (OSI, 2.94–99 [32–37])

Given the context—a contrast between God, who is pure form, and form-matter composites—the 'parts' here must be matter and form and, in his example, Boethius must be thinking, in the Aristotelian way, of the soul as the form of the body. The comment that (a) 'each thing has its *esse* from its parts' does not contradict the previous statement (b) 'all *esse* is from form' so long as (b) is taken as setting a necessary, but not a sufficient, condition. To be a man, a horse, or a stone means being a concrete whole, consisting of matter as well as form. One aspect of the contrast between God and other things, then, seems to be that, since God is pure form, there is no distinction between him and his essential form, whereas Socrates is not his humanity. Boethius goes on to bring out a further contrast. Another reason why God 'is that which he is' is that 'there is nothing in him other than what he is' (OSI, 2.103–104 [41–42]). Forms themselves, explains Boethius, have no accidental attributes: in a concrete whole, it is the matter subject to the form which also acts as a subject for the various accidents. Whereas God is great because greatness is an aspect of his substance, for Socrates to be wise requires the matter that already acts as a substrate to the essential form of humanity also to be a substrate for the accidental quality of wisdom.

What, according to Boethius, is the relationship between God, who is described as form,[23] and the essential forms that make things what they are (the humanity that makes Socrates a man, for example)? At the end of the section, he explains that the forms that are in bodies are improperly so called: really, they are not forms but images (*imagines*) of those forms that are not constituted in matter and from which they derive (OSI, 2.113–117 [51–56]). This comment suggests that Boethius wishes to keep the Aristotelian notion of a particular essential form (the particular humanity by which Socrates is a man), but to qualify it by adding that such forms are really images of genuine forms. Genuine forms exist independently and have no contact with matter. But, despite the plural, it also seems that in the final analysis there is not a plurality of independently existing genuine forms but just the one, true form, God. Boethius's language when he describes the study of theology (see below) bears out this view.

Boethius's world, therefore, seems to consist of God and of concrete wholes, each with an immanent Aristotelian-type essential 'form', that should not really be called a form but an image—an image of a true form that is itself an aspect of the divine mind.[24] These concrete wholes are the substrates for a whole variety of accidents. The division of the branches of knowledge (OSI, 2.68–83 [5–21]) which begins this section of OSI fits this metaphysical scheme well. Boethius draws on Aristotle's *Metaphysics* (VI, 1026a 6–19); Aristotle himself was probably drawing on Plato.[25] Each branch of speculative knowledge is concerned with forms. Both natural science and what he calls 'mathematics' are concerned with the forms immanent in particular bodily things. Whereas natural science studies them in the state in which they really occur—in changing things, mathematics considers them without the matter they inform and therefore without change. Both these branches of knowledge are sharply contrasted with theology, where (OS1, 2.81–82 [19–20]) we look at 'that form which is truly a form and not an image.'

At first sight, however, Boethius's remarks about numerical difference do not seem to fit in with the rest of this picture. He says it is the variety of accidents that make difference in number (OSI, 1.56–57 [24–25]; cf. OSI, 2.119–20 [57–58]). Such a comment could be taken to indicate a view (something like the material essence realism of the early twelfth century[26]) according to which a universal essence of, for example, humanity is shared by men, who are differentiated by their accidents—no one has quite the same combination, because—failing all else—no two bodily things can have the same accidents of place. Yet this view does not fit with his idea of the essential form as an image, nor with the way Boethius develops the notion of concrete wholes in OSIII. It is more plausible to imagine that Boethius thought of concrete wholes as intrinsically individual in virtue of the individuality of their essential, immanent 'forms' (that is to say, images), but that—as OSIII shows[27]—he considered that any concrete whole will have accidents and then reasoned that, at least for bodies, there was bound to be a difference at least in the accidents of place. Boethius may have considered that, in order for a difference in number to be established between x and y, there needs to be some feature in which x and y differ; in any concrete whole, variety of accidents will uncontentiously provide such a feature. Conveniently, because pure forms have no accidents, Boethius could then rule out any sort of numerical difference between the persons of the Trinity.

On the Trinity: The Argument

The metaphysical scheme set out in section 2 provides the background for the theory of predication, which Boethius will use to explain the doctrine of the Trinity. First, in section 3, Boethius locates more precisely the problem about God's triunity that needs to be resolved. The mere fact that when we talk about God we repeat the name of God three times, saying 'God the Father, God the Son, God the Spirit', does not imply that there is plurality in God. We can name the sun thrice—saying 'sun, sun, sun'—without thereby making there be three suns, or we can name the same one thing repeatedly using synonyms, as in 'sword, blade, rapier'. But these analogies merely show where the real difficulty about the Trinity lies. 'God the Father', 'God the Son', and 'God the Spirit' are neither the same expression nor synonyms. For instance, whereas the sword is the blade, he who is the Father is not the Son. Boethius's theory of predication will try to explain how this can be the case, although God is one.

In framework, the theory of predication is like that in Augusine's *On the Trinity*, part of which was used in OSII. Understanding how predications can be made about God requires a grasp of the differences between different sorts of predications about creatures There is a distinction between (a) predications in the category of substance, (b) those in the two accidental categories of quality and quantity, and (c) those in the other categories of accident. With regard to (b), predications of quality and quantity, the difference between those about God and those about creatures are exactly as Augustine said: in calling God 'just' or 'great', we are not just saying that he has this quality or quantity but that he is justice or greatness itself.[28]

Boethius elaborates the Augustinian framework in three ways. One of them is unimportant. Boethius wishes to insist that, in one sense, it is wrong to think of God as *substantia* at all. Of course, there is a sense of *substantia*—that which provides a substrate for accidents—in which, as OSV had made clear, the word does not apply to God. But that sense does not seem to be at issue here. The denial is, rather, that any predication even in the category of substance is true of God. It is motivated by Neoplatonic negative theology, according to which the One cannot be defined or limited by having anything predicated of it. But Boethius does not take this line of thinking very far, especially since it clashes with the view that God is more properly the subject of substantial predications than anything else and predications about qualities and quantities are substantial where God is concerned; rather, the negative theology becomes little more than a verbal gesture, as when he writes (OSI, 4.189–190 [16–18]) that if we call God 'just', we signify 'a quality indeed, but not an accident, but one which is substance, *but beyond substance*.'

The other two elaborations are more important. With his metaphysical scheme in the background, Boethius wishes to show how (leaving aside the idea that God is beyond substance) even in the category of substance there is a difference between predications about God and those about creatures. He writes

> . . . when we say 'substance' (either a man or God), it is said as if that of which it is predicated were that thing with regard to its substance (*ipsum sit substantia*)—for instance, 'A man/God is substance'. But there is a difference, because a man is not entirely the very thing which is man (*ipsum homo*), and so is not substance. For what he is, he owes to other things, which are not man, But God is the very thing which is God (*hoc ipsum Deus*). For he is nothing other than what he is, and so he is the very thing which is God (*ipsum Deus*). (OSI, 4.201–207 [29–36])

Although the language of this passage is difficult, Boethius's main idea is clear. A man—a standard example of a substance in Aristotelian logic—exists only as a concrete whole, in which the form of humanity is composed with matter, and this substrate also acts as a substrate for accidents. It is, then, in a sense wrong to say that the man—the entire concrete whole—is a substance. By contrast God, who is not a concrete whole and so entirely the very thing which is God, *is* rightly called a substance. (Boethius would presumably have accepted that second substances—genera and species—are genuinely substances. But according to his metaphysical scheme, these second substances do not exist independently, but only within God.)

The third elaboration is the most wide-reaching. Leaving aside for the moment the category of relation, which the next two sections will examine in detail, Boethius considers attributes in the six remaining categories (place, time, condition, doing, posture and being-acted-on). Whereas a predicate of substance, quality, or quantity 'points out the thing to which it applies and shows that it is something', predicates in these six categories show only 'as it were the external circumstances of the thing (*circumstantiae rei*)' and 'in a certain way attach something to it extrinsically' (OSI, 4.270–274 [100–104]). Boethius even goes so far as to say (OSI, 4.216–217 [44–45]), somewhat inconsistently, that attributes in these six categories are not predicated at all: presumably, he regards them as improper, measured by the standard of substantial, qualitative or quantitative predications.[29] Boethius's idea is that when I say 'Socrates is a man/ white/ six-foot tall', I am saying something about the thing itself which is Socrates, and that I could use a term such as 'the man', 'the white thing', 'the six-foot tall thing' to refer to Socrates. By contrast, when I say, for example, 'Socrates is in the forum' or 'Socrates runs wearing a toga', I am talking only about how Socrates relates to things other than himself. Although it would be hard to give a rigorous justification for this distinction, Boethius could argue that even if you pointed out someone by saying, 'Look at the thing in the forum, running and wearing a toga', if I wished to follow him I could not go on using those characteristics to mark him out, once he had stopped running, left the forum, and changed his clothes; I would need to use substantial and/or qualitative and/or quantitative attributes to go on identifying him.

Improper, extrinsic predications can be made both about creatures and God. But—and this is the central point for Boethius's argument about the Trinity—whereas all intrinsic predications, not just those in the category of substance but those of quality and quantity too, are substantial when applied to God, extrinsic predications are not. Indeed, they are subject to some special restrictions. Posture and being-acted-on cannot be predicated of God at all, and the only predications of place or time about God are 'God is everywhere' and 'God is always'.[30] Condition and doing can be attributed to God, as in 'He rules possessing all things' but, as in the case of a similar sort of predication about creatures, 'nothing is said of that which is the *esse* of either <God or his creatures>, but this predication is entirely concerned with exterior things and all of these in a certain way refer to something else' (OSI, 4.251–253 [80–83]).

When, in section 5, Boethius finally turns to the category of relatives, it is fairly clear that these sorts of predications will be extrinsic, since one of the marks distinguishing extrinsic predications is that they are not concerned with things themselves but with their relations to other things. He gives two arguments to bear out this view. The first (OSI, 5.283–294 [5–16]) contrasts a predication such as (*a*) 'Socrates is white' (an intrinsic predication) with a predication in the category of relation, such as (*b*) 'Socrates is a master (i.e., of a slave)'. In (*a*), there are just two elements involved, Socrates and whiteness. The whiteness informs him as an accident. If it ceases to inform him, he ceases to be a white thing. In (*b*), it is obviously not the case that the slave informs Socrates as an accident. Rather, Socrates is informed by a certain power of coercion over the slave. So there are three elements: Socrates, the slave, and Socrates's power of coercion over the slave. When the slave goes, Socrates ceases to be called a master, because this power of coercion no longer informs him. This power of coercion is, therefore, not something that informs Socrates as an accident through itself but through something extrinsic—there being at hand a slave or slaves. The second argument (OSI, 5.300–

306 [22–29]) points to the way in which a relation can become true of something without that thing doing anything or being changed in any way: if I stand on your right hand side, you thereby acquire the relation of being to the left of me.

Boethius draws the conclusion that relative predications, whether about God or creatures, not being concerned with the properties a thing has in itself, 'cannot alter, change or in any way vary any essence' (OSI, 5.308–310 [31–33]). It follows, he says, that if the Father, Son, and Spirit differ only in the relative predications that can be made about them, they will not thereby be made into different things, although there is some sort of difference that can scarcely be understood, which might be called a difference of 'persons'. Therefore, Boethius can conclude (OSI, 6.333–339 [1–7]), that

(3) There is number, threefoldness, in God, because relation entails there being more than one thing to be related, but
(4) There is unity also, because the terms of the relation do not differ with regard to anything that can be predicated intrinsically (*secundum se*).

Boethius ends by explaining (OSI, 6.345–356 [14–26]) that, although the relation of master to slave requires two different things, some relations such as similarity and equality are reflexive. On this basis, he claims that

(5) The relationship between the divine persons is like that of the same to the same.

Here, he admits, the parallel between predications about creatures and those about the creator no longer holds. We cannot find in other things relations of paternity, filiation and spiration that are like those between the same thing. But this, says Boethius, is the result of the 'otherness' attached to transitory things: 'we should not be guided by any imagination but raised up by simple understanding (*intellectus*).' As well as this—necessary and explicable—departure from logic, however, there is a tension between (3) and (5) that Boethius does not explain.

This worry aside, OSI can be seen as an ambitious and mostly successful attempt to build on Augustine's discussion of God and predication, and the adaptation of it in OSII. It is hard to see how the qualitative and quantitative attributes of the Christian God can be understood except as being substantial, but, as Augustine saw, if the personal attributes of Father, Son, and Spirit are construed in the same way, the three persons will not be one God.

Augustine offered a rather *ad hoc* solution, by making relations in God neither substantial nor accidental predications. Boethius, by contrast, not only spells out the metaphysics on which his theory of predication is based, but also draws his main distinction, not between substantial and accidental predications but between intrinsic predications (of substance, quality and quantity) and extrinsic ones. His treatment of relation is thus justified by the rest of his discussion of predication. Much more thoroughly than Augustine, Boethius follows through the parallel between the logic of statements about created things and the logic of statements about God, pointing to the precise moment where it breaks down—although even there, he suggests, the breakdown is more apparent than real, a result of our taking too much notice of the images of transitory things and not fully using our understanding.

OSIII: The Rules

The connections between OSIII and OSI and II are very evident. Like them, the main argument of OSIII concerns a difficulty about predication, involving God (although here, creatures also). And the metaphysical system set out as a series of definitions and rules near the opening is much the same, although refined and extended, as that presented in OSI. These connections have usually been obscured by two factors. First, the other *opuscula* are all discussions of Christian doctrine, whereas OSIII contains nothing explicitly Christian. As will become clear, this difference is superficial: OSIII is concerned with the same area of problems as OSI and OSII, but since the particular difficulty it tackles does not involve a specifically Christian doctrine, its language is neutral. Second, there are the rhetorical and allusive opening paragraphs of OSIII, which explain the purpose and occasion of the treatise. Many modern scholars have surmised from them that Boethius is replying to a request from John the Deacon for explanation of an obscurity in a work of his called the *Hebdomads* ('Groups of Seven').[31] In consequence, OSIII seems to be a surviving part of an area of Boethius's philosophical activity otherwise lost, rather than a close relation of the other *opuscula*. But Boethius's words cannot indicate the existence of an otherwise unattested work of his, the *Hebdomads*, since he explicitly says that he keeps the 'hebodomads' in his memory and thinks about them to himself, rather than share them with people who cannot tolerate anything that does not amuse them.[32] Perhaps John had used the word '*hebdomades*' as an example of a rather overblown, pretentious title for a philosophical treatise—as we might now ask a friend with philosophical pretensions whether he has treated a certain topic in his *Critique* or his *Tractatus*. John's tone might have been playful and teasing: he may well have already known that Boethius had no grand philosophical treatise hidden away in his top drawer.[33]

Boethius responds to John by explaining why he does not compose such a work, and why, for the same reason, the answer to his question will be put in a deliberately obscure and brief form, so as to make it inaccessible to the unworthy. To this end, Boethius says (OSIII.14–16 [14–17]) that, 'as is usual in mathematics and other subjects', he will begin by stating the 'terms and rules from which he will produce all that follows'. After the 'Rules' (as I shall call them for short), Boethius says (OSIII.47–48 [53–55]) that 'each will be fitted with (*aptabitur*) its arguments by the prudent interpreter of the reasoning'. Modern scholars usually take this to be a remark about using the Rules as axioms in the argument that follows, and they consider that the Rules themselves are common conceptions, of the sort defined in Rule 1. But Boethius might equally well have been asking the prudent interpreter to supply the arguments necessary to support the Rules (which do not appear to be self-evident, even to the wise). The Rules seem rather to set out the general metaphysical background and terminology for the argument that follows than to provide it with axioms in any thorough or rigorous sense.[34]

The meaning of the first and ninth Rules is clear. (R1) defines a 'common conception of the mind' (*communis animi conceptio*) as a statement that everyone accepts who hears it. They are of two sorts. For the first variety, 'everyone' is taken literally: for instance, 'If you take equals from equals, the remainders will be equal' is a statement that no one who understands it will deny. The second variety of common conceptions are those accepted not by everyone, but just by everybody who is learned; Boethius's example is 'Incorporeal things are not in place' (a dubious example in fact since, arguably, incorporeal things do have location, though not extension, in place). (R9) states the principle that things desire (he needs to add *only*) what is similar to them: when *A* desires *B*, *A* thereby shows that it is naturally like *B*.

The interpretation of the other seven rules/definitions is less simple.[35] (R2) states:

> *Esse* and that which is (*id quod est*) are distinct: *esse* itself is not yet (*nondum est*), but that which is (*id quod est*), having taken the form of being (*accepta essendi forma*), is and consists (*est atque consistit*).

What does Boethius mean here by *esse* and *id quod est*? On the most plausible interpretation, *esse* here means the immanent form that makes a thing the sort of thing it is, which in OSI Boethius had said should really be considered an image (for instance, the form humanity that makes Socrates a man). Although in OSI Boethius had said that all *esse* comes from form, he is not here so much changing his usage of *esse* as extending it, by synecdoche of effect for cause. By *id quod est*, Boethius means the concrete whole (for instance, Socrates). Immanent forms exist only in the concrete wholes they inform—hence the comment '*esse* itself is not yet'; and the phrase 'having taken the form of being' means 'having taken on the form which, by making it the sort of thing it is, allows it to exist'. The next rule adds to this picture of the structure of particular things:

> (R3) That which is (*quod est*) can participate in something, but *esse* itself in no way participates in anything. For participation takes place when something already is; now, something is, when it has taken on *esse*.

The second sentence here indicates that the participation considered here must be in accidental attributes, since it takes place after 'it has taken on *esse*'—after the thing exists by having an immanent form that makes it the substance it is. The first sentence makes the point that it is the concrete whole, *id quod est*, which is the subject for accidents, not the form. (R4) reinforces this idea by saying that *id quod est* can 'have something other than what it itself is' (for example, Socrates can be not just a man but a white man), whereas *esse* is just what it is (so, for instance, the form of humanity that makes Socrates a man does not have any characteristic except that of being the form of humanity).

The next two rules go on to make the distinction between substances and accidents clearer. In (R5), Boethius says that when (a) we say about a thing, *X*, that *X* is merely (*tantum*) something, we are talking about an accident; but when (b) we say that *X* 'is something in that it is' (*esse aliquid in eo quod est*), we are talking about a substance. The contrast, then, is between sentences such as (a) 'Socrates is white' and (b) 'Socrates is a man'; (b) but not (a) can be written more fully as 'Socrates is a man in that he is'. Going on with the same idea, Boethius says

> (R6) Everything which participates in that which is *esse*, in order that it is, participates in something else, in order to be something. And so that which is (*id quod est*) participates in that which is *esse*, in order to be; but it is, in order that it participates in whatever else.

Having an immanent form, which is what makes something exist, is here presented as a type of participation, but it is immediately distinguished from the participation by which a concrete whole has accidental attributes. (Probably, in line with OSI, when Boethius talks about accidents making a thing something, he has in mind only accidents of quality and quantity, not those in other categories.) (R6) also commits Boethius to the view that every concrete whole—a thing that exists in virtue of an immanent form—has accidental attributes: as well as a sentence about what it is in that it exists, there is also true about it some sentence about what it *merely* is.

In (R7) and (R8), Boethius turns from the everyday world of concrete wholes that we perceive with our senses. According to (R7), 'Every simple thing has as one its *esse* and that which it is.' A simple thing cannot, then, be a concrete whole, made what it is by having an immanent form: it must, presumably, be pure form. (R8)—'In every composite thing, *esse* is one thing, and it itself is another'—shows that lack of distinction between *esse* and *id quod est* (that is to say, not being a concrete whole) is not merely a necessary but also a sufficient condition for a thing's being simple.

Rules (R2)—(R8) have been read very differently. Pierre Hadot has argued that Boethius is following a terminology employed by Porphyry and Marius Victorinus, in which *esse* means the One/ the Good, who is pure act and is not limited by having being predicated of him and so 'is not yet', and where *id quod est* designates any thing other than the One.[36] It is hard to see how (R7) can be understood on this interpretation, but it may well be that Boethius had in mind a reading along Hadot's lines as a supplementary way of understanding some of the Rules.[37]

OSIII: The Argument

The problem John the Deacon posed to Boethius (OSIII.1–4 [1–4]) seems, at first sight, to be pernickety and unimportant. How is it that substances—all substances—'are good in that they are, whilst they are not substantial goods'? Once Boethius sets out the problem, however, it becomes clear that it presents a difficulty that threatens his whole metaphysics and view of the relationship between God and his creatures. A common opinion of the learned (cf. (R1)), says Boethius (OSIII.50–51 [57–58]) is that 'everything tends to the good.' This idea of final causality is precisely what, in the *Consolation*, Boethius-the-character has in his grief forgotten; the first three books will be mainly devoted to reestablishing it and the reasoning behind it in his mind. It is, then, a central feature of the author Boethius's understanding of things. Using (R9)—things are like in nature to what they desire—Boethius infers from the fact that everything tends to the good, that everything is good. This conclusion raises a problem (OSIII.53–54 [60–61]). If all things are good, it seems that they either they are good by participation ('*A* is good' would be an accidental predication, in the category of quality) or else they are good substantially ('*A* is good' would be a substantial predication, in the way that in OSI Boethius explains that predications of qualitative attributes to God are substantial).

Neither alternative, it turns out, can be true (OSIII.55–76 [65–85]). When *A* is F by participation, it is not F 'in that it is' (cf. [R5]). The attributes in which *A* participates are its accidents, not its nature. But (R9) established that *A* is *by nature* like that which it desires. If, then, things are good merely by participation, they are not good by nature and so they do not tend to the good. Are things good, then, substantially? This claim amounts to saying that the substance of everything is the good in itself, in which case all things are exactly similar to the first good, God. But nothing but God is similar to God. All things therefore are God—a wicked idea! And so it seems that things are good neither substantially nor by participation. How, then, can we say that they are good at all?

In order to answer this question, Boethius proposes a thought experiment (OSIII.77–107 [87–117]).[38] Suppose, he says, that

(6) God does not exist

and

(7) All things are good.

He considers that (6) is not merely false but impossible, but he believes that he can examine the consequences that derive from an impossible hypothesis.[39] Although, claims Boethius, (6) and (7) are consistent, (6) is not consistent with

(8) All things are good in that they are.

If, as (6) entails, all things do not flow from the First Good, then all things can indeed be good (in the sense of 'being merely something' defined in [R5]), but not good in that they are. Boethius argues for the inconsistency between (6) and (8) by considering two possibilities with regard to good things, which between them are exhaustive:

(*a*) they have other attributes as well as goodness,

or

(*b*) goodness is their only attribute.

In case (*a*), he argues, the various attributes—for instance, roundness, heaviness, whiteness, and goodness—cannot be the same as the thing in question's substance, otherwise these different attributes would be the same, 'which nature will not permit'. Therefore things would not be good (or round, heavy, or white) in that they are. (This is a bad argument, because there is nothing to prevent *one* attribute from being identical to the thing's substance. Boethius seems to take it for granted that all the attributes are logically alike.[40]) In case (*b*), a good thing would just be a form—the Good—not a concrete whole. Implicitly relying on his view that numerical differentiation takes place only when forms are embodied as concrete wholes, which receive other accidents, Boethius concludes that in case (*b*) there would just be one good thing. Case (*a*) clearly entails that (8) is false. Case (*b*) entails that it is true, since the one and only good thing would indeed be good in that it is. But what Boethius wishes to show is that (6) and (8) cannot both be true, and since (*b*) entails the existence of the Good, which is God, it contradicts (6).[41]

Boethius's thought experiment shows that, were God *per impossibile* not to exist, then the unacceptable position, which his initial arguments seemed to establish, that all things are not good in that they are would be inescapable. What this conclusion suggests is that, therefore, the way to escape from the unacceptable position is to consider the element of the real situation missing from the hypothesized impossible one: the existence of a First Good. And Boethius does indeed immediately turn his discussion to this point. He argues that

(9) Necessarily, whatever is derives its existence from the First Good,[42]

and

(10) Whatever derives its existence from the First Good is good in that it is/is good in its *esse*[43]

From (9) and (10), it follows that

(11) Every existing thing is good in that it is.

(9) is one of Boethius's underlying assumptions. Although Boethius would probably wish to press a stronger interpretation, for the purposes of the ar-

gument even the weakest reading is enough: the existence of the First Good is a necessary condition for the existence of anything else. (10) is not easy to interpret, and Boethius is not very clear about the exact nature of the relationship between the First Good and the goodness of creatures that he wishes to establish. Scott MacDonald has suggested that, according to Boethius here, for a creature to be good is simply for it to derive its existence from the First Good.[44] But Boethius does not seem to be content with this merely relational understanding of a creature's goodness. He has in mind both the idea that creatures derive from the *will* of the First Good (and therefore, since that must be a good will, are good), but also the notion that creatures will, in their very being, resemble the cause of their being, insofar as they can do so as concrete wholes rather than as pure forms. Creatures will, therefore, be good in that they are—but not white in that they are, because they do not derive from something white; and they will not be just in that they are, because although the First Good is just in that he is, for creatures justice is a matter of action, and so for them being just is not the same as being good and so not what they are in that they are (OSIII.140–64 [150–74]).

Why does Boethius go to the trouble of an elaborate thought experiment, especially since it does nothing to clarify how we are to understand (10)? Could he not just have explained that things are good in that they are because their existence depends on the First Good and added, as he does in fact remark in the course of the discussion (OSIII.135–36 [145–146]), that although the *esse* of created things is, therefore, good, it cannot be like that which is substantially good, for the very reason that it derives from it? No—such explanations would have been inadequate to the initial, difficult problem he addressed. Boethius undertook to explain how all things are good in that they are, but not substantially good. But, at first sight—and there is nothing in the Rules to suggest the contrary—'*A* is F in that it is' is equivalent to '*A* is substantially F'. A plausible modern translation of '*A* is F in that it is' is 'Necessarily, if *A* exists, it is F'—and that seems to be exactly what we mean by '*A* is substantially F' ('substantially' means, that is to say, what modern philosophers mean by 'essentially'; but I stick to Boethius's term here, since its exact meaning is under investigation). If Boethius had had only the ordinary grades of modality—necessary, possible, impossible—at his disposal, he would not have been able to solve the problem.

Boethius, however, distinguished between impossibility and inconceivability. Various states of affairs, he believed, are conceivable, although they are not possible. As Christopher Martin has shown, Boethius brings out this idea in his treatment of inseparable accidents when he is commenting the *Isagoge*.[45] There (*2InIsag.* 282:16–283:4) he makes it clear that although there could not be a white crow, if we imagine a crow that is white, not black, then we can see that it remains a crow. A white crow, that is to say, is an impossibility, yet it is conceivable. For Boethius, '*A* is substantially F' just in case it is inconceivable that *A* is not-F, whereas '*A* is F in that it is' just in case it is impossible that *A* is not-F. Since it is impossible that the First Good does not exist and necessary that the creatures that derive from it are good, it is indeed *impossible* that anything should exist without being good. Boethius wishes to insist, however, that it is conceivable that something should exist without being good, whereas it is *inconceivable* that God, the First Good, should exist and not be good. The thought experiment is designed to establish this point. Boethius does not pause to show the inconceivability of God's not being good; he takes it for granted. But he carefully shows that it is conceivable for a thing not to be good, by leading the reader in thought to these circumstances. We can conceive a world in which there is no First Good and, although we cannot be sure that in this world there is anything that is not good—it may be that everything in it participates in goodness, we can be sure, so Boethius tries to demonstrate, that things are not good in that they are, so that it is possible that, in such a world, something is not good.[46]

The Method and Character of the *Opuscula*

The apparently Neoplatonic metaphysics of OSIII turn out, then, to rest on a distinction within Aristotelian logic, although Aristotelian logic as presented by the Neoplatonist Porphyry and as extended by Boethius himself. In terms of theological method, Boethius's striking and deeply influential innovation in all the *opuscula* except OSIV is—as has been remarked already about OSV—his insistence on using the Aristotelian logical tradition, as developed within Neoplatonism, to tackle theological problems. Augustine had, indeed, anticipated this approach, in *On the Trinity*, but only fleetingly: Neoplatonic metaphysics remained his favored philosophical tool for understanding doctrine. Boethius takes for granted a good deal of Neoplatonic metaphysics, in a form that owes much to Augustine. But he sees Aristotelian logic (and even Aristotelian physics) as the way of tackling heresy, of resolving apparent incoherences in Christian belief, and of explaining doctrinal mysteries, insofar as they can be explained. In this respect, the great medieval theologians look back to Boethius more than any Church Father.[47]

Like that of his Greek contemporaries, Boethius's Aristotelianism fits easily into a Neoplatonic framework, and for him this synthesis can be accepted and used unproblematically by a Christian. When, as in OSIII, Boethius looks at a theological problem in terms that a pagan Platonist could also accept—because the particular problem is not a specifically Christian one, he does nothing to call attention to this feature. When, not long afterwards, Boethius wrote his *Consolation*, both his Christian faith and his passion for philosophy remained unchanged. But, as will become clear, the relations between the two, though still close, had become less simple. The *opuscula* show a calm, assured Boethius, for whom all the elements of his intellectual universe are in harmony. The shock of his sudden downfall would shatter that conception of harmony in a way that even Philosophy herself cannot completely restore.

6

THE *CONSOLATION*

The Argument of Books I–V.2

The *Consolation of Philosophy* is by far the best known of Boethius's writings and, in some ways, it is the most easily approachable. Unlike the logical textbooks and commentaries, written in a dry, technical style, and the *Opuscula*, which analyse the obscurities of christological and trinitarian doctrine, the *Consolation* treats subjects of obvious human importance—what true happiness is, and how the providential ordering of the world is consistent with the apparent prosperity of the wicked and oppression of the good—in a powerful dialogue, written in elegant prose interspersed with verse. It takes as its setting the dramatic circumstances of Boethius's last months of life: having been rich, powerful, and influential, he is suddenly condemned as a traitor, stripped of his goods, imprisoned, and sentenced to death. No famous work of philosophy, save those Platonic dialogues that tell of Socrates's trial, condemnation, and execution, is interwoven with so arresting a story. Yet, as with some of Plato's dialogues, the very features that make the *Consolation* attractive to read render its interpretation difficult. The *Consolation* is not, like a straightforward philosophical treatise, just an argument or series of arguments. It is a complex whole, made up of a variety of arguments (as will emerge, not always consistent with each other) presented in certain ways, and what requires interpretation is this whole, which is much more than the mere sum of its individual parts. In particular, neither the literary structure of the *Consolation*, nor the structure of argument, is linear: both might be better described as circular, as will become clear in the course of the following chapters.

Approaching the *Consolation:* Genre, Literary Form, Sources, and Argument

The *Consolation* draws on a number of generic traditions: the *consolatio*, the philosophical dialogue, and Menippean satire.[1] Earlier works in each of these genres not only provided Boethius with convenient models to imitate. Insofar as they were well known, these earlier works set up a pattern of expectations in Boethius's imagined audience, and part of Boethius's skill as a writer lies in *how* he chose to fulfil—or, indeed, to go beyond—them.

Works of consolation in the Roman tradition were addressed to those facing circumstances, such as bereavement, old age, death or exile, which distressed them. Books II and III of the *Consolation* fit well into this genre, but the work goes far beyond the conventions of the *consolatio* in the scope of its philosophical discussion (it is not *any* Consolation, but the Consolation *of Philosophy*) and, especially in Book V, in the technical intricacy of the arguments. Moreover, its form, in which the author consoles a representation of himself, through a fictional figure, is unprecedented. Usually, a consolation was addressed to someone else, although self-consolations were not unknown.[2] When Seneca wrote to console his mother, Helvida, about his own exile, he combined self-consolation with consoling another. This work might, in its formal complexity, provide a precedent for Boethius's *Consolation*, although here the pattern is different: it is Boethius himself, alone, who is consoled and does the consoling, but the fiction of the dialogue suggests that he is consoled by another.

For the dialogue form, Boethius could look back to many different examples of philosophical writing. Above all, there were Plato's dialogues: the personification Philosophy dominates the argument just as Socrates does, and her task of bringing back to Boethius's mind the philosophical truths he had known but forgotten echoes Socrates's self-professed function of midwife. Cicero's philosophical dialogues provided a (rather more distant) parallel in Latin and, nearer to Boethius's time, there was Augustine, who had written a number of his early works in dialogue form and also composed a *Soliloquy*, in which he and his soul engage in discussion—although it is not certain exactly which of Augustine's works Boethius knew.[3]

Boethius's very circumstances made the *consolatio* a natural choice of genre, and dialogue was a common form for philosophical writing. The decision to alternate prose with verse and adopt other characteristics of Menippean satire is less easy to explain at first sight—and turns out to be considerably more important in its implications for the reading of the *Consolation* as a whole. I shall discuss the question in detail when I consider how the *Consolation* should be interpreted.[4]

Most modern scholars acknowledge that the *Consolation*, although full of individual ideas, motifs, and arguments from the Greek and Roman philosophical traditions so well known to its author, is an original composition, in no sense narrowly based on sources.[5] The circumstances of its composition in prison make it unlikely that Boethius had access to many books while he was writing the *Consolation*.[6] Rather, he drew, as and when he needed, on a memory well stocked through a lifetime's study. In consequence, parallels can very often be found to many individual remarks and pieces of reasoning, although much less frequently to the whole shape and progress of an argument. The parallels are meticulously recorded in Gruber's commentary,[7] and I shall not in general pause over them. A few longer passages are, indeed, closely related to particular Greek texts, although they are almost never those of simple dependence.[8]

Unfortunately, modern discussion of the *Consolation* has tended to be *either* philosophical *or* literary. The philosophers have tended to be interested just in the individual arguments (and, in fact, predominantly in the arguments of Book V) and not in the overall pattern of argument or in wider questions of interpretation, the literary critics in matters of style, structure, and wider meaning but not in the arguments and their interrelations. In order to avoid such one-sidedness, I shall take a step-by-step approach. I shall begin with two chapters given over to analysing the arguments of the *Consolation*—the present one for all except the intricate discussion of prescience and contingency in Book V, which requires a chapter to itself. In these chapters I shall concentrate mainly on the prose sections; I shall raise questions about interpretation, and point out how arguments and conclusions intertwine or conflict, but I shall not discuss sources or draw conclusions about the meaning of the work as a whole. Then, in chapter 8, I shall look at the poems and their function, and discuss how the *Consolation* as a whole is to be understood, especially in the light of its being by a Christian author but containing no explicitly Christian material.

There is one other important preliminary—a matter of nomenclature, but one that connects with questions of interpretation. The *Consolation* was, so far as is known, Boethius's last work, finished not long before his execution. There is no good reason to suppose that the circumstances of its composition were other than they are described—those of a man in the condemned cell, with little hope of reprieve. But this is not to say that the states of mind attributed to the character Boethius need ever have been those of the real Boethius. Boethius the character is a persona, very possibly fictional in many of his thoughts and feelings, although sharing the events of Boethius the author's life. It is important that the two figures be kept distinct: in these three chapters from here onwards 'Boethius' will refer just to Boethius the character, and Boethius the author will be specially designated as such.

Posing the Problems (CI)

The *Consolation* begins with Boethius (the character in the dialogue) desperate at his sudden fall from prosperity and power and bewailing his state in an Ovidian elegy (I m.1).[9] He longs for death, which 'is happy for men when it comes, not in the years of sweetness, but often summoned, to those in sadness' (CIm.1.13–14). Philosophy, a lady youthful yet ancient, arrives and drives away the poetic muses—'theatrical whores' as she calls them (CI.2.8 [29]). Boethius, she considers, is a sick man and these muses will not cure him but make his illness worse. Boethius's sickness is portrayed in the following sections, not without an element of ridicule: he is struck dumb and, at first, does not know who Philosophy is (CI.2.4–5 [7–10]). When the 'clouds of his sadness' have been dissolved sufficiently for him to recognize 'the nurse whose house he had frequented since he was a young man', Boethius imagines that Philosophy, like himself, has been exiled as the result of false accusations (CI.3.1–3 [1–9]). Philosophy's reply makes clear that her followers, from Socrates onwards, have often been martyred in her cause, but their composure has not been at all affected by threats or violence done to them (CI.3.13–14 [43–49] and m. 4). Boethius, still in tears, does not respond: he is, says Philosophy, like an 'ass to the lyre'. Still taking the role of a doctor, she now asks Boethius to reveal his wound, so that she can cure it. Boethius now takes the chance to describe, in a long prose section (I.4), which observes the rhetorical form of a legal oration, the circumstances that led to his imprisonment, showing that he had been just and upright and that the charges against him were entirely false. Philosophy, though, is entirely unmoved by Boethius's complaint against what has happened (CI.5.1 [1–2]). She asks Boethius a series of questions (I.6) to establish how she should go about curing him and sets out the plan of treatment she will pursue.

To a considerable extent, then, Book I is devoted to scene-setting: introducing the personification of Philosophy (which I shall discuss in chapter 8) and giving Boethius the chance to justify his political record for posterity. But, additionally, one of the central themes of the following books is introduced by the attitude that Philosophy takes to Boethius's circumstances. She refuses to allow that, as a follower of hers, Boethius has suffered *any* loss. However much philosophers are persecuted by the stupid, they are able to retreat to an impregnable citadel: what their enemies can take from them—presumably their goods, their freedom, life itself—are 'altogether worthless', 'useless baggage' (CI.3.13–14 [45–47]). Boethius is not persuaded. Pointing to his prison cell, he asks Philosophy (CI.4.3 [10–12]): 'Is this the library which you yourself chose as your securest dwelling within my house?' Philosophy's retort (CI.5.6 [20–25]) is that her dwelling place is not in the ivory-and-glass-ornamented walls of his library, but in Boethius's mind. More generally, he cannot complain of being exiled because his fatherland is one from which he has been exiled only by himself: whoever chooses to be there cannot be exiled from it (CI.5.3–5 [6–20]). Philosophy, then, is saying that Boethius need only follow her and—in some way that is not at all specified—he will be entirely proof against real misfortune, as opposed to the merely imagined misfortune about which he has been complaining. She is holding that the correct view of what constitutes good and bad fortune, of what is and is not desirable, is completely at odds with common opinion. It is a view of things that the author Boethius had good reason to attribute to Philosophy, since it was widely represented in ancient philosophy: the Stoics were exponents of it, but it can be found in Plato and, in a very striking form, in the founder of Neoplatonism, Plotinus (*Ennead* I.4.6–8).

Book I also establishes the dual aim of the *Consolation*, which will govern the structure of the arguments that follow. Boethius is a sick man who needs the right sort of consolation—not that offered by self-pitying, elegiac poetry. One of Philosophy's tasks, then, is the personal consolation of Boethius, which she sees as the cure of a sick man through the administration of progressively more powerful and less easily palatable remedies (CI.5.11–12 [38–44]; 6.21 [55–62]). The underlying question, as will become clear, is about happiness. What is true happiness? Is it destroyed—is it even damaged—by a disastrous change of fortune such as that Boethius has suffered?

In Book I, Boethius also raises a more general question, which is not entirely answered by the arguments introduced for his personal consolation and goes beyond asking about happiness. The question arises from generalizing on Boethius's own experience. He is not the only good man who is oppressed while the wicked prosper. His case seems, rather, to be typical of human affairs. As Boethius says in metrum 5: 'the painful punishments that are the due for crime oppress the guiltless, whilst the wicked are enthroned on high' (29–31). Although God ('the maker of the star-bearing sphere' [1]) orders the movements of the stars and the changes of the seasons, he is unconcerned with human acts: there is no justice in human affairs, and human beings are left to be knocked about in the sea of fortune (45).

What, exactly, is the complaint Boethius is making? It may seem as if he is accusing God of failing to *intervene* as he should. But his point turns out to be significantly different, as three lines of the metrum (25–27) already indicate:

> You govern all things according to a determined end:
> Only human acts you, the ruler, refuse
> To constrain in the way they should be.

Here the mention of a 'determined end' (*finis*) suggests that what is lacking for humans is an end or goal at which to aim. The final prose section of Book I bears out this position. When Philosophy asks him whether he thinks that everything in the world happens merely by chance, Boethius emphatically rejects this position and insists that he knows and will never deny that 'God, the true maker, is in charge of his work' (CI.6.4 [9–11]). It then emerges that, although Boethius knows that God rules the world, he does not know how he rules it. He knows that everything originates from God, but in his sadness he has forgotten 'what is the end (*finis*) of things or to what the purpose of all nature inclines' (CI.6.10 [24–25]). As this passage suggests, the key to solving Boethius's second, more general complaint, about the apparent lack of a just order in human affairs, is for him to regain his knowledge of the *final* cause of all things. He knows that God is their efficient cause, but he needs to discover that to which all things incline as their ultimate goal.

To these two questions, Philosophy herself adds a third when (CI.6.15–17 [35–42]) she is diagnosing the cause of Boethius's sickness. She asks him whether he is anything other than a man, defined in the standard Aristotelian way as a 'rational, mortal, animal'. When Boethius replies in the negative, Philosophy remarks that she now knows 'another and the greatest cause of your illness, that you have ceased to know what you yourself are' (CI.6.17 [39–50]). He will need to find out again the answer to this question too, if he is to be cured.

It will turn out that Philosophy's final way (in Book III.9–12) of answering Boethius's first type of question, about happiness, and so of giving him personal consolation, involves showing what is the 'end' (*finis*) of all things. She is therefore also able by the end of Book III to give her answer to Boethius's second question, about how the world is governed and the apparent injustice in human affairs. And, in the course of the discussion, Philosophy also provides an answer to the extra question, about what Boethius is. Yet the *Consolation* has two more books. Book IV begins with Philosophy developing the position she has just reached, so as to explain how the wicked are in fact punished and the good are not really oppressed. But this explanation is inadequate, at least in Boethius's eyes. Philosophy is forced to offer a different solution, not apparently compatible with the position she had proposed earlier in the book, and with the view of things developed in the second half of Book III. Book V increases rather than resolves the tensions. And, just as the second half of Book IV and Book V do not fit neatly and unproblematically with the core arguments of the *Consolation* proposed from Book III.9 to Book IV.4, so too the approach of the section from the beginning of Book II to III.8 turns out to be at odds with them.

A Complex View of Happiness (CII–III.8)

Despite the severity of Boethius's misfortunes, Philosophy's initial approach to consolation in Book I had been a drastic one. She had suggested that, as a follower of hers, Boethius should find no cause whatsoever for unhappiness in his downfall. There seems to be no common ground between an everyday view of happiness, according to which Boethius has clearly suffered greatly, and a philosophical one. Once she begins her proper consolation, however, Philosophy's approach changes. For one and a half books, she develops a complex view of human happiness, according to which Boethius has genuinely lost by his misfortunes, but can be consoled because of what he retains and what, indeed, cannot be taken from him. Given her view of Boethius as a sick patient requiring gradual, at first gentle, treatment, not all Philosophy's arguments can be taken as representing her true opinions. The complex view of happiness, however, is developed through the light remedies with which Philosophy begins (II.1–4), the rather stronger ones (II.5–7), and the sharper, biting ones for which Boethius is ready by Book III (III.1–8).[10]

The light remedies are a discussion of the gifts of fortune, such as wealth and rank. Fortune is personified and allowed to defend herself against Boethius's charges of inconstancy: it is her very nature to be changing, and what she gives is hers to take away again (CII.1–2). Philosophy, at least at this stage, does allow that the goods of fortune do bring some felicity (II.3.4 [15]). She is careful to use the word 'felicity' (*felicitas*) here, rather than that which she will use for true, complete happiness (*beatitudo*—which I shall translate simply as 'happiness'), and she emphasizes that felicity is not the same as *beatitudo* (CII.3.8 [25–26]; CII.4.3 [8–9]).[11] But she does not try to show that felicity is worthless. Indeed, her argumentative strategy implies the opposite. First (II.3) she puts it to Boethius that, even given his present misfortunes, taking his life as a whole up until now he has on balance enjoyed felicity (CII.3.10 [39–41]). Boethius's reply—'in all the adversities of fortune, the most unhappy sort of misfortune is to *have enjoyed* felicity (II.4.2 [4–6])—makes the obvious point that past and future joys and miseries do not weigh equally in assessing a person's felicity *now*. This position makes it easy for Philosophy to argue that the goods of fortune cannot bring true happiness since, among other drawbacks, those enjoying these goods will, unless they are blindly ignorant, be in constant fear that they will lose them (CII.4.26 [84–89]). Such an argument would be pointless if *no* value attached to the felicity brought by transitory gifts of fortune. Philosophy's point is that such felicity is not the same as true happiness.

Moreover, a little before this (II.4.3–9 [6–34]), Philosophy has attempted to show Boethius that, although he has lost status, wealth, and power, and he faces death, he still has 'goods' (*bona*) which 'no one doubts are more valuable than life': his wise and virtuous father-in-law Symmachus, his sons, and his wife. Although these are gifts of fortune and might be taken from Boethius (indeed, Symmachus was executed shortly after his son-in-law), Philosophy ranks them higher than other goods of fortune; riches, status, and power are by comparison mere 'ornaments'.

The view that the non-ornamental gifts of fortune are genuinely valuable, although they can be lost, is one that Philosophy does not reject when, in the following sections, she goes on to administer her stronger remedies. She does, however, now (CII.5.2 [2–6]) start to argue that the ornamental gifts—she lists riches, status (high office), power, and fame—would be worth very little, even if they were not transitory. She has two main lines of argument. First, there are practical objections to excessive pursuit of these goods of fortune: people who accumulate riches are open to being robbed (CII.5.34 [100–102]); people who devote themselves to becoming famous will find that their fame, however great, is limited to part of the world and will last for no time compared to the inexhaustible length of eternity (CII.7.3–18 [10–63]). Second, there is the idea that the goods of fortune are external, as opposed to the good qualities that a person has, such as knowledge or the virtues (CII.5.24–29 [70–89]). Taking further this contrast between goods of fortune and internal good qualities, Philosophy argues that status or power (and the same point presumably applied to the other gifts of fortune too) can be possessed by wicked people and so it is evident that they do not have 'any natural good of their own' (CII.6.13 [40–42]). Both these lines of argument lead to quite a limited conclusion: not that the goods of fortune are entirely without value but that their value is limited and incidental: they should be sought only to a moderate extent (so, for instance, in the case of riches, to lead to sufficiency, not superfluity (CII.5.16 [44–46]; II.m.5), and they should not be anyone's ultimate aim.

By the beginning of Book III Boethius is ready for more powerful and bitter medicine (CIII.1.2 [7–9]). But here, even more clearly than in Book II, Philosophy brings out her complex view of happiness. She begins with a general theory about happiness:

> The efforts of all mortals . . . do indeed proceed by various different paths, and yet they strive to reach one end—happiness (*beatitudo*). Now the good is that which, once it is gained, nothing more can be desired. It is indeed the highest of all goods and contains all goods within it . . . It is clear, therefore, that happiness is the state made perfect by gathering together all goods. (CIII.2.2–3 [2–12])

Everyone, then, is trying to gain the same end: *true* happiness. (Note that Philosophy has introduced the idea of an end or aim (*finis*) for humans—precisely what Boethius had been ignorant of in Book I). Few people, however, succeed in gaining it. The reason, Philosophy explains, is not that they are unlucky or that they make practical mistakes in trying to acquire it, but that they pursue the wrong things: '. . . for desire for the true good is there naturally within the minds of men, but wayward error leads away to false goods' (CIII.2.4 [13–15]). To bear out this idea, Philosophy (CIII.2.14–19 [54–76]) lists the goods people desire—sufficiency, respect (*reverentia*), power, fame (*celebritas*), and joy (*laetitia*)—and argues that each is a true good, which a person must have in order to be truly happy. But, in the case of each of these true goods, people make the mistake of thinking they will gain it by acquiring what is, in fact, a corresponding false good. They mistakenly believe they will gain sufficiency by acquiring riches, respect through status, power by ruling kingdoms, fame by glory, and joy by sensual pleasures (*voluptates*). Philosophy's idea becomes clearer in her treatment of the individual false and true goods. Take, for instance, riches and sufficiency (CIII.3). People imagine that what they desire are riches, and it is riches they seek. But when they acquire riches, the desire that spurred them to the acquisition is not satisfied, because there are still things they lack, even if they are rich, and they are dependent on other people. What they really desired—and have failed to acquire because they have not known to seek it—is sufficiency. Philosophy applies the same sort of reasoning to the other pairs of true and false goods.

Philosophy's claim that people's real desires are not what they believe them to be may seem odd. We do, indeed, readily accept cases where, on the basis of someone's pattern of actions, we conclude that his real desires are not those that he (even sincerely) professes: Jim may believe that his main desire in choosing a car is to preserve the environment by buying a small, fuel efficient model, whereas we are sure, from the way he goes about making the choice, that what he really desires is to save money. Philosophy, however, is arguing that the very pattern of action that is directed to fulfilling the desires for false goods shows that people really desire the true goods. Her rationale becomes clear once it is seen that the false goods are each (supposed) means to acquire the true goods, which are ends. In the case, for instance, of riches, it can be asked for what end people wish to acquire them and the answer must be, Philosophy supposes, to gain sufficiency; whereas there is no further end beyond itself for which people desire sufficiency. Philosophy considers that, when we have a desire, our real desire is for the end, even if we believe our desire is for a means to an end. She is not making a psychological assertion about unconscious processes but rather, it seems, a logical one: just as desiring 67 silver coins and 138 gold coins entails desiring 205 coins altogether, so desiring riches entails really desiring sufficiency. Philosophy, therefore, thinks that people make a double error. First, instead of focusing their attention on the ends they desire, which are their real desires, they think only about supposed means to those ends. Second, they are mistaken in what they regard as means: the various false goods do not in fact lead, as means, to the true goods, the ends which people really desire.

Philosophy is not just going over the same ground as in II.5–8, although the false goods discussed are the same as the ornamental goods of fortune treated there, except for the addition of sensual pleasure. She has now introduced the idea of the true goods, which are really desired, and by doing so she has added to her complex conception of happiness. Although Philosophy concentrates on exposing the false goods, from her discussion it is possible, as she intends (CIII m.1.11–13) to gain a picture of the true goods and the happiness they bring, which needs to be combined with that provided in Book II.

According to this complex conception, true happiness is not entirely independent of the non-ornamental goods of fortune. The ornamental goods of fortune, the false goods that most people pursue, mistaking them for what they really desire, are of limited value, but they are not entirely valueless. When Philosophy shows that ornamental goods of fortune are not the means to the true goods, her point is that simply by pursuing these false goods we will not reach true goods: however much wealth we accumulate, for instance, we will not thereby be made sufficient. But she does not rule out that, in moderation, the ornamental goods of fortune can be useful as means to pursuing true goods. In order to be happy, a person should seek to have just the small amount of money and material goods needed for sufficiency. He should gain respect and fame by being virtuous and wise. He should not seek political power and should shun sensual pleasure. On such a view of happiness, Philosophy could not claim that Boethius had lost nothing through his misfortune, but she would be left with plenty of material for consoling him. His downfall has stripped him of most of his ornamental goods of fortune but not of much that contributes to his true happiness.

A Monolithic View of the Good and Happiness: The Climax of the *Consolation* (III.9–12)

Philosophy never draws together this complex conception of happiness or uses it to provide consolation. Although the argument appears to run on from the preceding sections, Philosophy in fact changes direction: she uses the ideas about the nature of the good and of happiness that she had put forward at the beginning of Book III, but in a way quite different from how she has just developed them.[12] She asks why pursuit of each of the false goods does not lead to the acquisition of the corresponding true goods. The preceding sections have already given a detailed answer to this question: the false goods are false precisely because they are not ends, and they are not even the means to any true goods. But now Philosophy answers it differently. 'Human error', she says, 'separates what is simple and undivided, and it perverts it from the true and perfect to the false and imperfect' (CIII.9.4 [10–13]). Previously, she had maintained that people erred by pursuing the false goods rather than true ones (riches instead of sufficiency, and so on). Now she claims that they err (the word is the same) by pursuing many goods rather than a single one. Her reason is that (CIII.9.4–14 [13–41]) power must, by its nature, have sufficiency and as such be worthy of respect and famous and so joyful. From this she claims (CIII.9.15 [41–44]) that 'sufficiency', 'power', 'respect', 'fame', and 'joy' are different names for one and the same substance.

In this argument, focuses not on the people who possess the true goods but on the goods themselves. She is not saying (at least, not primarily) that a powerful person will thereby also have sufficiency but that power has sufficiency. This way of talking suggests that she is talking about the goods envisaged putatively as things, like Platonic ideas which exist independently of the things that participate in them—power-in-itself, sufficiency-in-itself and so on, putatively, because the conclusion of the argument is that they are all really just one thing: the good. Now that the complex conception of happiness developed earlier in the *Consolation* has been pushed aside,[13] Philosophy's task in the rest of Book III will be to develop in its place a monolithic view of the good.

First, however, Philosophy underlines her change of direction by a change in tone. So that 'we may deserve to find where the highest good resides' (CIII.9.32 [101–102], divine help is needed, and she incants a solemn hexameter prayer (IIIm.9), closely linked to Plato's *Timaeus* (see chapter 8). The sections that follow, up until the end of Book III, give the climax of the work's argument: Philosophy not only provides the teaching that will, she claims, enable Boethius 'to return to his fatherland'—the fatherland from which she had said in Book I that he had exiled himself (cf. CI.5.3 [6–8])—'secure in happiness' (CIII.12.9 [28–29]).[14] She also shows Boethius what the end is to which all things, including humans, strive and so shows him how God rules the world, thereby answering the questions he had posed at the end of Book

I. The manner of III.10 and III.12 (III.11 is more relaxed) also stands out: these sections are dense with tight metaphysical reasoning, reminiscent of Proclus (and, perhaps, of OSIII), and, especially in III.12, there is also a scarcely suppressed excitement, as Philosophy weaves an ever more intricate web of reasoning, and Boethius's puzzlement becomes delighted wonder as she moves toward her promised conclusion[15]—although, as Books IV and V will show, it is a conclusion that is far from fully conclusive.

The aim of III.10 is to establish that the good—in the sense of perfect good—exists and that it is identical with God and with happiness. In III.11, Philosophy introduces the idea of unity or the one. Taking self-preservation to be the retaining of unity, she shows that everything, animate and inanimate, seeks the one and therefore, because they are identical with the one and each other, that they seek the good, happiness, and God. The good, therefore, is the end all things seek. In III.12, Philosophy takes the small step needed from this conclusion to explain how God rules the world: he rules it without using anything outside himself but rather through the good. In each of these sections, Philosophy is taking up schematically one of the points she raised in her diagnosis in Book I.6 of Boethius's sickness: his ignorance of his own nature, of the end all things seek, and of how God rules the world.[16] These are the broad outlines of this central portion of the *Consolation*: now it is time to look at some of the arguments in more detail.

God, the Good, and Happiness (CIII.10)

Philosophy begins (CIII.10.2 [4–7]) by raising the question of whether there really is a good of the sort defined earlier—that is to say, a perfect good, such that once it is gained nothing more can be desired (cf. CIII.2.2 [6–7]). She gives a positive answer, using the following argument (CIII.10.3–6 [7–22]):

(1) An imperfect felicity which comes from fragile good exists [premise established in Book II, cf. especially II.8.4 (13)]
(2) If an imperfect thing of a given genus exists, then there must exist something perfect in it too. [premise]
(3) There exists perfect felicity [2, 3]

The new premise (2) is a principle that can be traced back to Aristotle, where it was used—usually by subsequent philosophers—as an argument for the existence of God.[17] Philosophy's employment of it is a typical example of how traditional material is used to new purposes in the *Consolation*. The conclusion, (3), which Philosophy reaches using this premise, is not in itself the answer to the question about a perfect *good*. But Philosophy seems, at this stage, to assume that any sort of felicity derives from some type of good, and so that if perfect felicity exists, perfect good must exist from which it derives; soon she will show that *beatitudo*, the state of happiness in which perfect felicity is enjoyed, and the perfect good are one and the same.

Philosophy's next task is to show that the perfect good is God. Her argument begins from the position that God is good. That this is so is a 'common concept'—an obvious truth that is apparent to anyone who understands the words 'God' and 'good'.[18] Nonetheless, Philosophy adds a brief argument. Nothing better can be conceived than God and, surely, that than which there is nothing better is good (CIII.10.7 [23–27].[19] To show that God is good in such a way that 'there is perfect good in him', Philosophy argues as follows (CIII.10.9–10 [29–36]):

(4) If *a* is more perfect than *b*, *a* is prior to *b* [Premise]
<(5) The principal of all things (*princeps omnium*) is prior to everything else> [Unstated Premise, based on meaning of 'principal of all things']
(6) If the perfect good is not in God, something else possesses perfect good <and is therefore more perfect than God> [Premise, deriving from the previous argument, which showed that the perfect good exists]
(7) If something is more perfect than God, it is prior to God [Instantiation of (4)]
(8) If something is prior to God, he is not principal of all things [Instantiation of (5), and *modus tollens*]
<(9) If the perfect good is not in God, he is not principal of all things> [Unstated: 6, 7, 8 *modus ponens*]
(10) God is the principal of all things, because otherwise there would be an infinite regress [Premise, based on unstated argument—see below]
(11) The perfect good is in God [9, 10 *modus tollens*]

This is a tight and (with the unstated premisses supplied) valid argument, although it makes a number of assumptions that would have seemed perfectly obvious to the Neoplatonists of Boethius's day but now appear highly questionable. Behind (4) lies the idea that the universe consists of more and less perfect things, and that the order of perfection corresponds to a (logical rather than temporal) order of origin: what is less perfect derives from what is more perfect and never vice versa. The unstated argument on which (10) is based rests on an assumption going back to the earliest Greek philosophy and entirely accepted by the Neoplatonists. There must be some principal (*princeps*, in Greek: *archē*), some underlying determinant of all things, which, as (5) makes explicit, is prior to all things. But 'God' is the word we use to refer to such a principal. If we were to say that what we call 'God' is not this principal, then we should have to posit something else, call it 'God*', which is the principle from which what we call 'God' derives; and so on, *ad infinitum*.

After having shown that perfect good is in God, Philosophy then adds that 'we have decided that perfect good is true happiness (*vera beatitudo*)' (CIII.10.10 [36–37]). Philosophy must, it seems, be referring back to CIII.2.3 [10–12], where she had argued that 'happiness is the state made perfect by gathering together all goods'. Here, though, Philosophy kept apart two ways in which the idea of a highest good can be understood: as possessing every good—that is to say, true happiness, and as the good or goods that the truly happy possess. Now Philosophy not only substitutes the monolithic conception of the good, which is God, for the 'gathering together of all goods' she had previously envisaged; she also insists that there is no distinction between the highest good and possessing it.

So far, Philosophy has established only that perfect good and true happiness are in God—that is to say, that God is perfectly good and truly happy. Now she shows that they *are* God. Suppose the good were derived from *X*, and *X* were other than God himself, then *X* would be more excellent than God (because of the correspondence, mentioned above, between priority of origin and perfection). But that is impossible, because God is the most excellent of all things (CIII.10.13 [47–51]). Suppose, instead, that the good, although not derived from anything else, were different from him 'by reason' (*ratione*)—that is to say, were conceptually separable from God (in the way that, according to OSIII, goodness is conceptually, though not really, separable from anything other than God). What, in this case, could there be that would join together two such principals of things? (CIII.10.14 [51–53]). And, Philosophy adds, if the highest good were different in nature from God, God would not be the highest good; but it is 'wicked' (*nefas*) to think this of him, since he is more excellent than anything (CIII.10.15 [54–58]). Philosophy is therefore able to conclude that God *is* the good and, since the good is happiness, God is happiness (CIII.10.16–17 [58–67]).

It makes good sense, from a Platonic perspective, to insist that a supreme being is not merely good but is goodness. Otherwise, goodness would be something distinguishable from God from which he would derive his goodness, and he would therefore be in a certain sense inferior to it. Some Platonists would make the same argument about God's being justice, rather than just, wisdom rather than wise, and so on. It is harder to accept the same point with regard to happiness, since happiness (as discussed throughout the *Consolation*) consists in the possession of the good: how can God *be* happiness? Perhaps the motivation for this position is that by merely possessing the good, a thing is happy; and so, if it is the good, it must be happiness.

After some incidental developments, Philosophy will return with an additional argument for the identification of happiness with the good (CIII.10.27–43 [92–144]). One of these incidental points should be mentioned, because it provides an answer to the question raised on Boethius's behalf in her diagnostic passage in Book I. There Boethius revealed that he was ignorant of his being anything other than a man, in the sense of a rational, mortal animal. Now Philosophy argues (CIII.10.22–26 [80–92]) that since happiness, good, and God are identical, every happy person is thereby a God—an idea that would not have been as shocking, either to pagans or Christians, as it may sound.[20] Boethius is therefore, or at least can be, far more than merely a rational, mortal animal.

Philosophy's additional argument for identifying happiness with the good uses a distinction between different sorts of whole. Philosophy observes that just as it is true to say that 'The good is happiness', it is also true that 'The greatest sufficiency is happiness', 'The greatest power is happiness', and so on, for respect, fame, and pleasure.[21] Does this mean that good, sufficiency, respect, fame and pleasure constitute happiness as parts of an integral whole? No, because they are all the same and so, if they were parts of happiness, then a whole would have just one part, which—she says—is impossible. Rather, sufficiency, respect, fame, and pleasure are all sought because of the good. Philosophy goes further: nothing is sought except because it really or apparently has good in it, and 'since, therefore, all things are sought for the sake of the good, what is desired by everyone is not those things but the good itself.' (CIII.10.41 [134–35]). Then Philosophy takes the final steps in her argument, which are tighter than they might appear:

(12) Everything that is sought is sought for the sake of the good [Premise established by argument so far]
(13) Everything other than happiness is sought for the sake of happiness [Premise; asserted by Philosophy and accepted by Boethius at CIII.2.2 (4–5)]
(14) Happiness and the good are identical ('are one and the same substance') [12, 13; *reductio ad absurdum*—see below]

The grounds for deducing (14) from (12) and (13) seem to be that, if happiness and the good were not identical, then it would follow from (13) not merely that there are two different ends for which all things are sought, the good and happiness—a position which is strange but involves no contradiction—but also that the good (which would be contained in the extension of 'everything other than happiness') is sought for the sake of happiness, that is, *ex hypothesi*, for something other than the good—a position which clearly contradicts (12).[22]

By the end of III.10, then, Philosophy has completed her first task of consolation, by showing Boethius what happiness is and how it is not at all affected by the change of fortune he was bewailing at the start of the work. This consolation does, indeed, have an odd and large gap: there is no indication of how the individual man, Boethius, is supposed to relate to true happiness, which is God. I shall return to this point when discussing the overall interpretation of the work.

How God Rules the World (CIII.11–12)

In III.11–12, Philosophy uses the position she has established in III.10 to complete her other task of consolation, which requires her to show Boethius how God rules the universe. As her approach to Boethius's problem even in Book I showed, she will answer by pointing to the final cause of all things—the end which everything seeks. It might seem that she has already demonstrated it. The good (which is identical with happiness and God; like Philosophy, I shall just talk about 'the good' for brevity's sake) has been shown to be that for the sake of which all things are desired. But this conclusion does not go so far as to show that the good is the final cause of everything. Every desire is a desire for the good; but does everything have desires? Humans and higher animals do, but it is far from obvious in what sense a worm or a flower or a stone has desires that, really, are for the good. Although

Boethius's complaint had been that humans alone escaped from God's government, Philosophy is anxious to show how the same final cause rules *all* things, from inanimate objects to people. This is the gap that the argument of III.11 is designed to fill.

Philosophy's argument depends on the idea of unity (*unitas*) or, as she more often says, the one (*unum*). First, she establishes that the good and the one are identical. She has already shown, she claims (CIII.11.5 [8–17]), that the various individual true goods are not truly and fully good individually, but only when they are all one and the same. Since these things 'are not at all good' (*minime bona sunt*—an exaggeration of what she has just said she established!) apart, and become good when they are one, it is by acquiring unity that they become good. But everything that is good is good through participating in goodness. Therefore, since the good and the one both have the same effect, of making things good, and 'things which have the same natural effect have the same substance', the one and the good (and so happiness and God) are all the same substance.

In the second stage of her argument (CIII.11.10–37 [27–108]), Philosophy shows that 'all things desire the one'. Although the discussion is protracted by reference to a variety of empirical evidence, the structure of the reasoning is simple. First, Philosophy equates a thing's remaining in existence as opposed to its being destroyed with its being one: the idea is that if, for instance, an animal is broken up into its parts and so ceases to be one, it also perishes and ceases to be an animal. Next, Philosophy shows that everything naturally desires to persist, rather than to perish. The evidence is easy enough to find with regard to humans and other animals, and Philosophy also thinks that plants, by growing in habitats hospitable to them, and even inanimate things—fire by going upward, hard things by resisting pressure, and so on—show the same desire. So, since persisting is the same as being one, if everything desires to persist, everything desires to be one and so says Philosophy, desires the one. From these two stages, Philosophy's intended conclusion follows easily. The one is identical to the good, and everything desires the one; so everything desires the good (CIII.11.37–38 [110–12]).[23] The good, then, is the end of all things.

In III.12, Philosophy brings out how this conclusion presents the answer to the second, more general problem Boethius had raised in Book I: how does God rule the world? After Boethius himself has made a near approach to the answer, Philosophy explains that since sufficiency is part of happiness and God is happiness, God does not rule using anything outside himself

(CIII.12.10–12 [30–37]). God therefore governs all things through himself and, since God is the good, he governs all things through the good. The good is 'like a helm and rudder by which the fabric of the world is kept stable and without decay' (CIII.12.14 [40–42]).[24] Since everything naturally desires the good (as shown in III.11), God's rule is not in the least oppressive: everything wants it, and there is nothing that either wishes to resist it or could resist it, supposing it wished to do so.

In Book IV, Philosophy will try to explain how this conception of a benignly self-ruling universe is compatible with the apparent evidence of wickedness triumphing and goodness oppressed. She takes a first step in this direction even here, however, with a brief argument about evil (CIII.12.26–29 [74–82]). God is omnipotent and so there is nothing he cannot do. But he cannot do evil, and so evil is nothing. This reasoning has the appearance of fallacy, since it appears to treat 'nothing' as if referred to some given thing that God cannot do. But it can be construed like this:-Everything that is doable or makeable is doable or makeable by God, an omnipotent being. Evil is not doable or makeable by God and so evil is not doable or makeable: that is to say, the word 'evil' does not refer to things, actions or properties of things in the way its linguistic use suggests. On this reading, Philosophy is not failing to recognize the logical peculiarities of 'nothing', but rather pointing out the logical peculiarities of 'evil'.

The Impotence and Self-Punishment of Wickedness (CIV.1–4)

The account of God's government of the world, given with such a show of logical power in III.10–12, is a striking and very unusual one (although it has some important points of resemblance with Aristotle's view of *nous* and its relation to the universe). God is seen as completely non-interventionist: merely by being the highest good, which everything desires as its end, he regulates the universe. Even if the argument in III.12 to show that evil is not a thing is accepted, there still remains a puzzle about how this position can be compatible with the apparent power wielded by evil people, who go unpunished, and the suffering of good men such as Boethius himself. It is not at all surprising, then, that Boethius should begin Book IV by posing these problems to Philosophy, and that she should recognize (CIV.1.8–9 [31–

38]) that it is only after she has answered them that she will have succeeded in bringing back Boethius to his fatherland.

The challenge facing Philosophy is to fill in and make plausible the conception of divine government by final causality she reached at the end of Book III. Arguably, she will not succeed in making it plausible, but she certainly fills in the details with great consistency. In doing so, she borrows a number of arguments from Plato's *Gorgias*, but they are all put to her own particular use: to show how, merely because the good is the final cause, the wicked are impotent and self-punishing.[25]

Socrates is able to arrive at some strikingly counter-intuitive conclusions in the *Gorgias*—for instance, that a tyrant would be far happier being tortured and executed than continuing to live unjustly, enjoying his power and riches—by using as a premise the view that goodness (in the sense of moral goodness, involving in particular the practice of justice) is at least a necessary condition of happiness.[26] In the *Consolation*, Philosophy uses the same premise in a strong interpretation (people are happy by the very fact of being good: CIV.3.9 [26–28])—and it may seem that she is perfectly justified to do so, because in the preceding sections she has demonstrated the identity of happiness and the good. Yet there is a problem. In Book III, the good has not been discussed in terms of *moral* goodness. Rather, in the earlier parts of Book III, Philosophy talked about a variety of goods, such as sufficiency and power, which people really desire, and in the later parts she spoke of a single good, which is the final cause of all things. Here, however, by 'good people', Philosophy clearly means *morally* good people. Her previous argument has not given her grounds to identify being morally good with being happy. Indeed, as mentioned above, Book III is remarkably unclear about the links between any individual human and the good (which is God and happiness). Perhaps, by her line of reasoning now, Philosophy is trying to fill that gap (especially in IV.3: see below) and is suggesting that people become good and therefore happy by acting in a morally good way. But the way in which the good has been described precludes morally good behaviour from being a sufficient condition for goodness; nor does it seem to be a necessary condition, since Philosophy certainly does not seem to hold that God would not be good unless he acted well morally.

In IV.2, Philosophy's object is to show—purely in terms of the model of final causality—that, contrary to Boethius's complaint that the wicked have power over the good, the good are always powerful and the wicked always lack power (CIV.2.2 [3–5]). Her main argument (CIV.2.7–15 [17–42]), explicitly based on Plato (cf. CIV.2.45 [140]), runs as follows. Someone has power if and only if he can gain or bring about what he wants. Everyone, it has been shown in III, wants happiness, and happiness is the same as the good. And so everyone, the good and the wicked, is trying to reach the good. Since the good are good, they have gained the good. The wicked, however, have not gained the good, otherwise they would be good, not wicked. Therefore, the good have gained what they want and the wicked have failed to gain what they want, and so the good are powerful and the wicked are without power.

As she says (CIV.2.26 [74–75]), Philosophy 'heaps up' various arguments for the same conclusion besides this main one. The most interesting are those which link up with her point in III.12 about the non-existence of evil. To the common-sense objection that, despite what she has established, the wicked *do* exercise power (CIV.2.37 [113]), Philosophy responds that what they are able to do are evil things, and they are nothing. She also argues that those people who knowingly and without having been overcome by weakness of will do evil thereby cease to exist—that, indeed, the wicked, who are the majority of people, do not exist (CIV.2.32–33 [97–106]). Philosophy explains (CIV.2.34-35 [104-110]) this statement (which she admits will cause amazement) by distinguishing between the meanings of 'is' used as a copula ('*A* is tall') and 'is' used (apparently) absolutely, in a sentence such as '*A* is'. The copula can be used about wicked people, because they *are* wicked, but 'is' cannot be used about them in its apparently absolute form—the sense that she describes as being pure and without qualification. As a parallel, Philosophy gives the way in which a corpse is not a human being without qualification, but it is a dead human being. She goes on (CIV2.36 [110-112]) to give what is best taken as a further explanation of what is meant by the apparently absolute sense of 'is'. A thing *is* in this sense when 'it retains its order and preserves its nature'. The suggestion seems to be that, when we say 'John is' (without qualification) we mean that John is a human being (and so this use of 'is' is only apparently absolute). When, therefore, by behaving wickedly, John ceases to preserve his human nature, it becomes true to say that John is not, although 'is' as the copula can still be used to make true sentences about him ('John is wicked', 'John is a citizen of Cambridge' etc.).

In the next prose section, Philosophy answers the rest of Boethius's complaint about the seeming injustice of human affairs: the good, she claims, are always rewarded and the wicked always punished (CIV.3.1 [2–4]). The reward for good acts is the good, which is the same as happiness, and good people must have the good or it would be wrong to call them 'good' (note here the suspected equivocation between moral and more general senses of 'good' mentioned above). And not only will they be rewarded by happiness but also, as was established in III.10, by becoming Gods (CIV.3.2–10 [4–31]). Just as the good are rewarded simply by being good, so it is a punishment for the evil to be evil (CIV.3.11–13 [36–42]). Philosophy explains the nature of this punishment by drawing again on what she has said about evil and existence. By being evil, wicked people cease to be, and here she makes it explicit that they cease to be what they were—men—and become other, lower animals, although keeping the appearance of men (CIV.3.14–21 [42–69]).[27]

In IV.4, Philosophy confidently emphasizes the extremeness of her position by putting forward two of the most famous, counter-intuitive claims of the *Gorgias*: (1) that the wicked are less happy when they are able to carry out their plans than when they are prevented from doing so, and are made happier by being punished than if they escape punishment (CIV.4.3–21 [9–71]), and (2) that those who do injustice are unhappier than those who suffer it (CIV.4.32–37 [114–31]).[28] Both of these claims are established easily by the same moves Philosophy has used in the two preceding sections: just punishment—even if it is ineffective as a deterrent or for rehabilitation—adds an element of good, and therefore of happiness, simply by being just, and the wickedness of those who do injustice is something bad and so makes the perpetrators of injustice unhappy.

Fate and God's Providence: Philosophy's Change of Direction (IV.5–V.2)

Just as there is a break in the argument of Book III, so that from III.9 Philosophy follows a course of reasoning at odds with that of the previous sections, so too the argument of Book IV suddenly changes direction in IV.4. The break is more obvious than in Book III. In IV.1–4, Philosophy has single-mindedly elaborated the idea of divine rule by final causality: using the same argumentative moves over and over again, she has tried to show how a perfectly just order of things, where the good are powerful and rewarded, the wicked weak and punished, can and, despite appearances, does exist, without any sort of intervention by God: it is enough for him to be the highest good and the end that all things seek. Only for a moment does she waver in this approach, when, in response to Boethius's question, she refers fleetingly (CIV.4.23 [77–79]) to the punishments that will be inflicted on souls after death. Philosophy has all along freely admitted that her position, although rationally cogent, is completely at odds with people's ordinary way of thinking, and in IV.4 this disparity is repeatedly emphasized (CIV.4. 27, 38–39 [94–100, 131–140]). But Philosophy thinks it would be ridiculous to be swayed by what the common herd—she likens (CIV.4.30 [109]) the mass of people to beasts (*belvae*)—thinks.

In IV.5, however, Boethius is given nearly the whole prose passage to attack the counter-intuitive nature of Philosophy's position. He sees what Philosophy has argued, but he still thinks—what she has been denying since the middle of Book III—that there is 'some good and evil in fortune as it is commonly conceived' (CIV.5.2 [3–4]): that is to say that a person really gains some good by having the goods of fortune, such as wealth and status, and really suffers some evil by losing them. For, Boethius asks, 'which wise man would prefer to be a penniless, disgraced exile rather than stay in his own city and lead there a flourishing life mighty in wealth, revered in honour and strong in power?' (CIV.5.2 [5–7]). The prosperity of the wicked and their success in oppressing the good do not seem consistent with God's rule of the universe. The complaint is the same as that voiced at the beginning of Book IV, and indeed as that put forward in Book I, and Philosophy has already given the answer to it. All she need do now is repeat, once again, that an apparently oppressed good man, such as Boethius, is really, though exiled and imprisoned, in his own fatherland, and is truly happy, whereas the wicked are not really prospering but wretched. Instead, Philosophy mostly abandons the line of thought she had been developing from III.9 and begins a completely different (CIV.6.7 [21]: '. . . as if making a new start') train of reasoning.

'The coming-to-be of all things', she says, 'the development of mutable sorts of thing, and whatever is in movement in any way receives its causes, order and forms from the stability of God's mind' (CIV.6.7 [22–25]). This way of things being governed can be described from two different points of view. Envisaged 'in the purity of God's intelligence', it is called 'providence' and, as such, it is 'God's reason, which disposes all things'; seen in regard to the things which it moves and disposes, it is what the ancients called 'fate'—'the arrangement that attaches to all things subject to motion, through which providence links all things in their order' (CIV.6.8–9 [27–35]). Providence is the unified view in God's mind of the unfolding of things in time, whilst when it is unfolded and distributed in time it is fate (CIV.6.10 [36–42]).[29]

Philosophy is claiming that everything—or, at the least, everything on earth—is part of God's providence.[30] The distinction between providence and fate is designed to serve two purposes. First, a contrast is being drawn between the unity of providence and the way fate is distributed over time:

> For providence embraces all things, however diverse, however infinite, together, whereas fate orders individual, changing things, arranged in their places, forms and times. Consequently when all these things, unfolded in time, are united in the way they are seen by God's mind, they are providence; but when this unified providence is arranged and unfolded in time, it is called 'fate'. (CIV.6.10 [36–42])

Philosophy will take up this idea again and elaborate it in Book V. Second, Philosophy is excluding any ultimate cause of events other than divine providence: fate is not a separate causal force but merely the name for the unfolding of God's plan. She is deliberately vague about the mechanisms used by God, mentioning divine spirits, a (world) soul, the whole of nature, the stars, angels and demons—or some combination of them—as possible instruments of providence (CIV.6.13 [51–56]). Clearly, though, the picture is in stark contrast to that presented by III.9—IV.4. Rather than governing simply by being the goal for all things, God is now depicted as the planner of all things; indeed, he is explicitly compared to a craftsman, conceiving the thing in his mind (providence), which is then executed in reality (fate) (CIV.6.12 [44–51]).

Philosophy's explanation of providence and fate does not in itself solve the problem Boethius had put to her afresh: indeed, the emphasis on God as planner and efficient cause makes the injustices Boethius describes even more difficult to fathom. But the idea of providence opens the way to two different strategies, used together by Philosophy. On the one hand, she argues from the premisses that everything is part of providence, and that divine plans are beyond human understanding, to the conclusion that, although it may not appear to us, God so orders everything that the good is preserved, wickedness eliminated, and even evil is used by God to good effect (CIV.6.50–56 [184–206]). On the other hand, Philosophy does offer a sort of explanation that can be grasped by us. Boethius has complained about the misfortune of good men and the prosperity of the wicked. Philosophy argues that the good suffer misfortune so that God can test them or strengthen them, or so that by their behaviour in facing death or torture they can show how virtue is not overcome by evils (CIV.6.40–42 [147–57]). As for the prosperity of the wicked, Philosophy gives various reasons: to show the worthlessness of this sort of prosperity; to restrain evil people from doing even worse; to help the wicked to repent, or alternatively to bring them to ruin; to allow the wicked to punish the evil and 'exercise' the good (CIV.6.44–47 [164–179]).

This explanation is the one aspect of IV.5–7 that links closely with the earlier parts of Book IV, since it emphasizes the importance of a person's moral state as opposed to any other aspect of his well-being. Philosophy even speaks (CIV.6.28–29 [115–21]) of God using a medical simile: just as the doctor makes patients healthy by administering, as appropriate, bitter medicines and pleasant ones, so God cures souls of vices by dealing out to people the happy or sad experiences best suited to this aim. Nonetheless, there is an important difference from the earlier discussion. There, ordinary conceptions of happiness were of no account whatsoever: by being good—which in these sections seems to become equated with being morally good[31]—a person is happy and no explanation at all needs to be given as to why he is, for instance, imprisoned or being tortured, because these circumstances are quite irrelevant to his happiness. Now, however, Philosophy, by accepting that some explanation is needed for why a good person is subjected, for instance, to exile or execution, seems to accept there is some value in the goods that are usually regarded as bringing happiness, and some loss of happiness inflicted by what are normally regarded as evils, although the value of moral goodness is of a higher order altogether.[32]

In IV.7, Philosophy uses what she has now established to revisit the subject of fortune, discussed in Book II. What was seen then as an inexplicable, inconstant dealing out of prosperity and adversity is now seen to be the unfolding by fate of divine providence. All fortune is good, says Philosophy (CIV.7.3 [4–8]). Fortune is good by being just when it rewards the good with prosperity or punishes the evil. Fortune is good by being useful when it 'exercises' the good or corrects the wicked with adversity. When Boethius comments that this way of speaking, though persuasive, goes against the commonly accepted notion that there can be bad fortune as well as good, Philosophy suggests another formulation (CIV.7.15 [32–37]). For people who are either virtuous or becoming virtuous, all fortune is good, since adversity exercises or corrects them; for people who remain wicked, all fortune is very bad (CIV.7.15 [32–37]). Philosophy does not pretend that this conclusion is any less shocking to ordinary intuitions than the previous one, and there is a further awkwardness, which she does not notice. Presumably, wicked people who prosper materially and socially can be said to have bad fortune, because—from the true, philosophical point of view—nothing is worse than to persevere in wickedness. But, on the previous formulation, Philosophy needs to be able to say that they have good fortune, because all fortune is good; if so, 'good fortune' must be taken in the commonly accepted and misleading meaning of material and social success. At the same time, she needs to claim that the fortune of the wicked who are punished is good, even if not beneficial to the wicked themselves, because it is just.

Altogether, it is hard to read Philosophy's long and varied defence of the justice of human affairs without finding it incomplete. At the most, it gives an answer to the question posed by someone in Boethius's position—a good person in adversity—about his downfall is consistent with divine justice. It does not explain why God would have designed his providence as a whole in the way he seems to have done. In particular, it does little to explain the existence of wicked people, who may be justly punished but, because they remain wicked, receive no benefit from punishment.[33]

Providence, Chance, and Human Freedom (V.1–2)

Philosophy's change of direction in IV.5 introduces one new and very serious problem, which I shall call the 'Problem of Providence'. So long as divine government was explained solely in terms of final causality, there was no tension between acknowledging it and maintaining that humans have free will (although it was never made clear how anybody could know what is the goal of all things and not seek it[34]). Now, however, Philosophy is proposing that everything derives from divine providence. What room is left, then, for the freedom of the will? And, if human wills are not free, how can humans choose to act well? Yet Philosophy clearly attaches the highest importance to moral action, and she apparently believes it is open to humans to choose to act well or badly: indeed, she ends Book V exhorting, not so much Boethius, as people in general to virtuous behaviour.

Since, at least, the eighteenth century, some philosophers have held that there is no incompatibility between an act's being causally determined and its being free. On this view, the existence of the causal chain Philosophy calls 'fate' does not threaten human freedom of action and so the basis of morality. But Boethius the author makes it clear, in V.3, that he does not hold such a view (indeed, it is doubtful whether he would even have envisaged it). There the character Boethius asks (CV.2.2 [2–5]): 'In this series of causes that link up with each other is there any freedom of our will (*libertas arbitrii*), or does the chain of fate fetter even the very motions of human minds?' I shall return to the reply that Philosophy gives to this particular question. But the question itself supposes—and Philosophy does not query this supposition—that an act is not free when it is completely determined by a causal chain.

One way in which Philosophy might have solved this problem would have been to argue that, although there is indeed a causal chain, which is the working out in time of providence, it is not all-embracing. On this view, some events and actions would be completely determined by causes; others—acts of free will—would not be completely causally determined, although they might be to some extent constrained. In his second commentary on *On Interpretation*, Boethius seems to have proposed a theory on these lines. But Philosophy's treatment of the causal chain in the *Consolation* makes it clear that she does not share it. In Book IV, it is true, Philosophy is quite vague in her description of the extent of providence. Her comments (CIV.6.13 [51–60]: see above) about the possible ways in which 'the chain of fate is woven' leave open the possibility that this chain might be loose and incomplete, with God intervening to shape outcomes in accord with justice but not causally responsible for every event. At the beginning of Book V, however, she puts her position much more clearly and strongly. Boethius has asked whether there is such a thing as chance. In her reply (CV.1.8–18 [18–55], she asserts that if by a 'chance event' is meant an event that is not the result of a chain of causes, then there are no chance events. Every event has a cause. But a useful meaning can be given to the term 'chance event', following 'our' Aristotle.[35] When something happens due to a chain of causes that is not intended or expected, it is called chance, such as when a man digging his fields so as to grow crops in them discovers buried treasure. Philosophy's answer does not merely claim every event has an efficient cause. She also mentions at the beginning (CV.1.8 [23]), as reason for rejecting uncaused events, that 'God constrains all things into his order', and at the end of the discussion she says explicitly

> . . . what makes the causes coincide and run together is that order, which proceeds by inevitable connections and which comes down from providence as its source and arranges all things in their own times and places. (CV.1.19 [55–58])

Fate, then, which is the working-out of providence, *is* a completely tight causal chain that includes all events. Events, in this sense, include everything that happens with regard to earthly bodies and also celestial ones; they do not, though—as will become clear—include every sort of mental event.

The solution Philosophy does choose is not made clear until V.2. But she prepares the ground for it in a famous simile that is introduced shortly after her distinction between providence and fate (CIV.6.15–17 [65–82]). Providence, she says, can be compared to the axis around which a number of concentric circles revolve. The innermost circle covers the least distance in its motion and is like an axis to the others; the outermost covers the greatest distance and so is most unlike the undividedness of the central point. Thus, says Philosophy, whoever more nearly approaches the axis, the 'first mind', is the more free, and the farther a person departs from it, the more he is entrapped by the links of fate. Scholars have expended great energy in disputing the sources of this passage, which is a good example of how ideas common among Neoplatonists are fused together in the *Consolation* into a new form.[36] The main point proposed in the simile is that someone might be free from fate by 'sticking to the fixity of God's mind' (CIV.6.16 [76–77]). When (CV.2.3–10 [5–27]) she answers Boethius's question, quoted above, about whether the chain of fate binds the motions of human minds, Philosophy shows how this idea fits into a wider answer to the question about freedom of the will.

There *is* freedom of the will (*libertas arbitrii*), says Philosophy, and every rational being has it. Rationality includes the power of distinguishing one thing from another and judging that some things should be sought and some avoided in themselves. As a result, every being who is rational has the freedom of willing or not willing. Philosophy's point is that rational acts of volition do not belong at all to the causal chain of fate. They are not causally determined. If I rationally willed to do or not to do x, the correct explanation for this act of volition is not that it resulted from a certain set of causes, but that I willed so, because I discerned that x is desirable or undesirable in itself. Acts of will, then, are in principle unlike every other sort of act and event.

Philosophy goes on immediately, however, to explain how freedom of willing, which is supreme in 'divine and supernal substances', becomes limited for human souls when they cease to be occupied in contemplating God's mind, 'fall down to bodies' and 'are bound in earthly limbs', and is reduced still further when, given over to vices, they have lost possession of their own reason. When people are stirred up by 'destructive passions' (*perniciosos affectus*) and consent to them, then they are 'in a certain way made prisoners by their own freedom.' In this charged and highly Platonic language, Philosophy is explaining that an act of will is free only if it is fully a rational volition. Once the will is swayed by passions, which she portrays here as the result of the soul's embodiment, its volitions are determined causally—although this captivity stems, as she says, from its freedom, since by nature the will has the freedom to will rationally.[37]

Philosophy's position about the freedom of rational willing is consistent with her view that the chain of fate has no gaps because she does not extend the freedom to the effects of volitions. Events will take place exactly as providence, working through the causal chain of fate, decrees; only volitions themselves are, in principle, free. But the better and more penetrating a person's judgement, the closer what he wills to happen will be to what providence ordains. Philosophy does not make this point explicitly, but it is implied by her general position and is indicated by her simile in Book IV of the concentric circles (see above). It is for this reason that (CV.2.7 [14–16]) the divine and supernal substances, who have far-seeing judgement and uncorrupt will, also have the power to achieve what they wish.

Philosophy does, then, granted her Platonic assumptions about bodies and souls, at this stage give a sketchy but fairly satisfactory answer to the problem about human freedom. The final sentence of V.2 ties this answer back up more explicitly with her position on divine providence and the discussion in Book IV. God, she says (CV.2.11 [27–29]),

> looks at 'all these things' [that is to say, at people's volitions, both good and bad] from eternity with the vision of providence and disposes everything predestined according to the merits of each person.

Philosophy, then, imagines God as 'from eternity'—an expression Boethius will *initially* take as meaning something like 'from the beginning of time'—foreseeing how people will freely will and arranging his providential order, and so the chain of fate, with this in mind, rewarding, punishing, exercising, warning, improving (as set out in CIV.6.32–53 [126–196]). But, so far from rounding off her presentation, this comment occasions a question from Boethius that will need the rest of the *Consolation*—a dense discussion, stretching over four prose sections—to be answered.

7

THE *CONSOLATION*, V.3–6

Divine Prescience, Contigency, Eternity

The problem raised by Philosophy's final remark in V.2 is formulated at the beginning of V.3 by Boethius in this (ambiguous) way:

> (1) If God sees all things and can in no way be mistaken, then there necessarily happens what he by providence will have foreseen will be [*si cuncta prospicit deus neque falli ullo modo potest, evenire necesse est quod providentia futurum esse praeviderit*]. (CV.3.4 [6–8])

and

> (2) If things are capable of turning out differently from how they have been foreseen, then there will no longer be firm foreknowledge of the future, but rather uncertain opinion. (CV.3.6 [13–15])

Both of Boethius's formulations of the Problem of Prescience contain serious ambiguities, as will be discussed. But it would be hard to deny that Boethius has raised a genuine difficulty. If God knows the future now, surely the future is fixed; if the future is not fixed, how can God know it? In this chapter, I shall look in detail at the intricate argument Philosophy develops to solve the Problem of Prescience. I shall begin by explaining how this new problem fits with the Problem of Providence and Philosophy's solution to it, and at the end I shall return to the link between prescience and providence. In the course of my main analysis of the Problem of Prescience, I shall touch on the question of sources and make comparisons with Proclus and the Alexandrian Neoplatonist, Ammonius, who lived at roughly the same time as Boethius. Probably Boethius was not dependent on Ammonius's commentaries themselves, but both writers had access to similar material.[1]

Why Is the Problem of Prescience Important for Philosophy's Position?

Before examining how Boethius goes on to justify (1) and (2), and how Philosophy answers his case, it is important to be clear about what is the fresh difficulty that is now being addressed and why it is so important. Both (1) and (2) claim that there is an incompatibility between God's foreseeing all things and any event's being contingent. I shall call this the 'Problem of Prescience'. Clearly (although Boethius uses the word *provideo* in stating it), this problem is different from the Problem of Providence examined in the last chapter. The Problem of Providence concerns causal determinism, since divine providence is said to be exercised through the causal chain of fate. This causal determinism seemed at first to be incompatible with human free will, and Philosophy has just explained why it is not. By contrast, the Problem of Prescience does not involve causal determinism: it arises because, whether or not it causes them, divine prescience apparently makes all events necessary. When they describe events as 'necessary', Boethius and Philosophy mean that it is not possible, before it happens, that the event should not happen in the way it does, and they both accept that the will is not free if its actions are necessary in this sense.[2]

Granted that the Problem of Prescience is distinct, it still may be asked why Philosophy should regard it as a difficulty to be solved, given her way of treating the Problem of Providence. She has already allowed that every event is causally determined and so, in her view, no event is the effect of free will. Although divine prescience gives another, separate reason for denying that any event is the effect of free will—since all events will, Boethius argues, be necessary—what does this matter, since Philosophy has already conceded the position? The answer to this question is made clear by the way in which, in V.3, Boethius takes up the final comment in V.2. There, Philosophy, who has argued that the exercise of the will in itself is in principle free, was suggesting that God decides the course of providence, which is fixed, by foreseeing the volitions people will freely make. But if prescience makes events necessary, then these volitions themselves will not be free. Philosophy had been happy to accept that events are not the effects of free will, because she also claimed that the will itself can be free. But the Problem of Prescience threatens this freedom too. As Boethius says, very explicitly, after he has put forward (1): 'For this reason, if God foreknows from eternity *not just people's deeds but also their deliberations and volitions* (*consilia voluntatesque*), there will be no freedom of the will' (CV.3.5 [8–10]). The Problem of Prescience, then, has a place in the overall structure of the *Consolation* because the events that it suggests are necessary include purely mental events, such as volitions. But, once Philosophy sets herself to tackling the Problem of Prescience, she tends to forget this focus and concentrates on finding a counter-argument to show that divine prescience does not entail the necessity of any event at all, mental or otherwise—at least, not in the sense of necessity that is incompatible with freedom.

There is one further complication. At the end of his presentation and discussion of the Problem of Prescience, the character Boethius explains the consequences that seem to follow from it. Since there will not be any 'free and voluntary motion of the mind' (CV.3.30 [87])—precisely what Philosophy's concessions to the Problem of Providence had left untouched—there will be no basis for reward or punishment, or for considering one person virtuous, another full of vice. To this, however, Boethius adds (CV.3.33–36 [97–112]) that there will be no reason for hoping or for praying. But, except where hopes and prayers are about mental states or events (as I may pray to God to make me have certain wishes), this apparent consequence arises already from the position Philosophy has conceded about the causal chain of fate; indeed, Boethius even puts the point here in language that belongs to the earlier discussion of causal determination: 'for what may anyone hope or even pray for, when an unbending series links together everything that is wished for?' (CV.3.33 [99–100]). This point can be answered according to the general lines Philosophy uses to tackle the Problem of Providence: insofar as hopes and prayers are right (that is to say, in accord with providence), they will indeed be answered—just as volitions will be efficacious, when they are the right things to will. And Philosophy does answer it in this way, at the very end of the work.[3] It is not, then, really relevant to the main argument of V.3–6.

The Argument: Part 1 (CV.3.1–CV.4.23)

The argument of V.4–6 is divided into two main parts. The second part, stretching from just after the middle of V.4 (CV.4.24ff. [72 ff.]) to the end of the work, contains the argument, involving the idea of eternity and a distinction between types of necessity, which is generally recognized as Boethius the author's solution to the Problem of Prescience. The first part—all of V.3 and most of V.4—is usually neglected. Its argument is split in a rather complex way between Boethius and Philosophy. After Boethius has raised the Problem of Prescience in (1) and (2) above, he immediately brings forward a solution favoured by some but which he does not find satisfactory.[4] These people think that the problem is solved by noticing that the Problem of Prescience is not, like the Problem of Providence, one about divine causality. God's foreknowledge does not cause future events to happen; rather, God's foreknowledge is caused by the events (CV.3.7–9 [15–31]). Boethius accepts, for the sake of the argument, the point about the direction of causality (in the end it will be rejected: see below), but he insists that there still remains a Problem of Prescience. Whichever way the causation runs, if a person is sitting, the belief that the person is sitting necessarily is true; and if the belief that the person is sitting is true, then it is necessary that the person is sitting (CV.3.10–14 [31–46]).

Philosophy promises—looking forward to the second part of the argument—to clear up Boethius's problem by considering the simplicity of God's knowledge, but first she will consider the problems Boethius has just raised (CV.4.1–3 [1–11]). She thinks that Boethius is wrong to have rejected the counterargument based on the direction of causality, and she gives a number of arguments designed to show that the mere fact that God foreknows future events does not preclude their being contingent. According to one of them (CV.4.7–13 [21–41]), someone who claims that divine prescience entails determinism, although God's knowledge is not the cause of the future events, is committed to holding that everything would happen of necessity even if there were no divine prescience. Her point is that since God's knowledge does not *change* how things are but merely *grasps* how they are, they must be as it grasps them as being independently of it. The determinist must therefore be able to produce a reason independent of divine prescience why all events happen necessarily, which he cannot do. This is an ingenious argument, but an opponent could urge that divine prescience is a necessary condition for the necessity of all events, although not its cause.[5]

Another argument rests on an appeal to the common-sense acceptance that some events are, indeed, contingent. Philosophy observes (CV.4.15–20 [46–62]) that when we look at, for instance, a chariot race taking place in front of us, we have no doubt that the apparently voluntary actions of the charioteers, steering and guiding their chariots, *are* voluntary and that 'no necessity compels them'. Using the principle that what is at present the case, in the past was going to be the case, she then argues that, at some time before the present, these present contingent events were events that were going to take place contingently. There are, then, future contingent events. The weakness with this reasoning is that the Problem of Prescience challenges our common-sense acceptance that some events are contingent. Philosophy rounds off her case with a comment that may be a fresh argument, from analogy (CV.4.20 [60–62]): 'just as the knowledge of present things brings no necessity to what is happening, so the prescience of future things brings no necessity to those things that are to come'. Both this comment and the example of the chariot race before it anticipate the direction the second part of the argument will take, although there Philosophy will have reason to qualify what she states here.

Why is Philosophy made to give these somewhat unimpressive arguments, when she is about to produce a much more elaborate and convincing piece of reasoning? One explanation may be that she wishes to show, on the assumption that divine foreknowledge does not have causal power (an assumption she is not, in the end, willing to make), that the Problem of Prescience can be resolved without resort to any abstruse metaphysical ideas. Another reason is suggested by the passage that immediately follows this first part of the argument (CV.4.21–23 [63–71]) where, after concluding that 'prescience of future things brings no necessity to those things that are to come', Philosophy recognizes that Boethius will still want to ask 'whether there *can* be any foreknowledge of events, that do not have necessary outcomes', Philosophy seems to be thinking here as if the Problem of Prescience has two aspects. First, there is the question of whether, once it is accepted that God foreknows all events, it follows that all events are necessary—the difficulty put forward in (1). This is the question that Philosophy's arguments so far have been designed to tackle and which, to judge from what she has said, she believes they have resolved successfully. Second, there is the question of whether it is possible that God foreknows all events, since it seems—for the reasons just given—that contingent events cannot be foreknown: being uncertain, they are not possible objects of knowledge but only of opinion—the difficulty put forward in (2).[6] It is this question, perhaps, that Philosophy sees herself as addressing in the second part of the argument. Although the conclusions she will establish also help to deal with (1), and purportedly to do so even allowing God's knowledge causative power, the argument does indeed read as if it is specifically designed to tackle (2).

The Argument: Part 2—The Modes of Cognition Principle (CV.4.23–V.5)

The second part of the argument can be seen as itself divided into two stages. In the first stage, Philosophy puts forward the Modes of Cognition Principle, a general principle to which the author Boethius had appealed in his treatment of universals in the second *Isagoge* commentary, and provides it with quite an elaborate explanation, not immediately linked to the question of prescience. Philosophy then proposes an argument, not found in any other text and probably of Boethius the author's own invention, that develops the Principle in a rather different way and shows how it can be applied to the Problem of Prescience and used to solve it.[7]

The problem at issue is, as has just been discussed, that which Philosophy spells out just before she presents the argument to solve it. That passage reads in full:

> But, you say, there is a problem about this very point: whether there *can* be any foreknowledge of events that do not have necessary outcomes. For these things seem to be incompatible, and you think that, if things are foreseen, necessity follows; if there is no necessity, they are not at all foreknown, and nothing that is not certain can be comprehended by knowledge. If, then, things that are uncertain in how they will turn out are foreseen as if they were certain (*quasi certa*), this is the obscurity of opinion, not the truthfulness of knowledge. For you believe that it is foreign to the integrity of knowledge to judge a thing as being other than it is. (CV.4.21–23 [62–71])

At the basis of the problem are some assumptions about knowledge, certainty, and necessity, which should be made explicit or recalled. Knowledge, as opposed to mere opinion, can be had about future events only if they are certain, and they are certain only if their outcome is necessary. Necessity has not been explicitly defined, but Philosophy, as mentioned above, seems to take it that an event is necessary if, before it happens, it is not possible for it to happen otherwise than it does happen. Necessity, so understood, is considered to preclude freedom: if volitions are necessary, then the will has no freedom.

The argument that, in the quotation above, Philosophy sets herself to tackle can be set out more formally as follows:

(3) Future contingents are known. [Premise]
(4) All things that are known are certain. [Premise: meaning of 'know']
(4a) If someone knows something, he knows it as certain [considered to follow from (4)]
(5) Only what is necessary is certain. [Premise: see paragraph above on assumptions]
(6) Future contingent events are not necessary. [Premise: meaning of 'contingent']
(7) Future contingent events are not certain. [5,6; *modus tollens*]
(8) If future contingents are known, they are known as if they were certain [Instantiation of 4a]
(9) To know something as if it were certain when it is not certain is to judge it otherwise than as it is [Premise: meaning of 'judge otherwise than as it is']
(10) If something is judged otherwise than as it is, it is not known [Premise]
(11) If future contingents are known, they are not known. [8, 9, 10; *modus ponens*]
(12) Future contingents are not known. [3,11; *modus ponens*]
(13) Future contingents are known and are not known. [3, 12]

This argument leads to a contradiction and so, since it is valid, one of its premisses must be negated. The obvious premise to reject is (3), but (3) is precisely what Philosophy wants to maintain. (5), which is dubious to modern eyes, would have seemed obviously true, given the underlying view of modality in the *Consolation*.[8] Philosophy accordingly rejects the one other premise, (10), which does not follow obviously from the meaning of its words:

> The cause of this error is that each person considers that everything that is known is known just according to the power and nature of the things that are known. The truth is the very contrary. For everything that is

known is grasped not according to its own power, but rather according to the capacity of those who know it. (CV 4.24–25 [72–77])

This principle, which Philosophy cites as being contrary to (10), is the Modes of Cognition Principle.

In order to grasp what the Principle involves, it is best to start from the statement it is designed to challenge. Taken in isolation, (10) might seem merely to be asserting that what is true of how a thing is known is always also true of what is known. The Principle would, then, be a denial of this assertion: in some cases, what is true of how a thing is known is not true of what is known. On this reading, the Principle is uncontroversially true: for example, something made up of parts may be known in a way that is not itself made up of parts. But, in the context of the argument, (10) must have a stronger meaning (which entails, but is not entailed by, the weaker one). The particular judgement about which (10) generalizes is that an event *e* will happen certainly—that is to say, that it is a certain event—when, since *e* is contingent, and only necessary events are certain (cf. (5)), *e* is not a certain event. (10), therefore, is making the powerful claim that if something, *s*, is F, then a judgement in which *s* is taken as being not-F is not knowledge. Despite its apparent self-evidence, (10) can be challenged by saying that all knowledge claims must be relativized to the knower's mode of cognition: 'K knows *s*' means 'K knows *s* according to *k*' (K's mode of cognition). If K judges *s* as not-F, he is claiming *s* as not-F according to *k*, and this claim may well be true, even though *s* is F. For example, suppose I am colour blind. The only book on my desk is green, and yet it might be true that I know that the *blue* book on my desk is open, if by this statement it is meant: 'According to my mode of cognition, as a colour-blind person, I know that that the blue book on my desk is open.' The Modes of Cognition Principle involves just this sort of relativization of knowledge claims to cognizers. In the long discussion of the Principle, which occupies the rest of V.4, Philosophy develops a quite complicated scheme of relativization that does not apply directly to the main issue under discussion, how judgements about future contingents can be certain. In V.6, however, she proposes a rather simpler type of relativization, which is closely linked to the issue of future contingents. But, at the very end of the work, she fleetingly alludes back to the complicated scheme of V.4.

In V.4, Philosophy's main example (which harks back to the use made of the principle in the *Isagoge* commentary) is that of the four different cognitive faculties—sense, imagination, reason, and intelligence—considering a man. Sense considers a man as an enmattered shape; the imagination, as a shape without matter; reason is concerned with a universal form present in, and abstracted from, an individual; and intelligence (which is God's way of knowing) sees 'the simple Form with the pure keenness of the mind' (CV.4.27–30 [82–91]). (I capitalize 'Form' to distinguish it from the abstractable universal form that reason grasps.[9]) Each of the faculties, then, has a different object: for the senses, a particular, material thing; for the imagination, a sensible image; for the reason, an abstracted universal form; and for God's intelligence, the Form—that is to say, God himself. Yet Philosophy wishes to say that the cognitions of the thing, the image, the abstracted form and the Form (God himself) are all ways of cognizing the same thing, which is known in different ways—more perfectly by higher faculties, less perfectly by lower ones: 'the higher power of understanding', she explains, 'includes the lower one, but the lower one does not at all rise up to the higher one' (CV.4.31 [92–94]). So, for instance, the intelligence knows 'reason's universal and imagination's shape and the sensibly-perceptible matter, not by using reason or the imagination or the senses, but Formally in that one stroke of the mind, as I might put it, surveying all things' (CV.4.33 [100–104]). It comprehends the Form, which is beyond the grasp of any of the lower faculties—and in comprehending it grasps all the things below the Form, but in the same manner as it comprehends the Form (CV.4.32 [95–100]).

Philosophy's idea can be formulated schematically. There are the four different levels of cognizer: A = Intelligence, B = Reason, C = Imagination and D = Sense. Each type of cognizer has its own proper type of object—a = Form/God, b = abstracted form, c = image, d = particular bodily thing. Consider now the man, *h*, of Philosophy's example. Applying the scheme to this act of cognition, *h* is identical to d, and it falls under c (which is an image of it), b (which is the abstracted universal man), and a (the Form, under which everything falls). Each type of cognizer knows *h* by cognizing an object proper to it under which *h* falls or which is identical to *h*. In that act of cognition, the cognizer knows not only its proper object but through its proper object what the lower cognizers know through their proper objects. This might seem to be an impossible claim. Perhaps God, by knowing himself, knows all things in every way (since God might have powers we cannot fully explain), but how can the reason, by grasping the abstracted universal man, also know all the sensible particularities of *h*, which are cognized by the imagination and senses? But Philosophy may not be claiming so much. She explains (CV.4.34–36 [104–112]) that reason comprehends *h* by defining him as a mortal, rational, two-footed animal. This notion is a universal one, but the reason still 'is not ignorant' that *h* is a sensibly perceptible and imaginatively perceptible thing, although it considers it not in the senses or the imagination but in a 'rational conception'. According to this explanation, reason does not know that *h* is, for instance, balding and wearing a panama hat; rather, it knows that although it cognizes *h* through its proper object, an abstracted universal, *h* can be cognized also through an image (by the imagination) and as a particular bodily thing, by the senses.

Statements not unlike the Modes of Cognition Principle are found in Proclus and Ammonius, although there is no parallel to the way Philosophy works it out in V.4.[10] Rather, the two Greek thinkers are content to say, more vaguely, that the gods know what has parts in a way which has no parts, what is changeable changelessly, what is temporal eternally, and what is contingent necessarily (this list is sometimes longer or a little different).[11] All of these are indeed consequences of the Principle, worked out as Boethius, according to the interpretation here, conceived it, since the gods would know things through an appropriate object, unchanging, eternal, necessary and without parts. Boethius's working out of the Principle may well, then, reflect a wider understanding of it among Neoplatonists, although it is impossible to be sure.[12]

The Modes of Cognition Principle disposes of the challenge to (3), the claim that future contingents are known, posed by (4)–(13) by showing that (10) should be denied. It also, apparently, shows how God has certain knowledge of contingents. He has it through his proper object of knowledge, himself. Proclus develops exactly this sort of account of God's foreknowledge. He says that God can know future contingents with certainty because he is responsible for causing them. He is like the maker of a machine who knows how it will work,[13] or like someone who has made a ship and its sailors and controls the winds, and so knows what will happen to the ship just by considering his own thoughts,[14] or like a seed which, by looking at itself, can see all that will grow out of it.[15] As Proclus puts it in the commentary on the *Parmenides*, 'by the very fact of intelligizing himself he knows all things of which he is the cause'.[16] Ammonius too seems to move in the same direction.[17] At the very end of the *Consolation*, Philosophy too will take this line—with drastic consequences for her overall position, as will emerge (see below). But, for almost all of V.6, she takes her argument in a different direction.

Before then, though, Philosophy spends V.5 on a much easier argument, justifying the position that God does have a different method of knowing things from our way, as beings with reason but not intelligence. She asks Boethius to imagine sense and imagination contending that the universal, which reason grasps but they do not, does not exist (V.5.5–6 [21–30]). Reason's reply—that the same things are sensed, imagined and also grasped rationally, as universals; and that this rational cognition is 'firmer and more perfect' than the other sorts—is one which, Philosophy is sure, humans, endowed with reason, will accept. By the same token, she continues (CV.5.8–11 [39–50]), we should be willing to accept that God can grasp things in a different and better way than we can.[18]

The Argument: Part 3—Divine Eternity and Philosophy's Simplification of the Modes of Cognition Principle (CV.6.1–24)

In V.4, Philosophy's relativization of knowledge to knowers involved both different modes of cognition and the different proper objects of each mode. In V.6 she does not (until the very end of the section) consider the different proper objects; rather, she examines in detail God's mode of cognition in relation to time and what, in consequence, is the effect of relativizing knowledge claims to it. This new strategy does not merely allow Philosophy to escape the central difficulty which the other approach would—and, eventually will—present to her. It also brings about a demystification of the Modes of Cognition Principle as applied to divine knowledge. It shows how the relativization of knowledge to knower involved in divine prescience is exactly like a type of relativization of knowledge to knowers that takes place in our own, human cognition.

Philosophy begins her new approach by rephrasing the Modes of Cognition Principle ('everything that is known is cognized not from its own nature but from that of those who grasp it' (CV.6.1 [2–3]) so as to suggest that, in order to find out about a mode of cognition, we should investigate the *nature* of the cognizer. Therefore, in order to understand God's mode of cognition, which involves prescience, we need to consider how God exists (*divinae substantiae status*—the condition of the divine substance).[19] The way God exists, Philosophy goes on to explain, is to exist eternally. Divine eternity, she then makes clear, is not a matter of existing during an infinite length of time, as the universe does if it lacks beginning and end. Rather, God's eternity is 'the whole, simultaneous and perfect possession of unbounded life' (CV.6.4 [9–11]: *interminabilis vitae tota simul et perfecta possessio*). She continues:

> For whatever lives in time proceeds in the present from the past into the future, and there is nothing with its existence in time that can embrace the whole space of its life: rather, indeed, it does not yet grasp tomorrow but it has already lost yesterday—and in your daily life too you do not live in more than the moving, passing moment. (CV.6.5 [12–18])

Philosophy then goes on (CV.6.6–10 [18–38]) to draw a contrast between the state of what is 'subject to the condition of time' but has neither a beginning nor an end—as, she says, both Plato and Aristotle teach the universe to be[20]—and the genuine eternity of God, which involves not being spread out in time but 'having present the infinity of moving time'. In OSI (4. 231–48 [59–77]), Boethius draws a very similar distinction between what he calls the 'sempiternity' of the universe—the now of moving time stretched out for ever—and God's eternity, which is made by a now that remains still and unmoving.

Philosophy (and Boethius in his own voice in OSI) is clearly following a tradition in Greek philosophy, going back as far as Parmenides, according to which God is, or the gods are, outside time.[21] Modern commentators usually interpret her position to be that God is timeless or atemporal, in the sense that he cannot be placed in time at all—that he not only lacks any extension in time but also has no position in time.[22] This interpretation puts God alongside numbers and universals, which many modern philosophers regard as being similarly atemporal, in the sense that tense or temporal qualifications are inappropriate to them (no one says, except as a joke, '2 + 2 will equal 4 tomorrow'). But for Boethius, God's eternity is a way of *living*: 'the simultaneous, whole and perfect possession of unbounded life'. The comparison with numbers serves only to show how very different is Boethius's idea of divine eternity from anything we can envisage in the normal run of things—a point which at least some of the modern interpreters have acknowledged.[23] 'Life' also gives the clue to where Boethius's emphasis really lies. God's life is not, of course, that of a physical thing or something that has sense perception: it is a purely intellectual life, a life of thinking. When he describes God's eternity, Boethius is describing God's way of thinking. God is an infinitely powerful mind, which instantaneously grasps all that there is to grasp. Such a way of living leaves no room for time. Time is the condition of the life of less powerful minds, which have to grasp one thing after another.[24]

God's eternity is, then, more than mere atemporality in the modern sense, and it is even open to question whether Boethius the author (or his character, Philosophy) regarded it as atemporal in this sense at all. It is clear from both OSI and the *Consolation* that to speak of God using temporal or tense indicators ('God did that yesterday', 'God will think this tomorrow') is highly misleading. But neither text makes clear that such statements are false, which they would be if God were atemporal in the modern sense. All that these texts say is compatible with a different reading. According to it, God exists at all times in a way quite different from that of time-bound things and which is temporally completely unchanging.[25]

So far as her main argument is concerned, the important point Philosophy develops from her description of divine eternity is that God lives and knows in an eternal *present*. Indeed, this eternal present is the model of the ordinary present, with which we are familiar. We experience the presentness 'of this tiny, fleeting instant' (CVI.6.12 [50–51])—that is to say, of the moment that it is *now*. This presentness, says Philosophy (CVI.6.12–13 [40–56]), should be seen as an attempt to imitate God's eternal present. The attempt is unsuccessful, because whereas God is never changing, the only way in which our lives can be lived is not all at once, but by taking on 'the infinite journey of time'. Nonetheless, the ordinary, human present provides a comparison by which we can understand something of God's eternal present and so of God's way of knowing.

In a series of closely related statements, Philosophy emphasizes and re-emphasizes the point that God's way of knowing all that he knows is, although of course different from any human way of knowing, importantly *like* human knowledge of the present. God's knowledge 'remains in the simplicity of its presentness and, embracing the infinite spaces of the past and future, considers all things in its simple cognition as if they were now happening (*quasi iam gerantur*) (CV.6.15 [63–66]); 'just as you see some things in this temporal present of yours, so God sees all things in that eternal present of his' (CV.6.20 [78–80]); God's foresight 'sees present to it things in the way they will some time be in the future' (CV.6.21 [81–83]); and, Philosophy insists, it is not even right to talk about God's *fore*knowledge, his *praevidentia*, as if it were knowledge of the future: rather, one speaks of his *providentia*, the knowledge 'of an instant which never passes' (CV.6.16–17 [66–70]).

Modern commentators have tended to explain this idea of God knowing everything in the present by referring to God's atemporality. We know in the present what is happening simultaneously with our knowing it. Since God is atemporal, they have suggested, he can be considered to exist simultaneously with any moment of time, and so he does indeed know everything in the present. There then arises the problem that, since simultaneity is a transitive relation, everything that God knows—my typing this page and Nero watching Rome burn, for instance—is simultaneous.[26] An ingenious answer to this problem, not entirely free from suspicion of *ad hoc*-ery, has been worked out on Philosophy's behalf, according to which the simultaneity between an eternal thing and a temporal one (ET-simultaneity) is not a transitive relation.[27] Yet it may be that the whole direction of this explanation is misguided. There is some doubt (see above) about whether Philosophy's God is conceived as atemporal, and even if he is, it is highly questionable whether he would thereby exist simultaneously with all temporal things; a truly atemporal being would not be simultaneous with anything in time. In any case, Philosophy's idea does not seem to be that God exists simultaneously with events and therefore knows them in the present but that, although events are future or past, God knows them in the sort of way that we know present events. Indeed, she even talks (CV.6.40 [151–53]) of God's gaze outrunning 'every future thing and twisting and calling it back to the present of its own cognition'.

The Argument: Part 4—Simple and Conditional Necessity (CV.6.25–48)

After having shown that God's knowledge of everything is like (human) knowledge of the present, Philosophy's next step will be to show how, in the case of human knowledge of the present, contingent events, by nature uncertain, are necessary and so certain when relativized to their knowers. She does so by introducing a distinction between two sorts of necessity, which she calls 'simple necessity' and necessity that depends on a condition (*necessitas conditionis*) or 'conditional necessity' (CV.6.27 [103–106]. Simple necessity is exemplified by natural necessities—states of affairs which, given the laws of nature, cannot be otherwise—that, for instance, all men are mortal and that the sun rises. Conditional necessity is (CV.6.27 [105–106]) when, for instance , 'if you know someone is walking, it is necessary that he is walking.' Philosophy continues:

> (§28 [106–109]) For what each person knows cannot be otherwise <than it is known to be>, but this condition by no means brings with it that simple necessity. (§29a [109–11]) For it is not a thing's own nature that makes this necessity, but the adding of the condition: (§29b [111–113]) for no necessity compels a person who voluntarily is walking (*gradientem*) to be walking (*incedere*), but when he is walking (*graditur*), it is necessary that he is walking (*incedere*).

On the reading of Philosophy's strategy in V.6 I am advancing, her aim in §28–29a is clear. She is explaining that although an event—for instance, that John is walking—is contingent, when it is relativized to a human's present knowledge of it, it is necessary; but it is not necessary in the manner of a simply necessary event, such as that the sun is moving: it is necessary only given the relativization to the knower that is stated in the condition added to the simple sentence. §29b then goes on to introduce a new idea, which needs further explanation. Many scholars, however, have interpreted this whole passage about the distinction between simple and conditional necessity quite differently. Before looking at the new idea Philosophy adds at §29b, I shall pause, therefore, to consider and reject their interpretations.

To a reader today, it can easily seem as if Philosophy here is making here what, in modern terms, is called a scope distinction.[28] A sentence of the basic form 'If p, then necessarily q' is ambiguous, since 'Necessarily' can have either narrow scope, and apply to q alone, or wide scope, and apply to the whole 'If . . . then . . .' statement. In the first case, the sentence says that, if p is true, then q, the consequent, is necessarily true (later medieval logicians talked of *necessitas consequentis*—'necessity of the consequent'). In the second case, the sentence says that what is necessary is neither the antecedent p, nor the consequent q, but the whole 'If . . . then . . .' statement: 'it is necessary that if p, then q' (later medieval logicians talked of *necessitas consequentiae*—'necessity of the consequence, i.e., of the whole 'If . . . then . . .' statement).

This interpretation is tempting because, by applying the scope distinction, it is possible to resolve the Problem of Prescience, in the form in which Boethius puts it to Philosophy at the beginning of V.3. Consider again Boethius's first formulation of the Problem:

(1) 'If God sees all things and can in no way be mistaken, then there necessarily happens what he by providence will have foreseen will be' (CV.3.4 [6–8])

This argument depends on a hidden scope-ambiguity. (1) might mean either

(1W) Necessarily (If God sees all things and can in no way be mistaken, then there happens what he by providence will have foreseen will be.)

or

(1N) If God sees all things and can in no way be mistaken, then what he by providence will have foreseen will be happens necessarily.

1(W, i.e., 'wide-scope') is clearly true, because as a matter of definition whatever is known must be the case. But the truth of 1W does not entail that future events are necessary—the necessity applies to the whole 'If . . . then . . .' statement, not to the consequent. 1(N, i.e., narrow-scope) would, if true, state that all future events are necessary, because it claims that if the antecedent is true (as Christians and many others believe), then the consequent is not merely true but necessarily the case. But there is no good reason—at least, not without further argument—to accept (1N). And (2) is ambiguous in the same sort of way.[29]

The fact that the scope distinction disposes of Boethius's original problem is, however, one strong reason for not accepting it as an interpretation of Philosophy's distinction.[30] If Philosophy had understood the distinction between simple and conditional necessity in this way, she could be reasonably expected to have used it to unmask the ambiguity in Boethius's two formulations of the Problem of Prescience and so dispose of the problem. But she does not. She gives no indication anywhere of finding anything amiss with (1) and (2), and she does not reconsider them in the light of what she says about simple and conditional necessity. Moreover, if Philosophy did intend to solve the Problem of Prescience by making the scope distinction, then all the rest of the complicated apparatus she introduces—the Modes of Cognition Principle, God's way of existing in eternity, and his special way of knowing in the present—would be idle. Indeed, she would no longer make the assumptions about the connection between knowledge, certainty, and necessity on which the argument the Principle is designed to counter is based.

True, the scope distinction could serve towards answering a much more challenging formulation of the Problem of Prescience (the 'accidental necessity argument'), which takes account of the scope distinction. This accidental necessity argument is based on the idea that God does not merely know now what will happen in the future but has already come to know it: his knowledge of the future is a fact about the past and, so, irrevocable. By insisting that God is atemporal (if this is really what she does insist!), Philosophy would be providing a way to counter this argument by denying that God's knowledge of the future is a fact about the past, since no facts about God would be temporal.[31] But there is no sign at all of the accidental necessity argument in the *Consolation*. Moreover, it does not seem—at least from the indication of his logical works—that Boethius had even an intuitive understanding of how operators work on propositions, and so it is unlikely he could have even dimly envisaged the scope distinction modern thinkers make, let alone the accidental necessity argument.[32]

If these anachronistic readings of simple and conditional necessity are to be rejected, however, it still remains to explain what Philosophy is arguing in §29b (which, on the scope distinction interpretation, is another exemplification of the point already made). There she moves from considering conditions that relativize an event to its knower to those conditions that link an event simply to the fact that it is taking place at present: 'he is walking, *when he is walking*'.

The clue is given by the way the author Boethius used the distinction between two sorts of necessity earlier, when commenting on *On Interpretation* (*2InDI* 241:1—243:28).[33] Boethius is explaining Aristotle's point when he says in *On Interpretation* (19a23): 'what is, necessarily is, when it is.' This idea of the necessity of the present is characteristic of Aristotle (and, arguably, every philosopher up to the eleventh century, and many later), although it is at odds with modern approaches to possibility and necessity, which have their foundations in the later Middle Ages.[34] Aristotle took the view that the actual state of affairs exhausts the possibilities for what is happening at that given moment: there are no alternative synchronic possible states of affairs. Suppose I am sitting at the present instant, t*. On Aristotle's view, it is not possible that I am standing now—although it was indeed possible the moment before that I would be standing at t*, and it is possible now at t* that the next moment I shall be standing.[35] Boethius explains Aristotle's point by saying that there is a distinction between saying that something is necessary 'by a simple predication' or 'simply', which we do in cases of natural necessity—as when we say that it is necessary for the sun to be in motion, and saying that something is necessary 'depending on a condition'—as when we say that it is necessary for Socrates to sit, when he is sitting. He adds (using almost the same words as Philosophy will employ) that conditional necessity does not bring with it simple necessity.[36] The point he wishes to stress is that the necessity of the present is accidental to the thing that is necessary (*2InDI* 241:2), by contrast with simple necessity, which arises when something has no potency for opposites: the sun, for example, has no potency to be still, and so it is simply necessary that it moves (*2InDI* 243:13–15).[37]

In the *Consolation*, Philosophy's concern, as dictated by her overall argument, is the sort of necessity had by what is known relative to someone knowing it in the present. In §29b she suggests that this sort of conditional necessity is like that involved in the Aristotelian necessity of the present: suppose someone is walking voluntarily: his walking *is* indeed voluntary and 'no necessity compels it', yet when he walks, it is necessary that he is walking.[38] In effect, she is advancing a subsidiary argument to back up and clarify her position in §§ 27-29a. There she claims that conditionally necessary events are at once contingent and yet, relative to their present knowers, necessary. Being both contingent and (conditionally) necessary is nothing strange, she is now saying, because every present event is like this, whether or not it has a present knower. The important point here for Philosophy's argument is that no one thinks that the Aristotelian necessity of the present constrains freedom of action. In her example, the man is walking voluntarily, although it is conditionally necessary that he is walking; or, in another example she gives a little later (CV.6.38 [145–47]), a person is acting freely but 'cannot escape the gaze of an eye which is present'.

Philosophy has introduced human knowledge of the present only so as to be able to explain God's knowledge. She is now able to return to her main theme and state:

> (14) 'In the same way, therefore, if providence sees something present, it is necessary that it is, although of its nature it has no necessity.' (CV.6.30 [113–15])

What Philosophy has previously established about God's knowledge being like our knowledge of the present allows her to assert the minor premise:

> (15) 'But (*atqui*) God sees present those future things which happen as a result of free will.' (CV.6.31 [115–116])

And she can therefore draw the conclusion at which the whole of the second part of her argument has been aiming. Things that happen as a result of free will are, in their own nature, free, but in relation to God's vision of them they are necessary 'by the condition of God's knowledge'.[39]

To summarize. Philosophy's central idea, taken from the Modes of Cognition Principle, is that some events happen freely so far as their own nature is concerned but necessarily relative to their being known by God. This formulation is not logically problematic, but it does require explanation. Philosophy shows that when we humans know what is happening at present, then events that are contingent by nature are necessary relative to our knowing them. She adds that the sense in which these events are necessary is just like that in which (on her Aristotelian view) all present events are necessary when they are happening. Philosophy also shows that, because of his special mode of cognition, God's way of knowing all things, including the future, is like human knowledge of the present. And so future contingents, in relation to God, are necessary and can be known for certain, but they are contingent in their own nature and no more constrained than anything happening in the present.

This solution to the Problem of Prescience is probably the author Boethius's finest achievement in terms of philosophical argument. Each of the elements—the Modes of Cognition Principle (in some form), the idea of God's eternity as a life lived all at once, and even the distinction between conditional and simple necessity[40]—is found in other authors and so probably was not entirely invented by Boethius. But there is no evidence that anyone before had brought all these ideas together to solve the Problem of Prescience.[41]

Prescience and Providence

Right up until the final paragraphs, Philosophy keeps her discussion of the Problem of Prescience apart from what she has said about the Problem of Providence. But the results of the two lines of argument fit together. In both, she has been concerned to defend the freedom of the will. With regard to the Problem of Providence, she has argued that causal determinism does stop any event in the world from being free, but it does not prevent rational acts of the human will from being free. With regard to the Problem of Prescience, she has shown that God's foreknowledge is compatible with the freedom of any sort of event. Her overall position, then, will be that rational volitions are completely free, whereas other events are not free because they are causally determined.

But a section just before the end changes everything. Early in the discussion, the character Boethius had made it clear that he was not willing ultimately to give up the position that God not only foreknows what will happen but is causally responsible for it. In the course of rejecting the view of those who think that, so long as God's knowledge of future events is caused by those events and not the cause of them, the Problem of Prescience is resolved, Boethius had remarked parenthetically:

> Now indeed how back to front it is that the outcome of things in time should be said to be the cause of eternal prescience. What is it to judge that God foresees future things because they are going to happen other than to think that things which have once happened are the cause of that highest providence? (CV.3.15–16 [46–51])

As Boethius's phrasing indicates, his worry here is not about how an event in the future could cause a cognition in the past but that God's knowledge should be caused by something outside God. This worry is one that engaged Boethius as author, as well as the character Boethius.

For the moment, Boethius the character leaves the worry aside, for the sake of argument. But very near to the end of V.6, it is alluded to again, this time by Philosophy. After restating her point that God changelessly knows 'in one stroke' (*uno ictu*) all things', she goes on:

> God derives this presentness of understanding and seeing all things not from the future course of things, but from his own simplicity. From this is also resolved what you put forward a little before, that it is unworthy if our future actions should be said to be the cause of God's knowledge. For this power of knowledge, wrapping together all things in a present act of knowing, itself sets the measure for all things and owes nothing to things inferior to it (*posterioribus*). (CV.6.41–43 [155–63])

In this short passage, Philosophy suggests a way of using the Modes of Cognition Principle about God's foreknowledge nearer to his explanation in V.4, and to the thinking of Proclus, than to the line of thought he has developed in V.6. Although the language is vague, if God's power of knowledge 'sets the measure for all things and owes nothing to things inferior to it', then it seems to be that God knows everything by knowing himself: the proper object of God's mode of cognition will be, as in V.4, the 'Form'. The problem about this way of regarding God's knowledge is that, as Proclus's views illustrate, it seems to bring with it God's causal determinism of everything whatsoever that God knows: for how does God know all things through himself unless he sees himself as their cause? Certainly Philosophy, by presenting her comment as an answer to Boethius's objection that God's foreseeing must be the *cause* of future events rather than being caused by them, makes it clear that she is now acknowledging God as the cause of all that he knows and, so, the cause of the motions of the human mind as well as events in the world. But Philosophy had made it clear in Book IV that, in her view, what is causally determined is not free. On her assumptions, if God causes the events in our minds, including our volitions, then we have no free will.

Philosophy's long and impressive defence of human freedom is ruined—but she seems not to have noticed. She ends the *Consolation* (CV.6.44–48 [163–76]) by asserting that 'since things are thus', human freedom of choice is undefiled, and it is just for the laws to reward the good and punish the wicked. God, too, hears and answers our prayers, and gives out reward and punishment for good and ill behaviour. Since we act before his all-seeing gaze, there is a need for us to act well. Boethius does not reply. The final lines of the work are clearly designed to bring a resolution to the questions Boethius raised in V.3, but they leave the reader puzzled and dissatisfied. Philosophy has vindicated human freedom, only to sacrifice it in the space of a couple of lines.

8

INTERPRETING THE *CONSOLATION*

In the last two chapters I have shown that the individual arguments in the *Consolation* are more complex and sophisticated than is usually accepted. I have also suggested that, taken together, they offer an interpretative problem. Although Philosophy is presented as providing authoritative answers to the questions Boethius raises at the beginning of the work, the arguments she gives do not on scrutiny seem to fit together in supporting a single, coherent position. How, then, should the *Consolation* be read? To answer this question properly, analysis of the arguments alone is not enough. The *Consolation* needs to be considered as a whole, and as a complex literary artefact, and placed within its unusual cultural context. In the next four sections, I shall look at the poems in the *Consolation* and then examine the figure of Philosophy and the work's relation to Christianity. These discussions will reveal the full extent of the interpretative problem. Finally, I shall look to one aspect of the *Consolation*'s literary form—its alternation of prose and verse, in the manner of Menippean satire—which strengthens an interpretation that reconciles the various, apparently conflicting elements of evidence.

The Poems in the *Consolation*

By leaving the 42 verse sections aside until now, I may have given the impression that they are to be regarded merely as an ornament, irrelevant for an understanding of the *Consolation*'s philosophical content. Such a judgement would be misguided. Yet there is an important sense in which the *Consolation*'s argument is carried forward by the prose sections alone. Apart from the initial scene-setting poem, none of the other verse passages contains material essential either to the dramatic progress of the narrative of Boethius's cure or to the flow of reasoning. The poems repeat or, more rarely, even qualify or add to the arguments advanced in the prose, but they do not (with one exception) ever supply a premise missing in the prose or derive from premisses stated in prose a conclusion not given in a prose section. Indeed, only 14 of the poems—which I shall call the 'dramatic' poems—are part of the dramatic action of the dialogue in any explicit way.[1]

The remaining 28 poems all come directly after prose passages where Philosophy has been speaking, and they are always assigned by modern commentators to Philosophy.[2] There is good reason for the assignation: it has the merit of simplicity, and the way in which the final poems of each of Books I to IV are apparently mentioned specifically in the narrative suggests that Boethius the author is trying to link the poems as a whole into the fiction of the *Consolation*. Still, it is important to see that these 28 do not form part of the dialogue between Boethius and Philosophy; rather, they provide commentaries on the progress of the discussion, or interludes that divert from it but not irrelevantly. And these poems—along with some that *are* explicitly linked to the action but in a merely superficial way (those at the end of Books I–IV, and IV, m. 6)—provide a fuller view of Philosophy's outlook than emerges from the dialogue itself.

About half of these non-dramatic poems give summaries in figurative language of what has just been discussed in the prose section. Even these verse passages are not merely ornamental. In the majority of cases (I, m. 6; I, m. 7; II, m. 2; II, m. 3; III, m.1; III, m. 5; III, m. 8; III, m. 10; IV, m. 5; V, m. 1; V, m. 2), the imagery is natural—that, for instance, of the seasons, the weather, the sea, and the animal world.[3] When Philosophy found Boethius despondent in his cell, her initial complaint (I, m. 2) was that a person who once knew the secrets of nature—the motions of the stars and the reasons for natural phenomena such as the seasons—should now be staring, not heavenwards, but down at the ground. But her discussion in the prose passages of the *Consolation* leaves natural science aside: she concentrates on reawakening Boethius's metaphysical, rather than his physical, learning, conscious perhaps that a prison cell is hardly the place for making astronomical observations. The natural imagery of the verse passages, with its emphasis on natural order, reminds the reader that for Boethius the author a wise man sees the providential arrangement of all things reflected throughout the physical universe.[4] Often, explicit morals are drawn from the natural examples, and they are not always simple repetitions of what has been established in the preceding prose passage. I, m. 4, 6, and 7, all anticipate Philosophy's stoic teaching in Book II. And arguably, these poems, along with II, m. 3, and with two poems that move further away from the preceding prose passages, II, m. 4 and 5, make a special contribution to the overall meaning of the *Consolation*. They bring out positively, as a feasible ideal for living, the moderate stoicism that is advocated in more negative terms in II and III.1–8.

I, m. 4, drawing a general lesson from the exempla and the complicated metaphor in the preceding prose (CI.3.9–14 [31–49]) sets out how, spurning both hope and fear (l. 13) a person can live calmly whatever the persecution by tyrannical rulers. I, m. 6 argues that things should be done at the right time. The idea came up in the preceding prose in the context of Boethius's cure: he should start with gentle remedies. But in the poem it becomes a general rule for living. I, m. 7 picks up the idea from I, m. 4 of rejecting hope and fear and makes it into advice to anyone, not just those living under the sway of a tyrant. By freeing yourself from joys and sorrows, as well as hopes and fears, you are able to follow the right path (ll.20–28).[5] II, m. 3 relates the ever-changingness of fortune to the natural cycle of the seasons and to the 'eternal law' by which all things that come to be lack permanence (ll.17–18); whereas the prose discussion is limited to mere exculpation—Fortune cannot be blamed for its changeable nature and has been, all in all, good to Boethius—this poem presents it positively as part of a natural order to which humans can accommodate themselves. II, m. 4 promises that by building one's house not in the sand or on the top of a mountain but low down, on rock, one can be sure it will withstand any storms—a metaphor that supports the value of the modest way of life, not given over to pursuing the good of fortune, which will be advocated, negatively, in the following sections. II, m. 5 tells of the Golden Age, before there was trade or money. Whilst it links directly with the preceding prose, where the pursuit of riches has been shown to be foolish, the poem also suggests that there could in principle—as there was in a legendary time past—be a society living happily, were its members content with what nature provides.

A number of the commentary/interlude poems (like the last of the two just examined) add other ideas related, in some cases only indirectly, to the subject of the surrounding prose discussion. For example, two poems (II, m. 6; III, m. 4) use Nero as an exemplum of tyranny—a way of linking in to the *Consolation* the Roman past and of Boethius the author suggesting, as he had done already in Book I (CI.3.9 [31–33]), his place in a line of philosophers who die to uphold Roman principles against Imperial tyranny. II, m. 8, and III, m. 6 form, along with three of the dramatic poems, an important group concerned with cosmic order (see below). III, m. 11 and V, m. 4 are the most genuinely philosophical of the commentary/interlude poems. III, m. 11 gives a more explicit and detailed discussion of Plato's doctrine of *anamnēsis* than is given in the prose.[6] V, m. 4 fills in philosophical background for the prose discussion by supplying an exposition and critique of Stoic epistemology and so showing why Philosophy's approach in the prose, based on the Modes of Cognition Principle, is preferable.

Especially interesting are the poems that recount legends. II, m. 5, on the Golden Age, has been mentioned—it brings out its moral explicitly and clearly, but the others are more difficult to interpret. III, m. 12 tells the story of Orpheus and Eurydice. Orpheus so succeeds in charming the Underworld with his music that he is allowed to lead his dead wife, Eurydice, back to life. The one condition is that he should not turn back to look at her, and when, overcome by the power of love (ll. 47–48: 'Who can give a law to lovers? Love is the greater law for itself.'), he looks at her, she is lost. Although III, m. 12 dwells especially on Orpheus's achievement in winning back Eurydice, it remains a story of failure: figuratively, it tells of an unsuccessful attempt at mental ascent, at the very moment when Boethius has apparently regained true understanding through Philosophy's dialogue. The poem sets up resonances and tensions, both with other Latin accounts, such as Seneca's, of the same legend, and with other passages, verse and prose, in the *Consolation*.[7] Its comment on the power of love compares ironically with II, m. 8, a hymn to cosmic love and more widely with the whole argument of III.9–12, whilst there is a vivid contrast with the poem immediately following, IV, m.1. There Philosophy promises Boethius a successful ascent to his true fatherland and (ll.27–30) invites him to look back down at what he has left—precisely what III, m. 12 ended by forbidding.[8]

The two other poems based on legends are even less straightforward. In the case of IV, m. 7, the interpretative problem lies in seeing why Agamemnon's sacrifice of Iphigenia—an example of tragic, if resolute, action—is linked with the labours of Hercules. With regard to IV, m. 3, on Circe's bewitchment of Ulysses and his crew—an episode that already had a history of Neoplatonic allegorical reading—the difficulties concern especially the exact meaning of the moral drawn at the end. Literary specialists have debated at length their readings of both.[9] But the most important point for the understanding of the *Consolation* as a whole that all three legend poems bring out is one about the *complexity* of the *Consolation*. A casual reader might think that the work is complex only in its intricate philosophical arguments. These poems show that Boethius was capable, too, of contriving literary complexities. He writes so that his meaning emerges only when individual lines are placed in a wider context within and outside the *Consolation* and, even then, the meaning is not clear and unitary but suggestive and multifold.

Another aspect of literary complexity in the verse passages is structural. The poems often anticipate themes that the prose dialogue will treat later, or link back to earlier discussions. As mentioned already, poems in Book I (m. 4, 6, 7) anticipate Book II. III, m. 6, with its declaration (l. 2) that 'there is one Father of all things', foreshadows the conclusions reached in III.10–12 as well as the tenor of III, m. 9, the great hexameter prayer to God. In V, m. 2, it is stated (ll.11–12) that God sees all things which are, which have been and which will be 'in one stroke (*ictus*) of the mind'. It is this idea, and even the same word '*ictus*' (CV.6.40 [154]), that will be used in V.6 to resolve the problem about divine prescience of contingent events. Some poems look not forwards, but back to earlier parts of the discussion. IV, m. 4 begins by talking, disparagingly, about people who desire death and resort to suicide: Boethius himself, in the opening poem (ll.13–16), wished for death to come quickly. IV, m. 5, about how those ignorant of natural science are astonished or frightened by unusual celestial phenomena, links up I, m. 2, on Boethius's former mastery of astronomy.

Patterning is particularly evident with regard to the more important of the dramatic poems. Apart from the opening lament and the retrospective I, m. 3, just two poems are given to Boethius (the character): I, m. 5 and V, m. 3. They both share the same metre (they are acataleptic anapaestic dimeters), which is also that of III, m. 2 and IV, m. 6.[10] The four poems form a series, symmetrically placed around the central III, m. 9, with a special emphasis on the contrast between the two dramatic poems: I, m.5, at the beginning of the philosophical discussion, and V, m. 3, preceding the final topic, divine prescience and human free will. In I, m. 5 Boethius complains that, whilst God rules all the rest of nature, ordering it to a fixed end, humankind is left at the mercy of fortune. III, m. 2 and IV, m. 6 are closely related both in theme and organization, and by metre, to I, m. 5, and they show a distinct progression in thought.[11] III, m. 2 shows how all things in nature return to their origins and concludes (ll. 35–38)—in lines that anticipate III, m. 2—by optimistically affirming that everything thereby follows a fixed, circular course. IV, m. 6 reiterates the ideas of everything (including humans) following stable, circular courses and returning to their origin, now made clear (with echoes both of II, m. 8 and III, m. 9) as being God, who is also the end to which they are drawn by love.

The final poem of the series, V, m. 3, spoken by Boethius, is less easy to interpret. Perplexed by the apparent incompatibility between divine prescience and human free will, Boethius initially—in the tone of I, m. 5—considers the irreconcileability of the two truths as a fault in the constitution of the universe. But can truths really be discordant, he asks: is it not rather that his embodied mind—seeing, like the cave dwellers of Plato's *Republic*, by the light of a fire (l. 9)—does not see how they are linked? Why, then, wonders Boethius, do we 'blaze with such love' (l. 11) to find hidden truths, and he poses Meno's paradox of inquiry: we cannot seek to find out what we already know, but neither can we seek without knowing what we are seeking. As in the *Meno*, the paradox is answered by the theory of recollection—we learn by looking back to what we learned in a former, disembodied state. Commentators are no doubt right to see in the detached, philosophical manner of the poem, and its speaker's wish to enquire rather than complain, a pointed contrast with its pair, I, m. 5, and so a sign of how far Boethius's cure has advanced.[12] Yet the poem remains, just like I, m. 5, a confession of perplexity, and the air of uncertainty is thickened by an extra tension. Boethius's initial problem is that truths grasped as single things (*singula*)—God foreknows all things; humans have free-will—do not fit together with each other. He describes recollection, however, as proceeding from a knowledge of the whole (*summa*), which we retain, to that of the *singula*, which we have forgotten.[13] Altogether, the interpretation of the poem will depend especially on how the following argument is read. Philosophy, it might be argued, does not bear out even the limited optimism of Boethius about the success of human enquiry in this area.[14] Philosophy, perhaps, does not show even herself capable of fitting together the discordant truths.

Philosophy's dramatic poems mark the progress of her action in curing Boethius. I, m. 2 records the low state of her patient when she begins, IV, m. 1—closely linked to the *Phaedrus*—presents the remaining part of her discussion as a celestial journey that will return Boethius to his true fatherland. III, m. 9 is placed centrally in the *Consolation*; it stands out by its metre, solemnity, and its explicit announcement as a prayer, and the other poems are patterned, roughly symmetrically, on either side of it. In the past, commentators described this poem as an epitome of Plato's *Timaeus*. Although Friedrich Klingner's minute examination showed this view to be a simplification,[15] III, m. 9 remains, most obviously, a poetic allusion and tribute to the *Timaeus*, in the way that IV, m. 1 commemorates the *Phaedrus* and other poems present central themes of other Platonic dialogues: III, m. 10 the allegory of the cave, the fire, and the sun from the *Republic*, III, m. 11 and V, m. 3 the theory of recollection and paradox of enquiry from the *Meno*. Boethius the author, whose project of translating Aristotle and Plato had not gone beyond Aristotle's logic, obviously wished, through the poetry, to fill the *Consolation* with reminders of the Platonic positions and arguments that underlie the Neoplatonic arguments of the prose sections.

The structure of III, m. 9 follows the ancient pattern of a hymn. First, in the *epikleseis* (ll.1–6), God is invoked as maker and governor of things, eternal and good. Then, in the *aretalogia* (ll.6–21), God's works are described: how he makes an image of the ideal forms in his mind, binds the elements together, fashions the World Soul and also human souls, which return to him. Finally, in the *euchai* (ll.22–28), Philosophy makes her prayer to be allowed to see God, 'Disperse the cloudiness and weight of earthly mass and shine in your splendour' (ll.25–26), and then, as if that prayer had been granted, ends by again describing God (ll. 26–28):

> . . . For you are the serene heaven,
> The tranquil resting place for the good. To see you is their goal,
> You, at once the beginning, bearer, leader, path and end.

The whole opening of the poem, up to the end of the *aretalogia*, has close links with the *Timaeus*, although it is a *Timaeus* seen through the lens of Neoplatonic interpretation.[16] And the structure of the poem as a whole follows the Neoplatonic scheme of permanence (the initial description of God), procession (God's works), and return (the description of the return of human souls leads to the final prayer and the last lines, which evoke the soul back in its resting place). The *epiklēseis* and *euchai*, however, also draw more widely on the tradition of ancient hymnody, pagan and Christian. Some scholars have detected distinctively Christian elements in the description of God and in the ending of the final prayer. But, whilst the author Boethius's Christian background might well have coloured aspects of this poem, the prayer remains in all its obvious features—appropriately for its speaker,

Philosophy—a hymn to God as the Platonists understood him, and a God whose works are described in terms that every educated reader would recognize as those of Plato's *Timaeus*. Given the deliberate placing of III, m. 9 at the centre of the *Consolation*, the question immediately rises (as it did for commentators from the tenth century onwards):[17] why did a Christian author, Boethius, put at the centre of his last work around so strikingly non-Christian a hymn? It might help, in answering this question, to think about the speaker of the poem. III, m. 9 is, as has been said, one of Philosophy's few dramatic poems; indeed, it is presented as her most characteristic utterance. But who, exactly, is Philosophy? What does this personification represent?

The Personification of Philosophy

The *Consolation* is certainly not the first work where philosophy is personified as a beautiful lady: the idea was suggested by Plato himself and occurs often in, among others, Cicero and Seneca. Developing what was already implicit in these earlier personifications, Boethius the author described Philosophy's first appearance to Boethius (CI.1.1 [1–18]) in the manner of the arrival of a goddess in a vision.[18] Numerous details, from her position, seeming to stand above Boethius's head, her burning eyes, her vigour, her combination of youth ('fresh in her complexion') with great age ('she was so full of age that she would not at all be thought to belong to our era') fit into a tradition of divine manifestations, stretching back to Homer, as well as being appropriate characterizations of philosophy.[19] Philosophy's 'ambiguous' height—'now she kept herself back to the normal stature of humans, but now she seemed to strike against the sky with the very top of her head; and when she raised her head higher, it penetrated even the sky itself and cheated the gaze of the people who gazed at it' (CI.1.2 [8–13])—also has precedents in ancient descriptions of Gods, as well as indicating how the study of philosophy progresses from the easily graspable towards an intimation of what is beyond comprehension. And the dress 'that philosophy wove with her own hands' immediately conjures up that of Athene in the *Iliad* (V, 734ff.) when she appears to Achilles.[20]

Yet Philosophy's role and even her status, as it transpires, is something of an anti-climax. She has no supernatural powers to help Boethius. Rather, she must act as his doctor, and cure by helping him—through carefully graded and closely reasoned argument—to regain command of the philosophical wisdom he had already learned.[21] For, as is made clear at the moment when Boethius first recognizes her (CI.3.2 [5–6]), Philosophy personifies the tradition of philosophical thinking in which Boethius was educated. Her army includes the great philosophers of the past such as Anaxagoras, Socrates, Zeno, and Seneca (CI.3.9 [31–34]),[22] and she was there, by Socrates's side, when he was put to death (CI.3.6 [21]). She refers to 'our Plato' and 'my Aristotle'.[23] The description of Philosophy's dress, dirty from neglect and missing pieces torn off by the violent hands of Stoics and Epicureans (CI.1.3, 5 [16–17; 22–24]; 3.7 [21–27]), makes it clear that what Boethius has in mind is the tradition he had followed in setting out to translate Aristotle and Plato and show that their ideas were not in conflict—the tradition of Neoplatonism that, since Porphyry, had accommodated Aristotle as well as Plato. Although individual Stoic thinkers are commemorated as part of Philosophy's army, the Stoics and Epicureans in general are considered to be pseudo-philosophers.[24]

As leader and representative of the true tradition of philosophy, Philosophy—although imagined by Boethius her interlocutor to have come 'down from the pole on high' (CI.3.3 [7–8])—is not divine. Several passages make this point clear.[25] Describing providence and fate, Philosophy quotes the line from Homer (*Iliad* XII, 176), 'But it is hard for me to talk of these things as if I were a God' and adds—paraphrasing a famous comment from Plato's *Timaeus*: 'For it is not right for a human to grasp with the mind or explain in words all the contrivances of God's work.'[26] A little earlier (CIV.6.38 [144]), Philosophy has introduced another line of Greek—probably an otherwise lost fragment from the hermetic writings—with the comment: 'As one even more excellent than I says'.[27] Even when she is explaining the most impenetrable of problems, Philosophy's perspective is always that of the human searcher, trying to approach the divine in diffidence of his own powers.[28] And her great hymn, III, m. 9, is not a revelation of divine secrets but rather a prayer to God, offered by her for herself and for Boethius.

Christianity and the Consolation of Philosophy: An Interpretative Problem

Many readers of the *Consolation* have wondered about its author's Christian faith. From the earliest known of such remarks—in Bovo of Corvey's tenth-century commentary on III, m. 9[29]—to modern discussions, these queries have consisted in asking questions about the author, Boethius. For Bovo, there seemed an incongruity between the Christian writer responsible for the theological treatises and the doctrines of III, m. 9, inspired by Plato and some of them heretical. Later scholars, looking at the whole *Consolation*, have stressed, rather, the apparent lack of anything specifically Christian. In the eighteenth and nineteenth centuries, some scholars went so far as to deny that the author of the *Consolation* could have been the person who wrote the theological treatises. Contemporary evidence identifying Boethius as author of both works ended such speculations.[30] Instead, more recent historians have asked about the author Boethius's fundamental allegiances: was his Christianity merely superficial, a matter of form, whilst his fundamental intellectual and emotional allegiances, especially as he faced death, were to Platonism?

As the two previous chapters have shown, at no stage does the argument of the *Consolation* call on premisses known alone by Christian revelation. Indeed, there is no *large* or *obvious* feature of the argumentation or language that would mark it as the work of a Christian, rather than a pagan Platonist. Whether the *Consolation* contains small or hidden Christian features is a harder question. If a turn of phrase or argument is to be called 'Christian' simply because it shows the influence of Christian ways of thought or speech, then the answer must be positive. There are a number of biblical echoes in the work,[31] some traces of the language of the Christian liturgy,[32] and some turns of phrase which, arguably, are characteristic of Christian rather than pagan Neoplatonists.[33] In themselves, these features merely show what is already well known, that the author Boethius was familiar with Christian language, worship, and thinking. They do not reveal anything about his attitude to Christianity or his intentions in the *Consolation*. But one biblical parallel—much the closest—may show more. In III.12, Philosophy says, using the same words as Wisdom viii, 1, that 'it is the highest good that rules all things strongly and disposes them sweetly'.[34] Boethius responds to this comment in the following way:-'How does not only the conclusion of your arguments that you have reached, but *much more those very words that you use* delight me . . .'[35] As for the doctrinal positions developed, there is nothing in the *Consolation* that can be identified, with absolute certainty, as unacceptable for a Christian of Boethius's time. Nonetheless, the description of the World Soul given in III, m. 9 might have seemed dubious, and Philosophy's apparent acceptance of the sempiternity of the universe (CV.6.9–10 [31–38]) makes her take sides with the pagans on a matter on which there had been, and would be, controversy between them and the Christians.[36]

Faced by these conflicting indications, twentieth-century scholars fall roughly into three groups—'Christianizers,' 'Augustinists,' and 'Hellenists', as they might be called. The Christianizers emphasize, unduly, the traces of Christian thought and language throughout the *Consolation* and the visionary setting of Philosophy's appearance. Their leading representative, Klingner, concludes that the work is a sacred dialogue in which 'Philosophy, as the angel of God . . . leads Boethius step by step back to God.'[37] The Augustinists recall that Augustine, by his own account, was brought back to a full acceptance of Christianity through his encounter with 'the books of the Platonists' (treatises by Plotinus and Porphyry in Latin translation), and that his earliest works, dating from the period immediately before his baptism, are philosophical dialogues. Augustine, they believe, provided a source and a precedent for the author Boethius.[38] As one of the most recent, and subtlest, exponents of this approach, Henry Chadwick, puts it: '. . . there is nothing in the Platonic themes admitted to the *Consolation* which one cannot also find accepted in the philosophical dialogues and the *Confessions* of the young Augustine.'[39] The Hellenist approach has been championed by Pierre Courcelle. Courcelle does not wish to suggest that the author Boethius was not a Christian, or even that he was only superficially one. But the writer was, in his view, very strongly influenced by the Alexandrian Neoplatonism of his time, and he believed that by following it he could develop a purely rational theology, complementary to the Christian faith.[40] According to Courcelle, therefore, Philosophy is not an angel of God but rather a personification of human reason, and the author of the *Consolation* anticipates Aquinas' distinction between faith and reason.[41]

Perhaps, however, the approach for the twenty-first century should differ from all of these three and ask not about the author Boethius's faith but rather about how to interpret his work, the *Consolation*. The point of departure for interpretation is the knowledge that Boethius was a Christian writer who had a Christian audience in mind. Interpreters must consider, in this light, what was the view that the author wished to convey to his readers by his decisions on how to present himself, his choice of Philosophy as instructress, the arguments he gives her and their juxtaposition, the inclusion and content of the poems, and the structure of the work as a whole.

One point emerges quickly. The *Consolation* is a dialogue between a figure who is recognizably a Christian—Boethius—and a figure who is not—Philosophy. The reasons for making this assertion are almost too obvious to remark. Since the character whom Boethius represents, in the fiction of the dialogue, is the real Boethius, and the real Boethius was a Christian and known to be a Christian—because everyone of his class (and, indeed, almost everyone altogether) in the Italy of his time were Christians, Boethius the author would have had to give the clearest indications in the text had he intended the character Boethius to be taken as anything except a Christian. In fact, he takes the trouble to do just the opposite and insert some reminders that the character who is engaged in discussion with Philosophy is, indeed, a Christian. Boethius's approving comment in III.12, when Philosophy's words have echoed those of the Bible, must have had this implication for readers of the *Consolation*, who would have recognized the quotation from Wisdom; none of Philosophy's citations from pagan philosophers and poets receives a similar comment from her interlocutor. Also, the most characteristically Christian language in the whole work occurs in Boethius's complaint that if there is no free will, prayer will be useless (CV.3.33–34 [97–107]).[42] Moreover, none of the positions to which Boethius (as opposed to Philosophy) commits himself in the *Consolation* would have been in the least dubious for a Christian to uphold.[43]

The same considerations apply in reverse to Philosophy. She is introduced as the 'nurse' of Boethius's studies—and Boethius was well known to have dedicated himself to translating and expounding the masterpieces of ancient, pagan philosophy. For her to be considered as anything other than a non-Christian figure, the author Boethius would have had to include some very definite indications. Instead, the portrayal of Philosophy seems designed to underline her position as the figurehead for a non-Christian tradition of thought. She mentions Plato, Aristotle, Socrates, and Seneca, but no Christian writer, as being among her followers. Her allusions are to classical mythology and history. Her doctrines are, in some cases, ones that Christians would find dubious. True, there are aspects of her thought and language that show Christian influence, but these are merely the traces, detectable to modern scholarship, to be expected in a text written by a Christian author, not features that could have been intended as signs, against all other indications, of a Christian allegiance by Philosophy. And it is striking that Philosophy is at her most Christian in language and allusion precisely when she is directly echoing Boethius: when, for instance, her wording is close to the Gospel of Matthew in her summary of Boethius's complaint, or in the vocabulary of her very final remarks, about prayer, where she is answering the problem that Boethius had himself posed in even more characteristically Christian terms.[44]

The interpretative question to be asked, then, is what the intended (educated, Christian) reader is supposed to gather from this colloquy between a Christian, Boethius, and an authoritative non-Christian, Philosophy. The answer will depend on the arguments in the *Consolation* and how they are presented. Suppose, for instance, that there had been a concluding section, leading on from the ending as it now stands, in which the character Boethius expressed an explicitly Christian faith. In that case, it would be right to conclude that—just like Augustine in his *Confessions*—Boethius the author was showing how philosophy can provide the intellectual equipment for a genuine grasp of God, although not in isolation from Christian worship. Suppose, rather, that the *Consolation* ended as it does, but that it provided a coherent body of arguments that fully answered Boethius the character's questions. In that case, there would be strong grounds to advance as an interpretation what Courcelle and some others have put more as a biographical hypothesis: that the *Consolation* is written to demonstrate the scope and power of philosophy, which is to be kept distinct from Christian theology, although it is by no means opposed to it.

In the last two chapters, however, I have argued that Philosophy's arguments, although more complex and powerful than is often recognized, do not provide a coherent and full answer to Boethius's questions. To recapitulate. The line of reasoning Philosophy follows from III.9 to the end of Book III is at variance with that carefully developed in Book II and III.1–8, and the arguments of III.9–12 are strangely incomplete, since there is no account of how Boethius can enjoy the monolithic good that Philosophy has established. In Book IV, Philosophy's bold attempt to explain reward and punishment totally through final causality is suddenly abandoned for a scheme in which God arranges everything. Philosophy does succeed in showing how this scheme still leaves room for human free will, and in Book V she develops an intricate argument to counter another threat to the freedom of the human will, posed this time by God's prescience. But, at the end of her discussion, she suddenly concedes that everything is causally determined and so, by her assumptions, that the human will is not free.

Unless the analyses that have produced these conclusions about the failure of coherence in the *Consolation* are faulty, then there seem to be four possibilities:

(1) The incoherences are due to the ineptitude of Boethius the author.
(2) The incoherences are a typical feature of the genre of the *Consolation*: a consolatory work, intended for a general readership, in which arguments need not fit together rigorously.[45]
(3) The incoherences are merely superficial, because they can be explained by the structure of the *Consolation*, in which Philosophy gradually leads her pupil to the truth.
(4) The incoherences are intentional, and need to be taken into account in reaching an overall interpretation of the *Consolation*.

(1) is most improbable, given the intelligence displayed in the structure of individual arguments and chains of argument, and the very high degree of finish displayed by the *Consolation* as a literary construction, in its detail, its complex interweaving of imagery, anticipations, reminiscences and allusions, and its formal symmetry. (2) is unconvincing, because from III.9 onwards the *Consolation* so clearly enters into difficult and technical arguments, of a sort not usual in consolatory literature. (3) would be plausible if it were only the arguments in Book II (the lighter remedies) that did not fit with those in Book III (the stronger remedies). But the change of direction in Book III rejects the line that had been developed by both the lighter and the stronger remedies. In any case, if the truth is being gradually revealed, then by the end of the *Consolation*, a satisfactory answer to Boethius's problems should have been presented, even if it is not in consonance with all that has been established earlier in the work. But Boethius's problems are not satisfactorily resolved. Since (1), (2), and (3) turn out to be implausible, (4) is the best guide for interpreters and, as the next section will show, it is supported by the literary form of the *Consolation*.

Prose and Verse: The Consolation *as Menippean Satire*

The presence of verse passages alternating with the prose supports the idea that the *Consolation* is a more complex work to interpret than a straightforward philosophical treatise. The way in which the poems look forward and look backwards to the themes and positions of the prose sections, and the arrangement of the poems around III, m. 9, emphasize that the *Consolation* does not consist of a linear, progressive arrangement of arguments, leading from premisses through to conclusions. The fact that some of the poems, especially those on mythological subjects, call for sophisticated interpretation in order to see their appropriateness suggests that the whole *Consolation* may require such a careful and attentive reading. Most important of all, the combination of prose and verse (supported by some other features) places the *Consolation* in a particular genre: that of Menippean Satire. The *Consolation* is also, indeed, a consolation and a philosophical dialogue, but its links with these two genres do not affect its meaning. By contrast, to recognize the work as a Menippean Satire does, arguably, change how it should be understood.

As represented in antiquity by the work of, above all, Lucian—the writings of Menippus himself (ca. 300 BC) and the Latin author Varro (116–27 BC) are almost entirely lost—Menippean satires are short works, sometimes in dialogue, often aimed at ridiculing pretension, especially pretensions to wisdom, containing short snatches of usually borrowed verse. The satires are humorous but with a serious, educative point to make—examples of *spoudogeloion* ('ernest in game', in Chaucer's language), where the most serious questions are treated with lightness and wit. For example, in Lucian's *Icaromenippus*, Menippus recounts how, bemused by the theories and disagreements of the philosophers, he dons birds' wings and flies to heaven (a parodic allusion to the *Phaedrus*), where Jupiter shares his low view of the philosophical schools and promises to destroy them. In Latin, Petronius's *Satyricon* has links with the genre, and Seneca's *Apocolocyntosis*, a mock apotheosis of the emperor Claudius, is an example of it.

Scholars of an earlier generation noted, but dismissed as superficial, the formal connection of the *Consolation* with Menippean satire. Klingner, for instance, commented that the *Consolation* displays the piety and seriousness of sacred dialogues, rather than the playfulness of Menippean satire, with which it has only its prosimetric form in common.[46] More recently, it has been suggested that in late antiquity a new genre of prosimetrum developed, taking its origins from Menippean satire but diverging from it. Martianus Capella's vast, encyclopaedic prosimetrum, *On the Marriage of Mercury and Philolology*, the *Paraenesis didascalica* of Boethius's contemporary, Ennodius, and the *Consolation* itself would be the leading examples of this new form, which transforms the light-hearted, satirical instruction of Lucian into earnest didacticism, and where there is a regular alternation between prose and original (not borrowed) verse passages.[47]

Boethius clearly knew and was influenced by *On the Marriage*, and very possibly by the *Paraenesis*.[48] But careful reading of these works suggests that they may be far closer to the older Menippean tradition and its serious-humorousness than used to be thought. Certainly, *On the Marriage* cannot be regarded as unremittingly earnest.[49] At moments, Martianus deliberately makes the narrator or various personifications ridiculous. Although it seems far-fetched to suggest that the whole work is designed to demonstrate the failure of the encyclopaedic enterprise in which it is engaged, Martianus does appear to go beyond merely providing comic relief during a dull pedagogical grind: he takes his enterprise as an educator seriously, and yet—in true Menippean fashion—encourages us to see that it has its pretensions and absurdities.[50]

What about the *Consolation*? Two recent critics have brought out its links with the Menippean tradition. Peter Dronke draws attention to how Boethius ridicules himself, by having Philosophy undercut the self-pitying solemnity of his opening poem, and by presenting himself as dumbstruck. He also suggests that the *Consolation*, and especially the central poem, III, m. 9, is more deeply Menippean because it puts 'ultimate philosophical positions . . . to the test'.[51] Joel Relihan goes much further. Convinced that earlier prosimetra, including the works by Martianus and Ennodius, are self-undermining, he sketches a reading of the *Consolation* along the same lines. The work is intended, he argues, not to provide philosophical consolation but to show the failure of philosophy to achieve the goals it promises. He describes the arguments put by Philosophy in I–III as repetitious, obvious, and unconvincing to the character Boethius. In Book V, he says, Philosophy allows herself to be diverted from her main task of bringing her interlocutor back to his fatherland and ends the work without having given a satisfactory answer to Boethius's objections. This undermining of philosophy, Relihan believes, is in the service of the Christian faith. 'The *Consolation* is a Christian text', he writes, 'not because it advances Christian truths but because it allows a faith that has been glimpsed here and there to emerge as victor in a fruitless contest of opposing arguments.'[52]

Relihan's reading is as a whole unconvincing. Philosophy's arguments, taken individually, are far more powerful and conclusive than he allows, especially when they are read in the light of the intellectual assumptions of

Boethius's time. Moreover, it is as implausible historically that Boethius should have rejected wholesale, as Relihan seems to suggest, the tradition of philosophy to which he had dedicated his intellectual life, as that he should have rejected Christianity. Nonetheless, may there not be an important element of truth hidden in this extreme interpretation? The *Consolation* is not a work that rejects philosophy (as if its title had to be pronounced with ironic emphasis: 'that's the *consolation* you gain from *philosophy*!'), but it is one that—in the tradition of Menippean satire—explores its limitations.

In the last section, I argued that there is good reason to think that Boethius the author was conscious that individual stretches of argument in the *Consolation*, although cogent in themselves, do not cohere together, and that such incoherences are part of the work's meaning. The *Consolation*'s Menippean form strengthens this surmise and also suggests *how* the failures of coherence should be read. Philosophy's arguments go a long way to answering Boethius's problems, but Philosophy is seen as unable to establish by reasoning a fully satisfactory position, where every element fits together. To this extent, the pretensions of her goddess-like initial appearance are satirized in the *Consolation*. But the satire is combined with an evident respect for Philosophy and her deliverances, just as Martianus Capella was able to poke fun at learning whilst earnestly devoting himself to recording and propagating it.

The relationship between philosophy and Christianity is presented in a particularly subtle way. On the one hand, since the *Consolation*, as explained above, juxtaposes the Christian Boethius with a non-Christian Philosophy, any shortcomings in Philosophy's views can be read as pointing to the limitations of philosophy for Christians. On the other hand, there are two elements in the work that seem designed to remove the opportunity to find in it even this limited area of confrontation between Christianity and philosophy. The *Consolation* may indeed make the limitations of philosophical reasoning evident to the careful Christian reader: but they are also evident to Philosophy herself. Philosophy is always careful to acknowledge that she is no goddess, and that she cannot penetrate beyond the boundaries of human reasoning (perhaps her initial vision-like appearance should be taken as an illusion set up for Philosophy *herself* to deflate). And, as commentators have remarked, one of the uses Philosophy has for poetry is as a way of adumbrating truths that she cannot capture through straightforward philosophical reasoning.[53] Her frame of reference in looking beyond philosophical reasoning remains resolutely pagan and Neoplatonic. There is no open suggestion, however, that her point of view is any different in this matter from that of the Christian. What, of course, she cannot supply, or even acknowledge, is precisely what is wanting from the central climax of her exposition in the second half of Book III: a *way* for Boethius to grasp and gain the highest good to which she has led him. As a Christian author, Boethius might, like Augustine before him (*Confessions* VII.18.24—21.27), have written eloquently and movingly about this gap. Rather, he leaves the structure of his dialogue to make the point silently.

9

BOETHIUS'S INFLUENCE IN THE MIDDLE AGES

Boethius's influence in the Middle Ages was immense. Only Aristotle and Augustine had so great a direct influence over so wide a range of intellectual life. And because Boethius does not seem even to his warmest admirers to be on a level with two such giants of thought, there has been an inclination among scholars to allow this illustrious *Nachleben* to overshadow his own achievements rather than to vindicate them. One goal of this book is to correct that tendency. Medieval scholars turned again and again to the *Opuscula sacra* and the *Consolation* because they are complex, difficult and remarkable works; even the medieval enthusiasm for Boethius's logic, at least until about 1200, was not merely—although it clearly was in part—due to the unavailability of other sources. The present chapter is brief so as not to unbalance a study designed to focus on Boethius himself. It aims to indicate the main aspects of Boethius's medieval influence and to suggest how it reflects Boethius's individuality as a writer and thinker, as well as his role as a transmitter of ancient thought. I shall not consider the *Arithmetic* or the *Principles of Music*, although both works were widely read from the ninth century right through to the Renaissance, remaining a part of the syllabus in arithmetic and music despite the influx of new texts.[1] Rather, I shall look at the influence of the logical translations and commentaries; the logical textbooks; the *opuscula sacra*; and the different facets of the reception and use of the *Consolation*—the tradition of translation and commentary, the philosophical influence and the wider, literary influence among vernacular as well as Latin writers.

The Logical Translations and Commentaries

For Aristotle's logic, scholars in the West throughout the Middle Ages were almost entirely dependent on Boethius's translations,[2] with two exceptions.[3] One exception belongs to the very earliest period of medieval logic. The *Categories* was known first of all through a Latin paraphrase, the *Categoriae decem*, misattributed to Augustine. From the time of Alcuin, at the end of the eighth century, until the tenth century, the *Categoriae decem* was the most closely studied logical text. But it was gradually replaced by Boethius's translation, and had almost vanished from the schools by the twelfth century.[4] Boethius's translation of the *Isagoge* was known by the turn of the ninth century, and that of *On Interpretation* by later in that century.[5] The *Isagoge*, *Categories* and *On Interpretation*, in Boethius's translations, formed, along with Boethius's textbooks, the syllabus of the early twelfth-century logical schools. To this *logica vetus* ('old logic') were added, from the 1130s onwards, the texts of the *logica nova* ('new logic'): Boethius's translations of the remaining texts of Aristotle's logic (*On Sophistical Refutations*, the *Prior Analytics* and the *Topics*) and, the second exception, the *Posterior Analytics* in the translation by James of Venice, because Boethius's version had not survived.[6] Boethius's translations of the logical texts were used universally in the medieval universities, and they were copied in hundreds of university manuscripts. A typical such manuscript would include the whole set of Boethius's translations of Aristotle and of Porphyry's *Isagoge*, James of Venice's version of the *Posterior Analytics*, two of Boethius's textbooks (*On Topical Differentiae* and *On Division*) and the *Liber sex principiorum*, a twelfth-century work wrongly attributed to Boethius.[7]

On their own, the translated texts of the *Isagoge*, *Categories*, and *On Interpretation* would have been of limited value to early medieval scholars. They needed a guide to these terse and complicated works. Fortunately, through his commentaries, Boethius also provided one for them. The serious study of the translations, which began in the ninth century, is bound up with reading of the commentaries. In the period up to the twelfth century, some evidence of this study is provided by sets of glosses, written in the margins and between the lines of the texts. The earliest set to the *Isagoge* are found in several manuscripts and may be associated with Israel Scottus, a tenth-century grammarian of Irish origin; they consist mainly of carefully chosen extracts from both of Boethius's commentaries.[8] The few ninth- to eleventh-century glossed manuscripts of the *Categories* draw their material from Boethius's commentary, as for the most part does the one (tenth-century) glossed manuscript of *On Interpretation* (from the second, longer one).[9] The Old High German translations by Notker III of St Gall (ca. 950–1022) of the *Categories* and *On Interpretation* are, in fact, paraphrases, incorporating passages from Boethius's commentaries (including both of those on *On Interpretation*). When, at about the same time, a writer compiled what he called a set of 'expositions' of the *Isagoge* and *Categories* in question-and-answer form, he was also content mainly to excerpt from Boethius's *Categories* commentary and the two on the *Isagoge*.[10]

From the end of the eleventh century onwards (and especially in the period 1100–1150), logicians began to write their own commentaries on the *Isagoge*, *Categories*, and *On Interpretation*.[11] Boethius's commentaries were, however, initially as important to these commentators as they had been to the glossators. Many of the commentaries from the beginning of the century copy extensively from Boethius. Only gradually did the twelfth-century commentators assert their independence: they often provided a far closer, word-by-word reading than Boethius had thought necessary, and themes raised originally by Boethius took on a twelfth-century life of their own. The most famous of all logical discussions in the period—the debate over universals—illustrates both the formative role of Boethius's commentaries in twelfth-century thinking and how they were left behind by the developments they stimulated.

The medieval problem of universals centres on the passage in the *Isagoge* where Porphyry raises, but does not answer, three questions about genera and species, and the passage in Boethius's second commentary, where he proposes an answer to these questions. Yet the context for discussion of this problem was set by another of Boethius's commentaries—that on the *Categories*. The *Categories* commentary raises the question of what the *Categories* is about, words or things, and gives the nuanced reply that it is about words as signifiers of things. It gave rise to an eleventh-century controversy about how the *Categories* and *Isagoge* should be read: as about things or, as one group of interpreters, who apparently read Boethius too crudely, held, about words. William of Champeaux, who taught logic in Paris ca. 1100 when Abelard arrived there, opposed this interpretative approach, basing himself at least in part on a more careful reading of Boethius's *Categories* commentary. He also commented on the *Isagoge*, following Boethius's second commentary but drawing out a theory that was hardly Boethius's—material essence realism, according to which things of the same genus or species share a common essence—that, for example, of animal or of man—which is like matter to the *differentiae* that distinguish species of the genus or to the accidents that distinguish particulars of the species. In ca. 1107, Abelard attacked material essence realism so successfully that William was forced to adopt a different version of realism. Abelard went on, by the time he wrote his own long commentaries on the *Isagoge* and the *Categories* (ca. 1118–1119), to develop his own answer to the question about the subject-matter of the two texts, taking Boethius's views in a new direction. Abelard holds that Aristotle and Porphyry write sometimes about things (often through treating words) but sometimes—as when they are talking about genera and species—just about words. Abelard thus, looking back to Boethius but transforming his ideas, turned the exegetical question about the subject matter of the *Categories* and the *Isagoge* into a way of tackling the metaphysical problem of universals. Moreover, in elaborating the semantic theory he needed to support his nominalism, Abelard drew extensively on the semantics and psychology of Boethius's second commentary on *On Interpretation*. Despite such debts to Boethius, the effect of Abelard's own elaborate theories, here and on other matters of logic, and the responses to them, was to move the debate away from the areas considered by Boethius.[12]

From 1150 onward—and even more markedly in the thirteenth century—Boethius's logical commentaries were no longer of central intellectual importance. Not only had the debates they stimulated moved on, but also other logical texts, not commented by Boethius, had become available and fashionable; whilst from ca. 1255 the newly translated non-logical texts of Aristotle dominated the university syllabuses.[13] The *Isagoge*, *Categories*, and *On Interpretation* themselves remained a part of university courses and, indeed, many more manuscripts of these texts date from the thirteenth century than from any other time. By contrast, almost no new copies of Boethius's commentaries were made in the thirteenth century.[14] They were, however, still studied by some outstanding thinkers: Albert the Great and Aquinas used Boethius's second commentary extensively when commenting on *On Interpretation*; Aquinas also had William of Moerbeke's translation of Ammonius's commentary at his disposal, but it complemented

Boethius's work rather than replacing it.[15] Indeed, Boethius's commentaries were still used by fourteenth-century logicians, such as William of Ockham and Albert of Saxony, whereas the translations of Ammonius, and of Simplicius on the *Categories*, were little read.[16]

The Logical Treatises

Boethius's logical treatises seem to have been transmitted as a group (which usually, though not always, included not just SC (*On the Categorical Syllogism*) but also ISC (*Introduction to Categorical Syllogisms*))[17], and they were not copied or read from the end of the sixth to the end of the tenth century;[18] by contrast, the companion work to TD (*On Topical Differentiae*), TC (the commentary on Cicero's *Topics*), was available before 850.[19] Once the treatises began to be studied, they seem to have become quite popular: Gerbert, later Pope Sylvester II, taught them all at Rheims in the 970s to 980s;[20] at much the same time Abbo of Fleury made his own version of the treatise on syllogisms,[21] and a number of manuscripts from between the late tenth and the twelfth century contain the set of four treatises as a group.[22] In the early part of the twelfth century, the four treatises made up, along with Porphyry's *Isagoge* and Aristotle's *Categories* and *On Interpretation*, the seven texts of the logical curriculum in the schools, and they, like the textbooks of Porphyry and Aristotle, received commentaries.[23] As the logical curriculum changed in the course of the twelfth century, with the introduction of the rest of Aristotle's logic and the development of the branches of the *logica modernorum*, the treatises had different fortunes. The works on the categorical syllogism were outmoded by Aristotle's own *Prior Analytics*; the treatise on hypothetical syllogisms, too, fell into neglect. *On Division* and TD, however, remained as items in the standard later medieval university manuscripts of Aristotle's *Organon*,[24] and commentaries were still being written on TD in the thirteen century, though not later.

The different monographs were of varying importance to medieval logic. The treatises on the categorical syllogism gave a useful account of Aristotelian syllogistic that was quickly replaced by Aristotle's own, once it became known. *On Division* was cited often, especially when problems about mereology come up in discussing other logical texts. TD was influential both individually, and in combination with SH. The topics (as learned from TD, especially, and TC) were regularly used by twelfth-century commentators as a way of analysing the argumentative steps taken by Porphyry and Aristotle.[25] TD could provide a vehicle for semantic theorizing, but commentators also looked carefully at the doctrine itself of topical inference, and at what exactly the topics are. The thirteenth century commentators linked their answer to this question to the doctrine of first and second 'intentions' (first-order and second-order concepts). By the thirteenth century, Aristotle's *Topics* was available, and there is considerable interplay between the commentators' understanding of Aristotle's text and their interpretation of TD.[26]

But it was in combination with SH and TC that TD exercised its deepest influence on medieval logic. In studying SH with the theory of topics in mind, medieval logicians rediscovered the sentence logic that was at the basis of some of the ideas inherited in distorted form by Boethius. They also developed the theory of topics itself by linking to the discussion of hypothetical syllogisms. The earliest surviving medieval discussions of topics and hypothetical syllogisms, from the ninth century—written before SH and TD were known but indebted to Cicero's *Topics* and perhaps to TC—propose the idea, probably based on a misunderstanding of their sources, that the doctrine of the topics is concerned with hypothetical syllogisms.[27] Abbo of Fleury's exposition of hypothetical syllogisms draws on elements of TD and, in one chapter, gives the seven forms of hypothetical syllogism set out originally in Cicero's *Topics* and deriving from genuinely sentential stoic logic.[28]

In Abelard's *Dialectica* (ca. 1116) elements taken from SH and TD combine to provide a deep and sophisticated study of entailment.[29] Unlike Boethius, Abelard has a very clear grasp of sentence logic. He develops a semantic theory, according to which conditionals link what he calls *dicta* (roughly speaking, propositional contents).[30] Not surprisingly, therefore, he grasps the notion of a propositional operation, in a way Boethius could not do, distinguishing sharply, for instance, between the negation of an antecedent or consequent and that of the whole consequence ('if . . . then . . .' statement).[31] Abelard presents the study of topics as a preliminary to his discussion of hypothetical syllogisms (albeit a vast preliminary, far longer than the treatment of hypothetical syllogisms themselves). Hypothetical syllogisms themselves are valid in virtue of their form. The theory of topics shows which of the hypothetical sentences (conditionals) that make up such syllogisms are true, and why. Some conditionals, Abelard explains, are true in virtue of their form, because they conditionalize syllogisms (for example, 'If every man is an animal and every animal has a soul, then every man has a soul'). Such a conditional preserves its truth whatever other terms are uniformly substituted for those in the example. There are other conditionals that are true, he argues, although not in virtue of their form but because of the nature of things: for example, (C) 'If it is a man, it is an animal'. C does not remain true whatever terms are substituted for 'man' and 'animal', but it does remain true so long as the terms stand in the same relation, of species to genus, as those for which they are substituted. The theory of topical *differentiae* classifies these relationships, and the maximal sentences show the underlying principles on which the truth of such conditionals rests. It turns out, however, that only a few of the topics—a small proportion of Boethius's list—really serve to guarantee the truth of conditionals. Even those that seem to be likely candidates, such as the topic from immediate opposites (the topic that supports arguments such as 'he is not healthy, so he is sick') turn out to yield unacceptable conclusions when incorporated into arguments.

In the years after Abelard, his followers and the other schools of logicians debated vigorously the rules for sentence logic—an outcrop of the study of SH and TD, though not one that Boethius himself could have anticipated. It was not, though, until the fourteenth century that there developed a genre of treatise devoted entirely to the classification of consequences. Many historians of logic would regard these treatises as the outstanding examples of medieval formal, sentence logic.[32] It has been shown that there are links between this development and the study of TD and also with SH (despite its obscurity from the thirteenth century onwards). Although less prominent than in the twelfth century, Boethius's logical treatises seem therefore to have had an influence even late in the Middle Ages.

The *Opuscula Sacra*

The *Opuscula sacra*[33] were known to Alcuin's pupils Candidus and Fredegisus at the very beginning of the ninth century.[34] The earliest surviving manuscripts date from the 820s, and by the middle of the century the *opuscula* were being used in theological and philosophical debates. They feature in the controversy between Gottschalk and Hincmar of Rheims on trinitarian theology, and in the 860s Ratramnus of Corbie turns especially to some of Boethius's comments on universals in OSV.[35] John Scottus Eriugena, the greatest philosopher of the later ninth century, knew the *opuscula* well, although they were not central to his thinking.[36] At the end of the ninth or the beginning of the tenth century, a set of glosses was written to the *opuscula*, which circulated in a number of manuscripts over the next three centuries, with changes, omissions, and additions. Remigius of Auxerre was involved in the dissemination of these glosses, but it is by no means clear that, as often supposed, he was their author.[37]

The twelfth century was the period when the *opuscula* were most central to philosophical and theological life. When, ca. 1118–1120, Abelard first turned his energies to writing about sacred doctrine, he produced a treatise (the *Theologia Summi Boni*) which attempted, like OSI, to explain how it can be that God is both three and one. Although Abelard's individual arguments are not the same as those of OSI, he seems to have formed his theological method on Boethius's example, using logical analysis to reach, so far as possible, a rational understanding of the Trinity, but also showing where ordinary forms of reasoning are inadequate to this subject matter.[38] For Gilbert of Poitiers, perhaps the only twelfth-century philosopher to equal Abelard, the *opuscula* were even more important. Although Gilbert wrote commentaries on the Psalms and Romans, it is only in his commentary on the *opuscula* that he develops his characteristic philosophical and theological ideas.[39] The commentary is an extraordinary mixture of fidelity to Boethius's texts and original thinking by Gilbert. Gilbert incorporates every word of Boethius's text into the commentary, and he takes it upon himself to explain each nuance of Boethius's phrasing. The underlying approach to theology derives from Boethius's, but Gilbert takes it further, by making systematic use of OSI's division of the branches of knowledge into natural science, mathematics, and theology. According to Gilbert, the principles of reasoning appropriate for natural science do not apply directly to theology, but they can be transferred 'proportionately', so as to give humans some rational grasp of the Trinity.[40] Gilbert also systematizes and profoundly transforms Boethius's metaphysics, deriving from the notion of immanent forms a complex theory in which every concrete whole is made what it is by a structured group of forms (for instance, rationality, whiteness, six-foot tallness, humanity, animality, Socrateity) that are particular, not universal.

Despite an unsuccessful attempt by Bernard of Clairvaux to have the work condemned as heretical, Gilbert's became the standard medieval commentary on the *opuscula*. Another group of commentaries from the mid-twelfth century are associated with Thierry of Chartres and probably record his teachings mixed with the views of his pupils.[41] Whereas Gilbert developed Boethius's notion of immanent forms so as to analyse the structure of particulars, these writers—following the powerful current of Platonism in the period from 1150–1190—were interested in showing how all forms emanate from the one divine form. A rather simpler commentary on OSI and III, also influenced by Thierry, was written in the late 1150s by Clarembald of Arras.[42]

Although they remained respected patristic texts until the end of the Middle Ages, and OSV was the usual point of departure for scholastic discussions of the hypostatic union, the *opuscula* did not retain their position as a fundamental text for philosophical theorizing and theological method.[43] The reason was not just the Aristotelian syllabus of the universities. In the period from 1150 to 1200 Gilbert's theological method, linked to his exposition of the *opuscula*, was championed by many leading thinkers. But it was their opponents who eventually prevailed, establishing Peter the Lombard's *Sentences* as the one set text for theologians besides the Bible. There were, however, exceptions to the general pattern. OSIII was used as a set text in some central European late medieval universities.[44] And, as his use of the second *On Interpretation* commentary has already indicated, the most celebrated of all later medieval thinkers, Thomas Aquinas, had a special predilection for Boethius. Alone, it seems, of all important thirteenth-century writers, he commented on both OSI and OSIII (probably ca. 1257).[45] The work on OSI is an (unfinished) *quaestio* commentary, with very brief literal analysis of the text and free-ranging discussion, only loosely related to Boethius, in which some of Aquinas's most important ideas about the nature of theology and its place in the division of knowledge are developed. By contrast, OSIII is given a seemingly literal commentary. Aquinas's version of Boethius's argument is clear and links closely with his own views about the real distinction between being and essence; how faithfully it reflects Boethius's own ideas is much disputed.[46]

The *Consolation*

The *Consolation* was more influential in the Middle Ages even than Boethius's other works, and its pattern of influence is rather different. The commentaries, textbooks, and *opuscula* were studied intensively in the earlier Middle Ages and were among the texts that shaped twelfth-century thinking; from 1200, their importance diminished. The *Consolation* enjoyed a similar fortune up to the end of the twelfth century (though it was more widely read and had a distinctive literary influence). Its popularity did not, however, grow less after 1200. True, the *Consolation* was no longer one of the ancient texts studied formally in the universities, as it had been in the twelfth-century schools. But it continued to be read carefully, used, and commented on (right on through the Renaissance to early modern times); it was also translated into a diversity of vernaculars, and it influenced some of the greatest vernacular poets, such as Dante, Boccaccio and Chaucer.

I shall look, first, at the tradition of commentaries, then, very selectively, at some facets of the philosophical and theological influence of the *Consolation*, and, finally, at the translations of the work and its influence on medieval literature.

The *Consolation:* The Tradition of Commentaries

The tradition of commentary[47] on the *Consolation* began shortly after it was written. A learned edition of the work, with Greek rhetorical glosses, was compiled by Cassiodorus or in his circle; it can be reconstructed from a group of the earlier manuscripts.[48] Although the *Consolation* was used by Alcuin, at the end of the eighth century,[49] the earliest properly medieval commentaries date from the next century. In the middle of the century, Lupus of Ferrières wrote a short study of the metrical form of the verse passages.[50] There is much less clarity about the origins or form of the other, fuller ninth-century material. Pierre Courcelle, whose survey of *Consolation* commentaries is fundamental but needs much correction, identified a late ninth-century Anonymous St Gall commentary, but his attempts to isolate a pure form of it ignored the way in which early medieval glosses, even when written out as a commentary, are aids toward teaching and learning that vary in each manuscript.[51] A set of glosses in MS Vatican Lat. 3363 are related to this material.[52] At the beginning of the tenth century, Remigius of Auxerre brought together existing material with some of his own and produced a commentary that circulated widely over the next two hundred years, though often with changes and additions.[53]

One of the main problems for medieval users and commentators of the *Consolation* was how to accommodate within a Christian scheme of thought a text that considers God, death, and the aims of a good life without mentioning anything specifically Christian, and which contains some ideas that, at first sight, conflict with the faith. The preferred way of tackling this difficulty was already suggested by a miniature, which, the evidence suggests, accompanied the Cassiodorean edition, where Philosophy is depicted with the traits of the biblical Wisdom, herself often identified with Christ;[54] Alcuin makes the same identification, drawing in ideas from Augustine and from Cassiodorus's own writings.[55] Following this path, the Carolingian glossators and Remigius present Philosophy as a Christian figure and often offer explicitly Christian interpretations, even of passages which, taken literally, seem too hard for Christians to accept. Adalbold of Utrecht, commenting on III, m. 9 at the beginning of the eleventh century, took the same approach, although he drew more attention to the Platonic tenor of the poem.[56] Even these commentators could not fit every passage into their chosen, Christianizing interpretation, but the one figure to challenge this whole approach explicitly is Bovo, a monk of tenth-century Corvey, whose only surviving work is his commentary on III, m. 9.[57] He knows that Boethius is the author of the *opuscula sacra*, but he finds, to his surprise, that there are things 'contrary to the Catholic faith', both in the poem he is commenting and in many places elsewhere. For Bovo, Boethius's aim is to expound the views of the philosophers, especially the Platonists, as the fact that he makes Philosophy his interlocutor clearly shows.

The most ambitious and influential twelfth-century commentary (which continued to be read and used into the fourteenth) was that written by William of Conches probably in the early 1120s.[58] William would go on to write commentaries on Macrobius on the *Dream of Scipio* and on Plato's *Timaeus*. He viewed the relation between the *Consolation* and Christian doctrine in a way that already fitted his future work on genuinely pagan authors. Even more surely than Remigius, William considers the work full of valuable doctrine for Christians, and he is able to explain away apparently heterodox passages, sometimes by reading them as *integumenta*, extended metaphors. William sometimes even finds specifically Christian doctrine in them, as when he interprets the World Soul as the Holy Spirit. But, although he alludes to her parallels with the biblical Wisdom, on his reading Philosophy remains the personification of philosophy, as practised especially by Plato. William believes that, understood aright, Platonic philosophy, as followed by Boethius, accords—at least almost always—with the Christian truth.

William's was the standard commentary in the thirteenth century, and it was probably during this period that a revised version of it was made.[59] Little new exegesis was done in this century,[60] and there is some evidence of a dip in interest, by comparison with the earlier period and the centuries to come.[61] It is hardly surprising that the newly available translations of Aristotle and his Arabic commentators should have distracted thirteenth-century readers from the *Consolation*—although the greatest thirteenth-century Aristotelian of all, Aquinas, was an exception (see below). The tradition of commentary was revived in the fourteenth century, however: in his fundamental survey, Pierre Courcelle listed thirteen commentaries from between ca. 1300 and ca. 1500, but there are certainly many more, especially when vernacular commentaries are taken into account. Most of these commentaries are section-by-section expositions of the text. One of the most distinguished commentators, however, Pierre d'Ailly (writing ca. 1377–1381), sees the *Consolation* as posing two main questions—one about whether philosophical speculation, without revelation, can lead to true revelation, and the other on divine prescience and future contingents.[62] Pierre shows thereby considerable penetration into Boethius's intellectual concerns, but his discussion of these two problems, as a series of independent scholastic *quaestiones*, is not at all closely related to the text.

Despite the complexity of the late medieval exegetical tradition, it is dominated by a single commentary, still extant in over 100 manuscripts. It is the work of an English Dominican, Nicholas Trivet, written at the very beginning of the fourteenth century.[63] Trivet was read much more widely than any of the other commentators, and he influenced many of the other commentaries and glosses, and also some of the translations into the vernacular. Trivet himself used William of Conches's commentary as one of his sources, but he also drew on a wide variety of reading, including the Church Fathers, Plato's *Timaeus*, the Aristotelian works and commentaries on them studied in the universities, the Latin Classics and (most unusually) King Alfred's Old English translation of the *Consolation*.[64] Although Trivet's language and assumptions were formed by the Aristotelian curriculum of the universities (and his comments sometimes reflect controversies of his own time[65]), he approaches the Platonism of the *Consolation* sympathetically, using the *Timaeus* and Macrobius as background material—perhaps the ease with which the *Consolation* could be assimilated into later medieval scholasticism is not surprising, since Aristotle came to the universities via, and as moulded by, the late ancient Greek Platonism in which Boethius himself was intellectually formed. Trivet moves a little further than William away from the straightforward Christianization of the main earlier medieval tradition. Boethius is seen as speaking in the language of the philosophers.

The doctrines he proposes are, interpreted rightly, fully acceptable to Christians, but Trivet—reflecting a general shift of view about pagan philosophy from the twelfth to the fourteenth century—does not wish to interpret *integumenta* such as that of the World Soul in a *specifically* Christian sense.[66]

The *Consolation*: Philosophical and Theological Influence

Most of the outstanding medieval philosophers and theologians probably knew the *Consolation* and were affected by it to some extent, and so this aspect of Boethius's influence is even less open to summary than the proliferating tradition of commentary. I shall merely try to indicate two of the directions of this influence and, by taking as my main examples an outstanding early twelfth-century thinker, Abelard, and an outstanding one of the later thirteenth century, Aquinas, cast doubt on the generally accepted idea that the philosophical influence of the *Consolation* was powerful in the twelfth century but became faint when, from the 1250s, the Aristotelian curriculum was established in the universities.

The *Consolation*, at least in Books II–IV, is predominantly a work of ethics. It might be expected that, in the period before the mid-thirteenth century, when Aristotle's *Ethics* began to be widely studied, it would provide an important stimulus and source for moral philosophy. Yet it seems not generally to have been used in this way. Anselm of Canterbury (1033–1109), for example, despite his great debt to aspects of Boethian metaphysics and theology, developed his views on justice and evil without any apparent influence of the *Consolation*. He shared Boethius's Platonic view of evil as a privation and so, in a sense, nothing, but seems to have learned it from Augustine. In the twelfth century, Abelard—who knew the *Consolation* well—looked rather to Cicero's short rhetorical treatise, *On Invention*, as a treatise on ethics. In his *Collationes* (*Dialogue between a Christian, a Philosopher and a Jew*), Abelard presents an investigation into the highest good—just the subject of Boethius's dialogue with Philosophy in Books II and III. Yet the *Consolation* is not an important source for Abelard here; he prefers to use what he can gather about ancient philosophy from Augustine's *City of God* and from some of Seneca's letters.[67] Twelfth-century writers, it seems, were far more impressed by the Platonic cosmogony of Book III, m. 9 than by the ethical argument in the prose passages surrounding it.

In the next century, however, at least one great philosopher took the *Consolation*'s ethical ideas very seriously indeed. Aquinas seems to have had a special penchant for Boethius (see above on the logical commentaries and the *opuscula sacra*) and in his great study of ethics, the IaIIae of his *Summa Theologiae* (1271–1272), the *Consolation* has a special role. When, in q. 2, Aquinas considers in what human happiness (*beatitudo*) consists, he considers in turn (q. 2, a. 1–4, 6) each of Boethius's false goods: riches, honours, fame or glory, power and pleasure. The *Consolation* is clearly at the front of his mind, because in four out of the five discussions, a quotation from it is used to provide the '*sed contra*'—the short, authoritative statement for the correct answer to the problem. When, in the next question, Aquinas moves on to consider what exactly happiness is, the *Consolation* is still in his mind, though more as a source for apparently misleading positions (that God himself is happiness; that happiness is a state, not an activity (q. 3, a.1, arg. 1; q. 3, a. 2, arg. 2) that need to be explained away. It would be interesting to investigate whether Aquinas is unique in his blending of elements from the *Consolation* with ethical ideas from Aristotle's *Ethics*.[68]

By contrast with its ethical sections, the briefer but dense analysis of divine prescience and contingency in V.3–6 remained throughout the Middle Ages a classic treatment of this problem, as indeed it does to this day; and the definition of eternity in V.6.4 became standard in theological discussions. Yet, although everyone who approached the problem of prescience knew Boethius's solution, many philosophers chose not to follow it. In the early fourteenth century, William Ockham, as is well known, devised his own, un-Boethian approach;[69] but, nearly two hundred years earlier, Abelard had been equally independent, even while quoting enthusiastically from the *Consolation*. In his *Theologia Scholarium* (mid-1130s), Abelard proposes a solution of the problem of prescience that is based entirely on giving the correct analysis of the sentences in which it is stated, especially the scope of their possibility or necessity operators.[70] To give one example from his quite involved discussion. By making clear the scope of the possibility operator in a sentence such as 'If it is possible for a thing to happen otherwise than God has foreseen it, God can be mistaken', he believes that the sentence can be seen to provide no argument for determinism. God foresees with unfailing accuracy how things happen, so that it is no more possible for a thing to happen in one way and God to foresee it happening otherwise than for it to happen in one way and also in another different way. Nonetheless, suppose the outcome of an event is in fact *x*, and so God has in fact foreseen *x*: it is none the less possible that the outcome might not have been *x* (and so, of course, that God would not have foreseen it as being *x*). Abelard thinks that Boethius's introduction of simple and conditional necessity is designed to bring out a related distinction, between the necessity that can truly be predicated of the compound 'he is walking, given that I see him walking' but not of the simple 'he is walking'. Abelard is thinking far more propositionally than (as I have argued[71]) Boethius. As a result, he feels able to cite the authority of Boethius without bringing up the central feature of the solution in the *Consolation*: God's special way of existing and knowing in an eternal presentness.

Abelard does not consider—nor did Boethius himself—the strongest form of the argument from divine prescience to determinism, the 'accidental necessity argument': God's knowledge of the future is a fact about the past and so 'accidentally' necessary, and that necessity, along with the wide-scope necessity that if God foreknows *p*, then *p*, seems to entail that *p* is necessary.[72] But this argument was well known to Aquinas. One way of rejecting the argument is to claim that, because God is timeless, no facts about God are facts about the past. Such a solution is usually described by modern commentators as 'Boethian', although Boethius does not propose it (he did not even know the accidental necessity argument), and it is arguable whether he held that God is timeless.[73] Aquinas does not follow this (pseudo-)Boethian solution, although it would have provided a neat way out of the problem: evidence that, perhaps, he (too) did not consider that God is timeless. Rather, Aquinas's approach is much closer to the way Boethius himself actually presents the matter.[74] He accepts that in 'If God knew it will happen, it will happen', both the antecedent and the consequent are necessary, but then adds that because God knows all things as present, the necessity involved is merely conditional necessity—the necessity that applies to all present events while they are taking place and has no deterministic implications. He supports this argument by the principle—clearly related to the Modes of Cognition Principle in Boethius—that, as he puts it in *On Truth*, if in a conditional 'something about cognition is signified in the antecedent, it is necessary that the consequent is taken according to how the knower is, not according to how the thing known is.'

The *Consolation:* Literary Influence

Medieval readers found in the *Consolation* not only arguments and positions they valued, and information about Platonism they sought; the way in which it was written, its personifications, images, verse structure and vocabulary impressed and affected poets and writers of artful prose, some of whom were also interested by its philosophical ideas, others not. Incidental features of the *Consolation*, especially the personification of Fortune, were adapted in a wide variety of medieval writing.[75] Although there were also other models for the prosimetrum, such as Martianus Capella's *On the Marriage*, the *Consolation* helped to shape the medieval form—especially the twelfth-century prosimetra, such as Hildebert of Lavardin *De querimonia carnis et spiritus*, Adelard of Bath's *De eodem et diuerso*, Bernardus Silvestris's *Cosmographia*, and Alan of Lille's *De planctu Naturae*.[76] Alan's work, indeed, is designed with reference—and in partial contrast—to the *Consolation*. In form and in verbal detail, the *Consolation* is always in the background, although Alan tries to outdo even Boethius in the variety of metres he uses for the verses. Alan's description of his heroine, Natura, and of his, the narrator's, encounter with her very clearly echoes the appearance of Philosophy to Boethius; and Nature, like Boethius's Philosophy (but more explicitly) is attached to the realm of reason as opposed to that of faith. There is, though, a strong contrast with Boethius's work, marked even by Alan's title. So far from providing consolation, as Philosophy did, Nature is engaged in a *planctus*: she laments that humans have departed from her order by engaging in homosexuality. Her only solution is to issue a solemn proscription of such behaviour. The general tenor of Natura's complaint is close to that voiced by the character Boethius and rejected by Philosophy, that man has been left out of the order of nature. Perhaps Alan sensed and wished to underline some of the uncertainties and tensions contained (as argued above) in the *Consolation*.

The influence of the *Consolation* was not only, or even mainly, on readers and writers of Latin. It was one of the most widely and frequently translated works. In the last years of the ninth century, King Alfred translated it into Old English—often, especially in the later sections, very freely, and in the light of his patristic reading and his own concerns.[77] Around the year 1000, it was translated into Old High German by Notker III of St Gall.[78] The later Middle Ages, however, were the main period for translations of the *Consolation*. Over ten different versions were made in Old French (and its various dialects), all except one—the *Roman de philosophie* of Simund de Freine (ca. 1180), a poem freely based on parts of the *Consolation*—from the early to mid-thirteenth century or later.[79] The two most influential were the prose translation (*Li Livres de Confort de Philosophie*) made ca. 1300 by Jean de Meun (on whom see below), and a verse-prose translation, *Le Livre de Boece de Consolacion*, made in the mid-fourteenth century, to which translated glosses (based ultimately on William of Conches) had been added by the 1380s.[80] A number of translations into Italian were made in the fourteenth, especially, and fifteenth centuries; the most popular, that composed by Alberto della Piagentina in 1332, survives in 27 manuscripts.[81] There were three or four translations into Catalan and Spanish before 1400[82], translations into Dutch[83] and (from the fifteenth century) into German.[84] The *Consolation*'s first translator into Middle English was Geoffrey Chaucer himself; a little later (1410), John Walton finished a translation of it into verse.[85] The work was even put into Greek by Maximus Planudes at the end of the thirteenth century and into Hebrew early in the fifteenth.[86] Translation was often far from a merely literal rendering of the text. For example, some of the French versions engaged in various narrative elaborations.[87] Some translators tried to understand the text and bring out its meaning by using commentaries (and sometimes incorporating material from them into their version): the most studied case is Chaucer's use of Trivet.[88] And there are many manuscripts in which the translations are accompanied by an extensive page-by-page apparatus of commentary (taken from one of the popular Latin commentaries), whilst Trivet's commentary was itself translated twice into Italian.[89] Some vernacular, commented versions, such as the Ghent Boethius of 1485, engage in philosophical discussion at a highly sophisticated level.[90]

Not surprisingly, the *Consolation* was one of the ancient works most frequently borrowed from and alluded to in vernacular literature. Dante mentions it (*Convivio* II, xii, 2) as the book which, along with Cicero's *On Friendship*, won him to the love of philosophy; Boethius is placed in Paradise, alongside Augustine, Aquinas (and Siger of Brabant) (*Paradiso* X, 124–129), and the *Consolation* echoes at various points in the *Divina Commedia*. Although most of the writers themselves, like Dante, would have read the work in Latin, the diffusion of translations opened the possibility of using the *Consolation* in a more complex way than other learned texts, which would be unknown to almost all vernacular readers. Two striking examples of this complex use of Boethius are provided by two famous poets who also themselves translated the *Consolation* into the vernaculars: Jean de Meun and Geoffrey Chaucer.

Jean de Meun's original work consists in the continuation and ending he wrote to the *Roman de la Rose*, left unfinished half a century earlier by Guillaume de Lorris. Guillaume's poem described allegorically how a young man enters into courtly life, woos a lady (the rose) and is rebuffed. Jean's continuation finishes with the consummation of the lover's passion, but not until after 15,000 lines of mainly philosophical and satirical discussion. Near to the beginning of the continuation (4229–7184),[91] the lover is addressed by Reason, who adopts the tone and some of the ideas of Boethius's Philosophy in order to persuade the lover that he has lost nothing of value by his failure in love. But the Lover rejects Reason's advice. Boethian ideas and phrases recur near the end of the poem, in the first part of the confession (16729–17874) made by Nature to her priest, Genius. Nature and Genius are figures inspired, especially, by Alan of Lille, but Jean de Meun saw how Alan based his figure of Natura on Boethius's Philosophy and went back directly to the *Consolation* itself for much in this confession, including a long discussion of God's prescience, predestination, and human free will. Jean's treatment of these subjects, however, goes beyond the *Consolation* in various ways and links the treatment of providence and prescience differently. Moreover, Nature's role in the story is just the opposite of that taken by Reason, the other Boethian personification: whereas Reason wants to dissuade the Lover from his quest, it is Nature's help that enables him, finally, to win the rose.

The *Consolation* (often in combination with other works influenced by it, such as Alan of Lille's *De planctu Naturae* and the *Roman de la Rose*), is used by Chaucer in many of his works, from short lyrics such as *Fortune* and *Truth* to his most ambitious works, including the *Knight's Tale* and *Troilus and Criseyde*.[92] The way Chaucer uses the *Consolation* in *Troilus* is particularly fascinating and elusive. He took his plot from Boccaccio's *Filostrato*. Troilus, a Trojan prince at the time of the Greek siege, falls in love with Criseyde, daughter of Calchas who, foretelling the destruction of Troy, has defected to the Greeks. Troilus and Criseyde become lovers, but soon afterwards Criseyde is swapped for a Trojan hostage and sent to join her father in the Greek camp. She has sworn fidelity to Troilus but eventually even he has to accept that she has betrayed him for a Greek, Diomede. Although Boccaccio included Boethian allusions in the *Filostrato*, Chaucer introduces much, much more material from Boethius: many incidental passages and paraphrases, a song based on II, m. 8 sung by Troilus at the high point of his love affair, and an extensive paraphrase of part of the treatment of divine prescience, given to Troilus as he waits in vain for Criseyde to keep her faith after she has been sent to the Greeks. Usually, the adaptation or placing of the passages from the *Consolation* raises questions rather than answering them. For instance, what is the relation between the cosmic love presented in II, m. 8 and the type of love Troilus wishes to celebrate? And why is Troilus given just the character Boethius's arguments to show that all things happen of necessity and not Philosophy's reply? Some critics think that Chaucer intended his audience to use their knowledge of the *Consolation* to provide a sort of grid of authoritative, Christian doctrine, by which to judge the characters in the poem and their actions. On their view, Troilus's use—or rather, they would say, misuse—of II, m. 8 points out the disparity between his carnal and vulnerable love, and the love that unfailingly rules the universe; and the fact that he cannot go beyond Boethius the character's fatalistic arguments to Philosophy's vindication of human freedom is an indication of Troilus's limitations. One objection to this view, raised by other critics, is that it offers a rather generalized, simplistic reading, which does not respect the many nuances of the text. Another objection that should be raised concerns the *Consolation* and Chaucer's understanding of it. The *Consolation* may well be a Christian text, but only obliquely; and Philosophy is not a fount of authoritative *Christian* wisdom. The way Chaucer uses the *Consolation* suggests that, so far from seeing the *Consolation* as a stable, Christian authority, he was sensitive—even more than Alan of Lille and Jean de Meun—to the tensions and uncertainties in Boethius's text, the Roman author's literary and intellectual subtlety, and his awareness of the uses of obliquity.

NOTES

CHAPTER I

1. Courcelle (1967).

2. I do discuss them briefly in the next chapter, however, and give some indications for further reading. In his general book (1981), Chadwick gives them especial attention (see pp. 69–107).

3. I have tried to include rather full bibliographies in the notes to this chapter, for readers wishing to investigate this area further.

CHAPTER 2

1. See Obertello (1974) 4–15.

2. See Thompson (1982) 61–76; but cf. (for quasi-imperial role) Chadwick (1981) 2–3. There is a detailed and nuanced account of Theoderic's position in Moorhead (1992) 39–51. See also Heather (1996) 216–58 and Amory (1997).

3. On Rome, Ravenna and the different types of political career, see Matthews (1981) 26–30.

4. See Obertello (1974) 33.

5. See Obertello (1974) 30–31.

6. There is a thorough discussion of the primary sources for Boethius's trial and sentence, and their reliability, in Morton (1982), esp. pp. 108–9 and Moorhead (1992) 219–26; and see Obertello (1974) 85–138, Chadwick (1981) 48–68.

7. He may be the same as 'John the Deacon', to whom Boethius dedicated three of the theological treatises: see Chadwick (1981) 53.

8. Moorhead (1992) gives information that favours both interpretations—pp. 166–72, 220–22 (Boethius as leader of pro-Byzantines); pp. 226–32 (Boethius's enemies at court)—and ends (pp. 232–35) by seeing the attack on Boethius as mainly the reaction of a group of courtiers who saw their position threatened.

9. On Symmachus, see Chadwick (1981) 6–16.

10. *Anecdoton Holderi*, quoted by Obertello (1974) 22. On the *Anecdoton*, see Chapter 8, n. 30.

11. See Obertello (1974) 26–7.

12. Plotinus is an important figure in the intellectual background to Boethius, although Boethius may not have had any *direct* knowledge of his works. Two good, and very different introductions to his work are O'Meara (1993) and Hadot (1997).

13. See Sorabji (1990), Introduction, 2–3, Ebbesen (1981), 133–70.

14. See Damascius (1999) §118A (pp. 280–81), cf. Introduction, pp. 30–32; and Westerink (1990).

15. Cassiodorus *Variae* I, 45, 3 (Cassiodorus, 1973, 49:17–18) writes that 'from far away (*longe positus*)' Boethius 'entered the Athenian schools'; see Obertello (1974) 27–28.

16. Pierre Courcelle has argued for time spent at the Alexandrian school; Obertello (1974) 28–29 shows the weakness of the case. See also below, for links with Ammonius (and their indirectness).

17. See chapter 8.

18. The translation of the *Isagoge* was used by Boethius for his first commentary on that work (see chapter 3); *On Definitions* survives and was for a long time thought to be a work of Boethius's (in fact, Boethius devotes a section of his commentary on Cicero's *Topics* (TC324:45–327:8 [1098A–1100B]) to a critical account of it!); the commentary and the treatise on hypothetical syllogisms are lost but are attested by Boethius, Cassiodorus and Martianus Capella. In one version of his *Institutiones*, Cassiodorus says that Marius Victorinus also translated the *Categories* and *On Interpretation* and produced a commentary on the *Categories*; but probably this comment is the result of a confused revision of the text: see Hadot (1971) 108–112.

19. See Chadwick (1981) 115–119.

20. See chapter 5. Crabbe (1981) argues for the influence of Augustine on the *Consolation*.

21. See below, chapter 5, n. 46, for possible influence of more recent Greek theology on Boethius.

22. *Variae* I.45.4; Cassiodorus (1973) 49:23–50:32.

23. See Guillaumin (1995), Introduction , xlvii–l, lii–lvi and cf. *Ar* I, 1 #2–5.

24. II, vi, 3; Cassiodorus (1937) 152:10–13.

25. Folkerts (1970) 109–171, 173–217, edits the pseudo-Boethian *Geometry II* and the Euclidean material from *Geometry I*, which scholars have argued derive from Boethius's lost work. Pingree (1981) is sceptical about the identification. For a detailed discussion of evidence for these lost works, Obertello (1974) 173–96.

26. Guillaumin (1995) gives a detailed account of Boethius's divergences from Nicomachus's text: xxxix–xliv.

27. See the admirably detailed account of the *Principles of Music* in Chadwick (1981) 78–101, from which I have borrowed.

28. Cf. Chadwick (1981) 82–83.

29. Pizzani (1965) and, more emphatically, Bower (1978) and Bower and Palisca (1989), xxiv–xxix, see the treatise as being a literal translation of Greek sources; Caldwell (1981) argues that Boethius was more flexible in following his sources.

CHAPTER 3

1. See the comments in the Introduction (above) on the limitations of this chapter.

2. Obertello's dating (1984, 306); De Rijk (1964) suggests 504–505.

3. As Asztalos (1993) 372–77 convincingly argues.

4. See below, n. 22 to this chapter.

5. Cf. De Rijk (1964) 144, where he gives the date for *2InDI* as 515–16.

6. As, for example, at the beginning of the translation of *On Interpretation*. Boethius's choices as a translator here have been studied in detail in Magee (1989) 49–63.

7. In the case of the *Categories*, the two versions that survive are Boethius's final version and a 'composite' version, which is probably an earlier draft by Boethius, improved by using the lemmata of his commentary (close to his final version of the translation); see Asztalos (1993) 371–72. There is a very clear summary of scholarship on Boethius's translations in Chadwick (1981) 131–41; the fundamental work was done by Minio-Paluello—see Minio-Paluello (1972) and the introductions to the *Aristoteles Latinus* editions (*Aristoteles Latinus*, 1961–).

8. See Chadwick (1981) 139, who cites *2InDI* 190:13, 458:27 and TC 1152B.

9. I discuss this commentary in chapter 4 below, because it is closely related to Boethius's treatise on topical reasoning.

10. As Obertello (1974) 229 has noted, Boethius refers to a commentary by him on Aristotle's *Topics* in his *On Topical Differentiae*, 1191A, 1216D. But none has survived. He also clearly refers to having expounded 'the Analytics' (cf. Obertello (1974) 229–30); Minio-Paluello has discovered marginal annotations

in a medieval manuscript of the *Prior Analytics* which, he argues, are Boethius's: see *Aristoteles Latinus* (1961–) III 1–4, lxxix–lxxxviii and (for edition of the scholia) 295–372.

11. See Ammonius (1996) 2–3.

12. See Shiel (1990)—a revision of an article first published in 1958, and the replies to his thesis by Chadwick (1981) 129–31 and Ebbesen (1990) 375–77.

13. Cf. De Libera (1999) 164–48 and Magee (forthcoming).

14. See De Libera's introduction in Porphyry (1998) VII–XII; according to Strange (1987), the contrast between Porphyry and Plotinus in their approaches to the Aristotelian Categories is less sharp than it might at first appear. On the *Isagoge*, see below.

15. See Porphyry's question and answer commentary to the *Categories*: Porphyry (1887) 57:20–59:2. [Tr: 1992] Many of the later Greek commentaries on Aristotle have been translated, with valuable notes and introductions, in a series edited by Richard Sorabji. I list them in the Bibliography, where relevant, under the name of the commentator, with the date of publication. For ease of reference, these translations divide up the text according to the pages and lines of the CAG edition of the original. In references, I simply give, therefore, as here, the date of the translation, which appears in the bibliography under the Greek author's name (e.g., 'Porphyry (1992)') along with a full reference to the Greek text.

16. Porphyry (1887) 90:2–92:2. [Tr: 1992]. For the reconstruction of Porphyry's semantics and his treatment of primary substances, see Ebbesen (1981) 133–70, Lloyd (1990) 36–75, Strange's Introduction to Porphyry (1992), and De Libera (1999) 85–100.

17. Ammonius (1895) [Tr: 1991]; Dexippus (1888) [Tr: 1989]; Simplicius (1907); [a French translation, with commentary, is in progress, 1990–]. For an account of the Greek commentary tradition on the *Categories*, see Simplicius (1990–), Fasc. 1, 21–23.

18. Asztalos (1993) 394–98.

19. See Asztalos (1993) 385–89.

20. Ammonius (1895) 14:1–2 [Tr: 1991].

21. Cf. Simplicius (1990–), Fasc. 1, 7, n. 20.

22. The text of 160A–B in Migne contains an inauthentic reference to a second commentary, but even without this reference the passage fairly clearly sets out Boethius's intention to write a fuller commentary for the more learned. Asztalos (1993, 384–88, including a new edition of *InCat* 159A–161A) makes a convincing case that the passage was inserted after Boethius was some way further on in the commentary. On the existence of a second commentary, see Chadwick (1981) 141–43, Ebbesen (1990) 387–88. De Rijk (1964, 132–141 is more sceptical. Hadot (1959) believes that a fragment in a medieval manuscript comes from this commentary.

23. Asztalos (1993) 379–81 argues that a reference in *2InDI* (7:18–31) to how the scope of the *Categories* is described in his commentary may be evidence that a second commentary was written, because it differs from the scope as defined in *InCat*. But it is not clear that the scope really is described differently but merely envisaged from a different point of view, because of the comparison being made with that of *On Interpretation*. I give a more detailed discussion of the question of Boethius's second *Categories* commentary in Marenbon (Forthcoming-4).

24. In Porphyry (1998), Alain de Libera and Alain-Philippe Segonds provide the Greek text of the *Isagoge*, with Boethius's Latin translation, their own French translation and very full and important commentary.

25. Porphyry (1998), 1 (section 2).

26. One is by Elias, who taught at Alexandria in the earlier sixth century (Elias, 1900); another is the work of David 'the Invincible' (David, 1904) who wrote later in that century, or at the beginning of the seventh. The third is related to the work of Elias (Pseudo-Elias, 1967). This tradition is still seen as one strand in Ibn al-Tayyib's Arabic commentary from the eleventh century (Ibn al-Tayyib, 1979). On the Alexandrian tradition, see Westerink (1990).

27. Cf. Ammonius (1881) 110–13 and Boethius *1inIsag.* 100–102, *2InIsag.* 280–83.

28. Ammonius (1881) 41:10–42:26; Elias (1900) 48:16–30; David (1904) 120:8–14; Pseudo-Elias (1967) 68–69 (§29.31–35); Ibn al-Tayyib (1979) 38–40; cf. Hoffmann (1992–93) and De Libera (1996) 103–105.

29. De Libera (1999) 199–202.

30. De Libera (1999) 187–88 also finds traces of this approach in the first commentary.

31. De Libera (1999) 159–280 (on Boethius), 25–157 (on Alexander). There is also a useful, if rather disparaging, discussion in Tweedale (1976) 63–86.

32. See above, n. 13.

33. See *2InIsag.* 163:6 and 163:21–22 (. . . *omnis haec sit deponenda de his quinque propositis disputandi cura*). Boethius is right to think that MAU applies equally to any sort of universal, whether or not it is in the category of substance. It would not, however, apply to a particular *differentia*, *proprium*, or accident.

34. On these arguments, see Spade (1996) and De Libera's convincing points against it (1999, 206–207).

35. See De Libera (1999) 209–214.

36. See especially Alexander's *Quaestiones* (Alexander of Aphrodisias, 1892), nos. I, 3; I,11; 2, 14. These questions are translated, with useful notes, in Alexander of Aphrodisias (1992). I am basing myself on the presentation in De Libera (1999); see also pp. 51–55 of that book for full details of the corpus of Alexandrian material on the problem, including works available only in Arabic.

37. The position expressed here (that will not be Boethius's final position in this discussion) seems to correspond exactly to Boethius's view in his *Categories* commentary: (*InCat* 183C): 'For genera and species are not understood from one single <member of a species or genus>, but from all the single individuals, conceived by the mind's reason.'

38. Cf. De Libera (1999) 244–49.

39. Cf. Tweedale (1976) 63.

40. Boethius uses the word *propositiones* to refer to what syllogisms consist of (e.g. 'Every man is rational' is a *propositio*. It is tempting to translate *propositio*—as most historians do—by 'proposition', since many modern logicians talk of arguments as being made up of a sequence of propositions. But 'proposition' is a word by which some of its modern users mean, not a linguistic item, but rather what a group of linguistic items, express: the proposition, John is writing, is what 'John is writing' said now, 'John was writing' said in five minutes time, and 'Joannes scribit', and many, many more sentences, all express. For Boethius, by contrast, a *propositio* is a linguistic item.

41. See above, and n. 11.

42. See Ammonius (1996) 4–5.

43. Ammonius (1897) 34:10–41:9 [Tr: 1996]

44. See chapter 7.

45. For a detailed study of the textual and interpretative problems of Aristotle's text, and Boethius's choices in translation, see Magee (1989) 7–63.

46. The Latin reads here *quorum autem hae primorum notae*—literally 'But the first things of which they are signs.' The *primorum* here indicates that Boethius's text read *prōtōn* (genitive plural), rather than *prōtōs*, the adverb, found in some manuscripts and chosen by some modern editors. None the less, as Magee puts it (1989, 53) 'the burden rests on the commentator to find adverbial force in the genitive.' The commentary shows that he understands *primorum* adverbially because Boethius usually uses an adverb such as *principaliter* (e.g., *2InDI*, 24:12, 33:28, 43:19; see Magee (1989) 52, n. 8, for a full list) when paraphrasing Aristotle's remark. For a full discussion of the textual problem, see Magee (1989) 21–34.

47. *2InDI* 21:18–22: 'Nam cum Romanus, Graecus ac barbarus simul videant equum, habent quoque de eo eundem intellectum, quod equus sit, et apud eos eadem res subiecta est, idem a re ipsa concipitur intellectus, sed Graecus aliter equum vocat . . .' Note here how, although Boethius remarks that the complex thought or judgement 'It is a horse' that they make is the same, the only sense in which he considers that the simple thought of the horse is the same is that it originates from the same thing.

48. *2InDI* 34:13–17: 'This passion is like the impression of a figure of some sort, but in the way that is usual in the soul. For its own figure is within a thing

in one way, but its form is transferred to the soul in another way'; cf. De Rijk (1981) 145–47.

49. For a detailed discussion, see Magee (1989) 98–105. My interpretation owes a great deal to Magee's, although I differ in some of my emphases and conclusions.

50. See, e.g., Kretzmann (1967) 367–68

51. Cf. Magee (1989) 118.

52. See Magee (1989) 120 for a discussion of the text and translation; I do not agree that the passage need be translated, as he does, involving a reference to an inner, mental speech.

53. Cf. Magee (1989) 138–40.

54. Kretzmann (1998) 29–37.

55. See chapter 7.

56. Kretzmann (1998) 39–40 identifies the apparent contradiction and uses it as evidence that Boethius is putting forward a theory about the *assertion* of propositions.

57. For Ammonius's discussion of divine prescience and determinism, see chapter 7 (in connection with Boethius's treatment of the problem in the *Consolation*).

58. There is a good analysis of this theory in Kretzmann (1985).

59. For some brief indications of this influence, and bibliography, see chapter 9.

60. See Marenbon (Forthcoming-4).

CHAPTER 4

1. See D877B and Magee (1998) 67. References to D are to Magee (1988), but I use the column numbers and letters of Migne, *Patrologia Latina* 64, which are also given by Magee, for ease of reference.

2. See Magee (1998) xviii–xxxiii.

3. For an evaluation of the meaning of Boethius's comments on his sources, see Magee (1998) xxxiv–lvii, and cf. Magee (1994).

4. Porphyry (1998) 15–16; *2InIsag*. 282:4–283:4.

5. For Boethius's interest in separable accidents, see also chapter 5, n. 45.

6. Confusingly, SC is sometimes called *Introductio in syllogismos categoricos*, almost identical to the common title of ISC (*Introductio ad syllogismos categoricos*).

7. See Obertello (1974) 234–48. De Rijk (1964) 6–44, 159, 161 proposes a very early date for SC (505–506) and a very late date for ISC (ca. 523).

8. For a succinct account of modern interpretative debate (with full bibliography) and a formal model of syllogistic, see Robin Smith's Introduction to his translation of the *Prior Analytics* (Aristotle, 1989).

9. This makes it seem as if predication was regarded as a relationship between words. But Boethius, in line with the ancient tradition, seems not to have made a sharp distinction in this matter between the words of a sentence and what they stand for, and he would have been perfectly happy to think of philosopher being predicated of Plato.

10. Nowadays, only arguments formulated according to Aristotle's syllogistic tend to be called 'syllogisms'. Aristotle himself defines *sullogismos* (*Prior Analytics* 24b18–22; *Top.* 100a25–277) very widely, in a way which applies to many sorts of valid argument. Boethius's own explicit definition (SC 821A–2B) falls between these two extremes. Syllogisms, he considers, are valid arguments, with two premisses and a conclusion that does not merely repeat one of the premisses. I shall follow this definition in talking of 'syllogisms', although Boethius himself does not always stick to it, since he sometimes calls an invalid argument in syllogistic form a syllogism.

11. On the *Prior Analytics* as a natural deduction system, see Corcoran (1974) and Smiley (1973).

12. See *Prior Analytics* 53a3–14 and 29a19–29 (which would warrant more additional syllogisms than Boethius's five); Alexander of Aphrodisias (1983) 69:5–22, where Theophrastus is credited with introducing the extra syllogisms; and the note in the translation (Alexander of Aphrodisias, 1991), p. 136, n. 157.

13. SC 819B, cf. 827C. Beginning with Theophrastus (see Alexander of Aphrodisias, 1991, p. 168, n. 18 for a discussion and full references), some had claimed that, as well as 'Every *B* is *A*; Every *B* is *C*; therefore Some *C* is *A*' (accepted by Aristotle, *Prior Analytics* 28a17–18), there was a distinct syllogism, with the same premisses but the conclusion 'Some *A* is *C*'. Since 'Some *C* is *A*' and 'Some *A* is *C*' are equivalent, this is a very weak case. But, as presented by Boethius, the case is even worse! His alternative syllogism, which is given using terms (good, just, virtue) rather than letters, reverses the order of the premisses, as well as transposing the terms in the conclusion: the result is a syllogism which, if the terms were replaced by letters to bring out the logical form, would be seen to be *exactly the same in form* as that of which it is supposed to be a distinct variant.

14. See Patzig (1968) 69–73 and Alexander of Aphrodisias (1991) 75, n. 141.

15. Patzig (1968) 75–76.

16. See ISC 787 A–C, SC 806 CD. He calls both these sorts 'conversion by accident', since the conversion is made possible by the fact that just one of the pair can itself be converted: for example, because 'No *A* is *B*' is itself convertible to 'No *B* is *A*', Boethius concludes that 'Some *A* is not *B*' (the particular negative which follows from the universal 'No *A* is *B*') converts with 'No *B* is *A*'. He talks here of the two sentences both being true—a way of speaking which

does not make it as clear as might have been expected that while from 'No *B* is *A*' it follows that 'Some *A* is not *B*', the implication does not hold the other way round.

17. See Prior (1953).

18. De Rijk (1964) 145–54.

19. See Dürr (1951) and, much more intelligently but still misguidedly, Barnes (1981) 83–84.

20. The point is made in Green-Pedersen (1984, 80) and developed powerfully in Martin (1991). It is borne out in Speca (2001), which fills in the background detail.

21. See above, chapter 3, n. 40.

22. References are to the Books, sections, and subsections as given in Obertello (1969).

23. Boethius uses two different conjunctions, *si* and *cum*. *Si* is the usual Latin word for 'if'; *cum* might be translated rather as 'since' or 'given that'. But it seems that Boethius uses two different words for the sake of stylistic elegance, so as to prevent having ugly and confusing doublings (*Si si* . . .). In my translation, I render both by 'if . . . then . . .'. The 'then' does not correspond to any Latin word, but helps to make clear the structure of antecedent, consequent.

24. See Barnes (1981) 83–84.

25. See especially Martin (1991) 279.

26. The argument goes: 1) p –> (q –>r) [1st premise]; 2) p –> q [constraint 3]; 3) p [supposition, for *reductio*]; 4) q –>r [1,3 *modus ponens*]; 5) q [2, 3 *modus ponens*]; 6) r [4,5; *modus ponens*]; 7) q –> ~r [2nd premise]; 7) ~r [5, 7; *modus ponens*]; 8) r & ~r [6, 7]; 9) ~p [by indirect proof].

27. I am very grateful to Dr. Christopher Martin for having discussed this whole topic with me and explained the views indicated briefly in his publications.

28. 1) (p –>q) -> (r –>s) [1st premise]; 2) p –> r [constraint]; 3) q –>s [constraint]; 4) r –> ~s [2nd premise]; 5) ~s –> ~q [3; contraposition]; 6) r –> ~q [4,5; transitivity of predication] 7) p –> ~q [2,6; transitivity of predication]. I leave it to others to see if similar proofs can be constructed for the sentence logic analogues of the other 15 four-term syllogisms.

29. Speca (2001). I am very grateful to Dr Speca for sending me a complete copy of his manuscript before it was published.

30. Cf. Striker (1973) who, while making a good case for the dependence on Book I on more than one source, allows (75) that Boethius's claims for the originality of Books II and III may be justified.

31. There is a critical edition of TD included with the edition of the Byzantine Greek translation (Nikitas, 1990). The best edition of TC is still Cicero (1833). Useful translations of both works with notes and introductions have been

made by Eleonore Stump: TD: Stump (1978); TC: Stump (1988). I use the colum numbers and letters of *Patrologia Latina* (Migne, 1847, 1173–1216) for references to TD, because these are reproduced in both Nikitas's edition and Stump's translation. For TC, I give the page and line(s) in Cicero (1833) followed by the column numbers and letters of the edition in Migne (1847) 1039–1169.

32. Cf. Stump (1988) 10–12 on range and interest of TC.

33. See Stump (1988) 11.

34. It is not known exactly what was the form of the material from Themistius that Boethius knew; some quotations from Themistius about the topics are preserved in Averroes' middle commentary on Aristotle's *Topics*; see Stump (1978) 212–13 and Stump (1974) 89–91.

35. See chapter 9.

36. See Stump (1978) 205–214, Green-Pedersen (1984) 37–38.

37. I shall use 'plausible' (cf. *endoxon* = 'plausible argument') to translate Boethius's *probabilis* and *verisimilis*: TD 1182A illustrates clearly that Boethius regards these words as synonyms, while at TD 1180C Boethius defines a *probabile argumentum* in the same way as Aristotle defines *endoxon* (*Topics* 100b20–22).

38. See Stump's good exposition: Stump (1978), 195–99.

39. Cf. Stump (1978) 195–99.

40. See also below, n. 43, for a further example.

41. See the useful discussions in Stump (1978) 181–89 and Green-Pedersen (1984) 68–71.

42. Green-Pedersen (1984) 38, 63–64, 71.

43. TC 1185 CD. The *differentia* of this argument is 'from definition'. In TC, Boethius phrases the maximal sentence differently ('Things which have diverse definitions necessarily have diverse substances' 1052AB); elsewhere, Boethius gives a variety of maximal sentences for this topic, some designed to back a positive and some to back a negative conclusion: 'Everything which is conjoined to the definition of something is also necessarily tied to the those things of which it is the definition' (TC 288:33–34 [1060AB]); 'That to which the definition of the genus does not apply is not a species of the genus which is so defined' (TD 1187A) 'Where the definition is absent, that which is defined is also absent' (TD 1196D).

44. See Stump (1978) 182–84 for an attempt at formulating this argument. As Stump (1978, 183–84) points out, when they use a conditional, sometimes Boethius's examples do present a perfectly valid argument. For instance, at TD 1188D–89A, he argues from (i) If it is useful . . . for diseases to be driven out, for health to be preserved and wounds to be healed, then medicine is useful, and (ii) It is useful for diseases to be driven out, for health to be preserved and wounds to be healed, to the conclusion (iii) Medicine is useful. But, as Stump

goes on to show, the maximal sentence in question—'What is in the single parts is necessarily in the whole'—is required as a support for the argument, since it warrants the truth of the conditional (i).

45. See chapter 3.

46. See Blumenthal (1990).

CHAPTER 5

1. On the identification of John the Deacon and his relations to Boethius, see Chadwick (1981) 26–29, Daley (1984) 162, n. 17, and above. On John as compiler of the collection Chadwick (1981) 255; he refers to Boethius's comment (OSV, 45–46 [Intr. 48–49]) that John already had copies of a number of his works.

2. The manuscript tradition, it is now agreed, indicates that Treatise IV was part of the original collection, although there are occasional suggestions of unease from medieval copyists about its inclusion (see Obertello, 1974, 261–70). The case for Boethius's authorship has been convincingly made by Bark (1946) and, on stylistic grounds, in Chadwick (1980); Obertello (1974, 270–75) remains uncertain whether the treatise was written by Boethius or by someone else in his circle, but his doubts are unnecessary.

3. As Chadwick (1981, 180) suggests, and Merle (1991, 85) takes as being 'certain'.

4. Cf. the excellent preface in Merle (1991) 25–28.

5. The *opuscula sacra* are now available in a critical edition (Moreschini, 2000), but I shall also give, for convenience, references to the edition of Stewart, Rand, and Tester (1973), with parallel English translation, which has until now been the most commonly used. The capital roman numeral designates which of the *opuscula* is being cited; for OSI, II and V, which are divided into sections, the section number then follows, after a comma; then, after a period, there follows the line number(s) in Moreschini and, in square brackets, the line number(s) in Stewart, Rand, and Tester. So, for example, 'OSV, 7.585–87 [1–3]' is a reference to *Opusculum Sacrum* 5, section 7, lines 585–87 in Moreschini (who numbers his lines continuously) and lines 1–3 in Stewart, Rand, and Tester (where the line numbering restarts at the beginning of each section).

6. Chadwick (1981) 180.

7. Cf. Daley (1984) 188–89.

8. See Chadwick (1981) 183–84.

9. On Boethius and the letter from the Eastern Bishops, see Schurr (1935) 108–127, Chadwick (1981) 181–83, Daley (1984) 178–80.

10. See Hadot (1973), which I have used extensively in this paragraph.

11. See chapter 2.

12. See *AL* I, 1–5, *Index Graeco-Latinus*, p. 205 for this translation of *ousia*; by contrast, the (earlier) *Categoriae Decem*, a paraphrase from the circle of Themistius which was thought in the Middle Ages to be by Augustine, usually uses a transliteration, *usia*. For Boethius's rendition of *ousia* in OSV, see below.

13. Note here—as John Magee has pointed out to me—that, in formulating this definition, Boethius does not follow the usual logical procedure of giving a genus and *differentia* (or *differentiae*) but combines two separate divisions of the genus Substance, one from the *Categories* (where substances are divided into universal and particular/individual substances, the other from the *Isagoge* (where one of the divisions of substance is corporeal, living, sensible rational substance).

14. Cf. Schlapkohl (1999) 25–26, 120, who sensibly suggests that the function of the word *naturae* in the definition is syntactic rather than semantic.

15. OSV, 3.215–20 [51–55]. Here Boethius regards distinguishing properties (*propria*)—a man's ability to laugh—as distinct from accidents, whereas in Porphyry's *Isagoge* and his commentaries on it, distinguishing properties are a type of accident.

16. Cf. Chadwick (1981) 197.

17. Boethius says (OSV, 6.488–93 [10–14]) that, were divine nature transformed to human nature, 'human nature would remain, and its substance would be immutable, and divine nature would change, so that what is naturally changeable and passible [human nature] would exist for ever immutable, and what is naturally thought to be immutable and impassible [divine nature] would be turned into a mutable thing.' This suggests that he also thought it, in principle, objectionable that changeable human nature should become unchangeable. But when he turns, immediately, to consider (*ii*), he does not write as if he thought that human nature's becoming divine, and hence unchangeable, can be rejected without further argument, which he goes on to give.

18. For shared matter underlying change, see 314b7–5a3 (cf. Chadwick, 1981, 199—but his reference is wrong); for qualities acting, or not acting on each other, see 328a19–b14 (here Aristotle gives the very examples of wine being mixed with both a small and a very large quantity of water). Questions about the mixing of liquids were certainly debated in post-Aristotelian philosophy (cf. Plotinus, *Ennead* II.7, which debates with Stoic as well as Aristotelian positions); but the framework on which Boethius relies here seems to be Aristotelian, although he may well have known later commentaries or discussions of the subject.

19. This analysis is put forward in Schlapkohl (1999), 3–5, 10–123; see esp. 97–107.

20. See Schurr (1934) 136–227.

21. On OSII, cf. Schurr (1934) 210 and Chadwick (1981) 212–213.

22. Gersh (1986) 647–718 (see esp. 705–707) makes a strong case for Augustine's work as the main influence on Boethius's metaphysics.

23. In so describing him, Boethius shows his tendency to merge the Neoplatonic One, the first hypostasis, with the second hypostasis, the Intellect, in which the Ideas or Forms exist. Some parallels for calling God a form can be found in pagan Neoplatonists, but the closest thinker to Boethius here is Augustine: see Gersh (1986) 689–90.

24. On the links between this view of concrete wholes and OSV, and the parallels between this view and Greek writers of Boethius's time, see Daley (1984) 181, n. 95.

25. For a discussion of Boethius's use of Aristotle here, see Jacobi (1995), 513–516. On the Platonic background to Aristotle's division and its use by Neoplatonists, see Merlan (1968) 59–87. Cf. also Maioli (1978) 59–82.

26. See chapter 9.

27. See below.

28. OSI, 4.187–96, 206–215 [14–24, 36–44]. Whereas Augustine talks of God being, e.g., greatness (*magnitudo*), Boethius here prefers to say that 'God is that very thing which is just' (*Deus . . . idem ipsum est quod est iustum*) and 'God is the Great' (*Deus . . . ipsum magnus exsistit*).

29. The translators, however, try to explain Boethius's apparent inconsistency by adding glosses that have no textual justification. Tester (Stewart, Rand, and Tester, 1973) 20, adds a footnote, '*i.e.* according to their substance.' Merle (1991) 137 translates: 'Les autres catégories ne sont attribuées ni à Dieu ni même aux autres choses (substantiellement). Obertello (1979) 370–71 translates: 'Ed anche le altre categorie non si predicano nello stesso modo di Dio e delle altre realtà.'

30. On Boethius's discussion of divine eternity here, see chapter 7.

31. See, e.g., the translation in Stewart, Rand, and Tester (1973) 39: 'You ask me to state and explain somewhat more clearly that obscure question in my *Hebdomads* concerning . . .'; cf. Chadwick (1981) 203; Elsässer (1988) 122.

32. OSIII, 7–11 [Intr. 8–11]. Another reason why Boethius cannot be referring to the title of a work of his is that there is a variation in the form of the word used in its two mentions (in the first and third sentences). John requests to have made clear 'from our *hebdomadibus*' (l [1]): ablative plural of *hebdomas*, 3rd decl.; Boethius refers to his '*hebdomadas*' (7–8 [8]): accusative plural of *hebdomada*, 1st decl. *Hebdomas* and *hebdomada* both have the same meaning. But if the title of a book were in question, the form of the word would not be changed between two mentions of it by its author.

33. A different explanation made by Chadwick (1981) 203–204 and taken up by Merle (1991) 88–91 (translation 99) is that the 'hebdomads' refer to the group of 'terms and rules', on which his argument will be based, that Boethius

sets out immediately after the preface. Although there are nine of these, these scholars suggest that they are intended to be seven, and that John the Deacon's request is that Boethius should use these rules and definitions to solve a problem he finds difficult. But the arguments for regarding the nine rules as seven are not compelling. Recently (Hudry, 1997) a quite different interpretation of *hebodmas/hebdomada* has been proposed, according to which the terms mean a day (of philosophical debate). Boethius would therefore be referring back to a discussion he had with John the Deacon during such a day of philosophical disputation. Although the arguments Hudry uses to establish this thesis are highly speculative, the interpretation is itself quite plausible and escapes my objections to the other readings.

34. The most thoroughgoing attempt to fit the Rules to the argument that follows is in De Rijk (1981) 152–53.

35. The literature is very large. The interpretation I give in general follows Maioli (1978) 13–38 who develops the course of thinking advanced by Brosch (1931) 37–73; MacDonald (1988) 247–50 also seems to be thinking on these lines. See the following note for further literature. See especially Brosch, 103–105; Hadot (1963), (1970). Obertello accepts this MacDonald (1988) 247–50.

36. See Hadot (1963), (1970). See also Schrimpf (1966) 3–29, for a complex reading that does not correspond exactly to any of the others, and De Rijk (1981) 152–56; (1988) 17–25; McInerny (1990) 161–98 for a wide-ranging survey of the various interpretations.

37. In a recent, detailed discussion (Nash-Marshall, 2000, 225–73), Siobhan Nash-Marshall has advanced a very different interpretation of the axioms and of Boethius's ideas on participation, both in OSIII and in the *Consolation*. I shall explain why I do not accept her conclusions in a review of the book in *The Thomist*.

38. For my understanding of the thought experiment, I am greatly indebted to Martin (1999) 287–91, and also to my discussions with Christopher Martin and his kindness in letting me see a longer version of his article than the published one.

39. The impossibility of God's nonexistence is not established by the facts that (OSIII.83–86 [92–95]) 'it is clear that he exists' and that 'the opinion of all learned and unlearned people, and the religions of barbarian peoples' holds him to exist. But Boethius introduces the discussion (OSIII.76–82 [87–91]) by comparing the thought experiment to the separation of things—such as the shape of a triangle from its matter—which cannot be separated in act. From this it is clear that the hypothesis of God's non-existence is considered to be an impossibility. Martin (1999) 287–91 gives a detailed discussion of the argument, concentrating on the fact that it rests on a hypothesis accepted as being impossible, and he compares

other passages where Boethius argues *ex impossibili*. Martin takes the Rules as axioms, and he believes that Boethius sets them out so as to give him a guide about what principles to employ in reasoning under the very strange circumstances of starting from an admittedly impossible hypothesis.

40. MacDonald (1988) 257–58 points out the invalidity of the argument and gives a good explanation of how Boethius might have been able to derive the conclusion validly from other premisses, which he held but does not state here.

41. Cf. Martin (1999) 289, although I think Martin is wrong to suggest that in case (*b*) Boethius has in mind a *composite* substance.

42. E.g., OSIII.122–23 [131–33]: '. . . non potest esse ipsum esse rerum nisi a primo esse defluxerit, id est bono' (The very *esse* of things could not be unless it flowed from the first *esse*, that is from the Good). The same claim is repeated a number of times, in different forms.

43. See (i): OSIII.114–18 [124–27]: 'Sed ipsum esse omnium rerum ex eo fluxit quid est primum bonum et quod bonum tale est ut recte dicatur, in eo quod est, esse bonum. Ipsum igitur eorum esse bonum est . . .' (but the very *esse* of all things flows from that which is the Highest Good and that good is such that it may be rightly said to be good in that it is. Therefore the very *esse* of them is good); (ii): OSIII.150–52 [161–62]: '. . . quia vero voluit ea esse bona, qui erat bonus, sunt bona in eo quod sunt' (because he, who was good, willed them to be good, they are good in that they are).

44. MacDonald (1988) 264–67. One strong reason for rejecting this interpretation is that if Boethius's thought experiment is to be of relevance, 'good' must have the same meaning within it as within the discussion which it is supposed to illuminate. But in the thought experiment, we are to suppose that there is no First Good, and so 'good' could not mean 'deriving from the First Good' in the context of the experiment. For some other critical remarks, cf. Aertsen (1991) 63–64.

45. Martin (1999) 282–83, 290–91.

46. As Martin (1999, 289) puts it: 'Casting the conclusion in modern idiom, in that impossible world either some substances are not good or there is another accessible impossible world in which substances which are good in the first impossible world are no longer good.'

47. See chapter 9. Daley (1984) might seem to cast doubt on this judgment about Boethius's methodological originality. Daley points out that Boethius's use of Aristotleian logic and physics in theology is typical of the Greek writers of his time. But, as Daley also admits, hardly any of the Greek material is earlier than the *opuscula sacra*. Boethius was one of the leaders of the trend, rather than a later follower. And the influence on the method of later Latin theology was from the *opuscula* rather than any Greek works.

CHAPTER 6

1. Gruber (1978) discusses the *Consolation*'s sources and allusions in detail in the course of his commentary; he draws together material on the genre of the *Consolation* at pp. 16–32. See also Reichenberger (1954) 1–7. The *Consolation* has also been considered along with protreptic works—texts designed to lead a reader to the pursuit of philosophy. Although Boethius may use some arguments originating ultimately in Aristotle's *Protrepticus* (see below, n. 5), there is a wide gap between the situation assumed by a protreptic work—of a novice being brought to engage in a life-long study of philosophy—and Boethius's—someone who has spent his life studying philosophy and is now facing execution and so the end of his philosophical studies.

2. See Gruber (1978) 27.

3. Apart from *On the Trinity*. Lerer (1985, 56–69) also draws a parallel with Fulgentius's *On Virgilian Continence*, where Virgil himself takes part in a pedagogic dialogue. Lerer also contends (esp. 203–36) that the work moves away from dialogue altogether, to the private study of texts, in its closing parts. This view is very questionable. Although Boethius's exchanges with Philosophia are fewer in Book V than previously, it is in this book that he plays the role of a serious philosophical contender, not only presenting Philosophia with a very difficult problem, but anticipating a possible solution and giving reasons why it is unacceptable.

4. See chapter 8.

5. In the nineteenth century, Usener (1877, 51–52) proposed that the *Consolation* consisted of a section translated from a lost adaptation of Aristotle's lost *Protrepticus* (roughly II.4–IV.5) and a section translated from a lost Neoplatonic work (roughly IV.6–end) with only Book I and the beginning of Book II, and the poems, being Boethius's own work. Usener's theory was well criticized in Rand (1904) and Klingner (1921). Balanced assessments of Boethius's access to and use of source material are found in Gruber (1978) 38–40 and Crabbe (1981) 238–41.

6. Courcelle (1967, 333–34) considers that he must have had at least a few books at his disposal.

7. Gruber (1978). Gruber collects and greatly adds to the material which had been assembled over many years, especially by Klingner (1921), Fortescue (1925), Courcelle (1967; 1969, 295–318).

8. They are: III m. 9—*Timaeus* and commentary on it; IV.1–4—*Gorgias*; V.1—Aristotle, *Physics*; V.4–6—Ammonius, Proclus, or related texts.

9. For the text of the *Consolation*, I use Moreschini (2000). The translations are my own, although I have consulted with profit those by Tester in the Loeb edition (Stewart, Rand, and Tester, 1973) and Sharples (1991). In references, I use a Roman numeral for the Book and Arabic ones for the prose sections within

each book (the numbers of metrical sections are prefaced by 'm.'); and, where necessary, Arabic numerals for the short subsections numbered by Moreschini (the same numbering is used in some other editions, e.g., Bieler, 1957, rev. 1984; Sharples, 1991). Where a precise passage of prose is being cited, for ease of reference I also add in square brackets the line numbers of the reference in the prose or metrical section as found in the parallel text Loeb edition (Stewart, Rand, and Tester, 1973). For example, 'CII.2.2 [4–5]' means lines section 2 of prose 2 of Book II in Moreschini's edition, or lines 4–5 of Book II, prose 2 in the Loeb edition. In the case of verse, the line numbers are given ('CIII m.9.2–3' means Book III, metrum 9, lines 2–3).

10. For a more detailed discussion, see Marenbon (Forthcoming-2).

11. *Felicitas*, as used by Boethius, is a neutral word for happiness: it might be taken as referring to the experience of being happy. Felicity may be false in the sense that it is transitory or that pursuing it is detrimental to reaching happiness (*beatitudo*). The person who has gained felicity may well not have gained happiness, but the person who has gained happiness will thereby have gained felicity. In translating or summarizing, I have tried to use 'felicity' to render *felicitas* (and phrases involving it to render *felix*), leaving 'happiness' for *beatitudo*. 'Happiness' might be thought a little weak for *beatitudo*. But words like 'bliss' or 'blessedness', which are sometimes used for it, have too many overtones of the afterlife. Note (see below in the present chapter) that Boethius is willing to talk about *perfecta felicitas*, by which—if he is not using the phrase merely as an equivalent for *beatitudo*—he means the experience which goes with *beatitudo*.

12. John Magee has pointed out to me, however, a formal way in which III.1–8 is made to form a unit apart, which is closed at the very beginning of III.9, by a use of chiasmus: (A1) C III.1.5–7 [17–26]: veram . . . felicitatem . . . verae beatitudinis; (B1) CIII m.1.11–13: falsa . . . bona . . . vera; (C1) CIII.2.2–3 [4–11]: diverso . . . calle . . . bonorum omnium congregatione; (C2) C III.8.12 [33–35]: omnium bonorum congregatione . . . quidam calles; (B2) CIII m.8.21–22: falsa . . . vera . . . bona; (A2) CIII.9.1 [1–3]: mendacis . . . felicitatis . . . vera.

13. For a more detailed discussion, see Marenbon (Forthcoming-2).

14. The Latin texts reads: '. . . ut felicitatis compos patriam sospes revisas'. For the use of *felicitas* here, cf. n. 11 above.

15. Cf. CIII.12.30 [82–86]: 'Ludisne, inquam, me inextricabilem labyrinthum rationibus texens, quae nunc quidem qua egrediaris introeas, nunc vero quo introieris egrediare, an mirabilem quendam divinae simplicitatis orbem complicas?' ['Are you playing, I said, and weaving me an inextricable labyrinth with your arguments—now entering where you will come out, now coming out where you entered—or are you knitting together some wonderful circle of divine simplicity?']

16. I am grateful to John Magee for pointing out the tightness of the *Consolation*'s structure here.

17. Aristotle, Fragment 16 (from *On Philosophy*); cf. Gruber (1978), 291.

18. See chapter 5, on common conceptions.

19. Readers familiar with Anselm's ontological argument may find the transition here from 'can be conceived' to 'is' worrying. But God's existence is not in question. For Boethius (see chapter 5), 'inconceivable' is an even stronger term than 'impossible', and Philosophy's point here is that it cannot even be conceived (and so, *a fortiori*, it is impossible and thus not actually the case) that something is better than God. The weakness in the argument is the final proposition, that that than which there is nothing better is good, because it makes the assumption (probably held by Boethius himself) that all things could not be evil.

20. The idea that truly happy people are Gods can be traced back to Stoic (Cicero, *De natura deorum* 2, 153) and Neoplatonic pagan texts (Proclus, *Platonic Theology* III.7), but there are also biblical and other Christian precedents for the idea of humans making themselves into Gods (e.g., Psalm 81, verse 6; John x, 34–35; 2 Peter i, 4); cf. Fortescue (1925) 88, Gruber (1978) 295.

21. Surprisingly, Philosophy uses the word *voluptas* here (CIII.10.30 [105]), rather than *laetitita*, for pleasure, although she is clearly talking about a true good, not a false one; perhaps this is a sign of how completely she has abandoned the arguments of III.1–8.

22. Philosophy does not spell out this reasoning, but after saying that all other things are sought for the sake of happiness, she remarks, rather laconically, 'quare sic quoque sola quaeritur beatitudo' (CIII.10.41 [137–38])—'and so happiness too is the only thing which is sought in this way'—i.e., sought in the way she has just said the good is sought.

23. The argument is not valid on some interpretations of 'desire'. It might be held that (*a*) one cannot desire *x* without believing that one desires *x*, or—more weakly and more plausibly—that (*b*) the criteria for ascribing a desire for *x* to someone involve at least hypothetical beliefs by the person about something under the description of *x*. On either interpretation, (*a*) or (*b*), 'desire' creates an opaque referential context, and so it does not follow from 'I desire *x*' and '*x* = *y*' that I desire *y*. But Philosophy clearly does not interpret 'desire' according to (*a*) or (*b*); cf. her implicit views about truly desiring earlier in Bk III.

24. Philosophy uses the phrase 'veluti quidam clavus atque gubernaculum': *gubernaculum* echoes the question she had asked Boethius at CI.6.7 [18–19] about whether he knew *quibus gubernaculis* the world is ruled. In the plural, as used there, *gubernacula* takes on the figurative meaning of government; in the singular, as used here in a simile, it means rudder.

25. In Marenbon (Forthcoming-2) I show the extent to which Boethius the author is willing to adapt Socrates's arguments and to depart entirely from his

view that punishment is valuable only as a way of reforming the character of wrongdoers. Courcelle (1967, 173–75; 1969, 307–308) argues that the main source here is a Neoplatonic commentary on the *Gorgias*, perhaps the lost commentary of Ammonius, although he does not rule out some direct reading of Plato (1967, 175). Although it is probable that Boethius knew one or more Neoplatonic commentaries on the *Gorgias*, and his approach to this dialogue, as to Plato's work in general, was shaped by the Neoplatonic tradition, Courcelle has no good grounds for doubting or minimizing Boethius's direct reading of Plato during his long life of learned leisure (cf. the apposite criticisms in Dronke, 1969, 125–26). Indeed, the only surviving Neoplatonic commentary on the *Gorgias*, that by Olympiodorus, does not parallel the particular ways in which the dialogue is used and altered in the *Consolation*.

26. *Gorgias* 470e9–11. It is unclear whether Socrates holds merely this position, or the stronger one that happiness consists in being good: see Plato (1979), 149.

27. Philosophy also adds the idea of the one to her argument: by ceasing to be good, things cease to be one and so to exist (CIV.3.14–15 [44–48]). This addition is rather confusing. The way in which a set of disunited limbs fails to exist because it is not one thing at all seems to be different to the way in which a bestial man fails to exist because he is not a human.

28. On how the *Gorgias* is adapted, see Marenbon (Forthcoming-2).

29. A distinction between providence (*pronoia*) and fate (*heimarmenē*) is made by Plotinus (*Ennead* III.3.5) and repeated or elaborated by later Neoplatonists: cf. Courcelle (1967) 204, (1969) 304–305, who also points to passages in Calcidius's commentary on the *Timaeus*. The distinction that Philosophy makes is, however, rather different from Plotinus's hierarchical arrangement. For Plotinus, although providence extends to all things, fate orders lower things, providence alone higher ones. Philosophy's distinction is, rather, between two ways of regarding the same, divine ordering.

30. When providence, and later in Book V divine prescience, is discussed in the *Consolation*, it is usually 'things' that are said to be providentially arranged or foreseen, rather than events, although events are sometimes mentioned (as in the discussion of chance at CV.1.8 [19]—where *eventus* can (unusually) be translated as 'event'). If we now were arguing that God had predestined John to be writing his book this morning, we should probably want to insist that it is the event—John's writing at this time—that is predestined, but Boethius would be happy to talk about the thing being predestined, leaving it unclear whether the thing is a loose word for the event or whether, rather, John himself and his book are the objects of this predestination.

31. See above, for the possible equivocation involved here.

32. Two rather clear pieces of evidence for this change of position are: (1) the acceptance that too much adversity can lead to the moral degradation of

some people (CIV.6.35–36 [133–40] (and cf. CIV.7.20 [48–49] on danger of being oppressed by adversity), and (2) the idea that providence judges it wicked that someone who is entirely virtuous, holy, and near to God should be touched by any adversity at all, even by illness (CIV.6.37–38 [140–45]).

33. On Philosophy's rejection of Plato's view of rehabilitative punishment, see Marenbon, Forthcoming-2.

34. Philosophy's main line of argument seems to be that people fail to seek the true good out of ignorance (cf. CIII.2.4 [13–15]: '. . . For desire for the true good is there naturally within the minds of men, but wayward error leads away to false goods'). But at CIV.2.32 [97–98] Philosophy talks of people who 'knowingly and willingly desert the good and turn away to vices.'

35. See Aristotle, *Physics* 2, 196b10–35, *Metaphysics* 5, 1025a14–29. Courcelle argues (1967, 218–19; 1969, 311–12) rather unconvincingly that Boethius is borrowing from a lost commentary by Ammonius on the *Physics*; cf. Sharples (1991) 214–15 for a full discussion and references.

36. Plotinus often speaks of the Good or the One as the centre of a circle (e.g., *Ennead* I.7.1; VI.5.5; VI.8.18) and at one point of the soul moving round its source and centre (VI.9.8). In his *Ten Problems* (I.5), Proclus uses the image of a circle and its centre in describing providence. No known source, however, anticipates the main feature of the simile in the *Consolation*—that where concentric circles are revolving, any point on the circumference of a circle travels further, the farther out the circle is, and so there is more in common between the stillness and fixedness of the central point and something at the innermost circle, which does not therefore travel far, than between it and something on the outermost circle, which travels over vast distances. See Patch (1929); Courcelle (1967) 206–207, (1969) 305–307; and Sharples (1991) 205 for a judicious discussion and full references.

37. There are close parallels between Philosophy's discussion here and Plotinus, *Ennead* VI.8.6.

CHAPTER 7

1. See above and below for Courcelle's different view.

2. See CV.6.32 [120–24], where after having put forward her solution to the Problem of Prescience, Philosophy says that future things are foreknown by God, but this does not prevent some being due to free will since, although they happen, they are such that before they happened they were also able not to have happened (*prius quam fierent etiam non evenire potuissent*). The view of necessity seems, then, to be as follows. Let E be some event (e.g., a sea battle) and O the outcome which the event in fact has (e.g., the Greeks win): E is a necessary event iff there is no time at which it is possible that the outcome of E is not-O.

(Usually, Philosophy and Boethius do not use a special word for 'event(s)' but just the neuter (e.g., in (1) *cuncta* = all things; *quod providentia* = that which providence). The word *eventus* normally means the outcome of an event.

3. CV.6. 46 [170–72]: 'Nor are hopes and prayers directed to God in vain: when they are right, they cannot fail to be efficacious.'

4. On the identity of those who held this unsatisfactory solution, see Sharples (1991) 218–19.

5. Although talk of possible worlds seems anachronistic when discussing the *Consolation*, this argument is clearly based on the sort of considerations that are nowadays discussed using this terminology. It could be spelled out in more detail, using this terminology, as follows. According to the opponent, in the actual world, w*, God foreknows all events, and all events are necessary. Philosophy asks us to consider the possible world, w1, which is the possible world closest to the actual world in which it is not the case that God foreknows events. He then calls on the following principle:

> (P) If w* includes A and B, and w1 is the closest possible world to w* without A, and A is not the cause of B, then w1 includes B.

(P) seems plausible since w1 must be like w* in every way consistent with its lacking A. Applying (P) to the case in hand, with A = God's foreknowledge of all events and B = the necessity of all events, it follows that at w1 all events are necessary, because at w* all events are necessary and God's foreknowledge, it has been agreed, is not the cause of their necessity. But (P) needs modification if it is to be accepted, because if A, even though not a cause of B, is a necessary condition for B, then w1 would not include B (it could not, because it would lack a necessary condition for B). (P) therefore needs to be changed to

> (PP) If w* includes A and B, and w1 is the closest possible world to w* without A, and A is neither the cause of B, nor a necessary condition for B, then w1 includes B.

The problem with (PP) is that an opponent might well claim that God's foreknowledge *is* a necessary condition for all events being necessary. (I am grateful to Jonathan Evans for his comments on an earlier version of this analysis, which led me to revise it.)

6. From the perspective of modern logic, it is strange to divide up the solution of (1) and (2) in this way. Since any proposition follows from an impossibility, by showing that there is some proposition *q* that does not follow from *p*, a modern logician also shows that *p* is not an impossibility. Therefore, from the modern point of view, once Philosophy has succeeded in showing that from God's foreknowledge of events it does not follow that they are all necessary (i.e., refuting (1)), she will also have shown that it is possible for future contingent

events to be known (i.e., will have refuted (2)). But Boethius certainly did not acknowledge that from an impossibility anything follows.

7. My analysis of the overall structure of the argument of V.4.23–V.6 owes most to Sharples (1991), 27, 44–45. For a discussion of analyses that, I believe, are misleading, see below.

8. We would say that, arguably, I can be certain, e.g., that my computer is now on the table, although it is not necessary that it is there now—there is some possible world in which it is now in its travelling case. For Boethius, however, the present is necessary, in the sense that there are no synchronous alternative possibilities. For an event to be contingent, it must have not yet happened and there must be the possibility that it turn out in one way *or* in another (or others)—hence, it seems, there cannot be any certainty about it.

9. On the double form, cf. Sharples (1991) 224, n. 30.

10. See Proclus, Commentary on *Timaeus* (Proclus, 1903, 352:15–16) '. . . the way of knowing differs according to the diversity of knowers' [there is a translation of this commentary into French: Proclus, 1966–68]; Proclus, *On Providence*, (Proclus, 1979, 82:26–27): 'the type of cognition is not like the thing cognized but like the cognizer'; Ammonius, Commentary on *On Interpretation* (Ammonius, 1897, 135:15–16 [Tr: Ammonius and Boethius, 1998]): 'knowledge is intermediate between the knower and the known . . .' Ammonius credits 'the divine Iamblichus' with proposing this Principle.

11. See Proclus, *Elements of Theology*, §124 (Proclus, 1963, 110); *Commentary on Parmenides* IV (Proclus, 1864, 957) [there is a translation of this commentary: Proclus, 1987]; *Commentary on Timaeus*, to 29cd (Proclus, 1903, 352:5–8); *Ten Problems* II, 7–8 (Proclus, 1977, 62:20–25, 63:11–64:20; *On Providence* XII, 64 (Proclus, 1979, 82:12–16). Ammonius, Commentary on *On Interpretation* IX (Ammonius, 1897, 136:15–17 [Tr. Ammonius and Boethius, 1998]).

12. Mignucci (1985) apparently interprets the Principle, as proposed by Proclus, in the weak manner rejected above so far as the *Consolation* is concerned. He suggests that Proclus's position amounts to saying that the gods' knowledge consists of Quinean eternal truths—statements that associate truth values with times and so remain true without change. Mignucci also assumes (p. 245, n. 39), without argument, that Boethius's position was the same. While Mignucci is right to see Proclus and Boethius rejecting the idea, which was accepted even by Plotinus, that what is changing cannot be known unchangingly, there is no need to accept his explanation of why they thought they could do so: there is no evidence for it in Boethius, whereas there is an explicit discussion in the *Consolation* to ground the different interpretation given above.

13. *On Providence* XII, §65 (Proclus, 1979, 82:1—83:10).

14. *Commentary on Parmenides* IV (Proclus, 1864, 958).

15. *Ten Problems*, II, 8 (Proclus, 1977, 64:30—65:46; cf. 139).

16. *Commentary on Parmenides* IV (Proclus, 1864, 958).

17. Ammonius (1897) 137:1–11.

18. See also the valuable discussion of this passage in De Libera (1999) 247–48.

19. There is, as it will be made clear, a sense in which is incorrect to say that God has *pre*science. Indeed, on some readings of Philosophy's argument, according to which God is atemporal (see below: I question whether such a reading is necessary), it is straightforwardly wrong to talk of God's *pre*science, because no temporal qualification applies to God. On other readings, the idea of divine *pre*science is, at least, misleading, because all God's knowledge is like our knowledge of the present. None the less, the expression 'divine prescience' is needed in order to set up the problem. It need be taken to imply no more than that God knows, in some way or other, the outcomes of contingent events that are future, at least so far as we are concerned.

20. The view that the universe lacks beginning and end is central to Aristotle's physics. Plato probably thought that the universe had a beginning but would have no end, but from early on many of his successors interpreted his position as being the same as Aristotle's. Philosophy points out (CV.6.9–10 [31–38]) that to accept that the universe is eternal in this sense does not amount to claiming that it is coeternal with God, whose eternity she has just established is of a quite different sort. As a Christian, however, Boethius himself would have been committed to the view that the universe had a beginning and will have an end. But Philosophy is not Boethius. See Sharples (1991), 228 and, on disputes over this issue in Boethius's time, Courcelle (1969), 312–15.

21. See Sorabji (1983), esp. pp. 98–130 for a full discussion.

22. See Sorabji (1983) 115–60, 119–20 for a very clear and detailed exposition of this view. On atemporality as lack of spatial extension and position, see Pike (1970) 6–15.

23. Two discussions that emphasize the difference between mere timelessness and eternity as simultaneous, perfect possession of unbounded life are Stump and Kretzmann (1981) and Gale (1991) 47–56.

24. Plotinus (*Ennead* III, 7; it has been edited, with full discussion and a detailed comparison with Boethius, in Beierwaltes, 1967) considers eternity as the life of the Intellect and time as the life of the Soul. Later Neoplatonists hypostasized both time and eternity (see, e.g., Proclus, *Elements of Theology* §53 (Proclus, 1963, 51); cf. Siorvanes, 1996, 134–35). Although neither OSI nor the *Consolation* provides enough evidence for a definite answer, it seems that Boethius's view was nearer to that of Plotinus than to the later Neoplatonists.

25. I discuss this idea at greater length in Marenbon (Forthcoming-1) and (Forthcoming-5). A modern objection to the view proposed on this interpretation is that it implies that God has temporal parts and so is not simple: I do not,

however, know of any evidence to suggest that Boethius would have considered such a problem.

26. See Kenny (1976) 264.

27. See Kretzmann and Stump (1981).

28. A number of modern philosophers have interpreted Boethius in this way. See, for instance, Henry (1967) 178; Sorabji (1980) 122; Kirwan (1989) 96–98; Paul Spade in Kenny (1994) 72. By contrast, Knuuttila (1993) 60–61 and Weidemann (1998) reject this interpretation.

29. The ambiguity is best shown by setting out (2) as an argument rather than a conditional:

(2.1) Things are capable of turning out differently from how they have been foreseen

so

(2.2) There will no longer be firm foreknowledge of the future, but rather uncertain opinion

(2.1) can be interpreted in two different ways: as

(2.1W) The following is possible: an event that does not take place is foreseen as taking place

or

(2.1N) An event is foreseen as taking place, and it is possible that it might not take place.

(2.2) follows from (2.1W), but (2.1W) is clearly false (given that the foreseer is infallible). (2.1N) is true but (2.2) does not follow from it.

30. For a reading of Boethius's argument that supports the conclusion urged here but uses different evidence, see Weidemann (1998).

31. More precisely, the accidental necessity argument (ANA) runs:

(t1, t2, and t3 standing for three successively later moments of time, and the time now being t2; and L meaning 'necessarily' in its ordinary logical sense, L* meaning 'necessarily' in the sense of unchangeably):

(A1) L (God has the belief at t1 that *e* will take place at t3 –> *e* will take place at t3)

(A2) Facts about the past have necessity in the sense that they cannot be changed (= L*)

(A3) God's belief at t1 that *e* will take place at t3 is a fact about the past

(A4) L*(God has the belief at t1 that *e* will take place at t3)

(A5) L(p –> q) –> (L*p –> L*q) [Transfer of Necessity Principle]

(A6) God has the belief at t1 that *e* will take place at t3 –> L*(*e* will take place at t3) (A1,A4,A5)

The type of necessity defined in (A4) is usually called 'accidental necessity', and it seems hard to deny that there is this sort of necessity about the past. A Transfer of Necessity Principle is contained even in the simplest modal systems. The one controversial feature of (A5) is whether a Transfer of Necessity Principle applies to necessity in the sense of unchangeability (L*); intuitively, it seems that it should, but what sort of necessity is entailed: in A5, is it correct to write 'L*q', or should it be 'Lq' or is q shown to be necessary in some other way, different from ordinary logical and from accidental necessity?

Boethius the author is taken to have provided a solution by denying (A3), because no fact about God is a fact about the past. A strong rejoinder, however, is that God's timelessly eternal belief that *e* takes place at t3 is a fact about the eternal present, and that an accidental necessity attaches to facts about the eternal present just as it does to facts about the past. For a thorough, recent discussion, see Zagzebski (1991) 36–65. All of the following (and many other) modern writers treat *Consolation* V as providing a solution to ANA: Sorabji (1980) 125; (1983) 255–56; Kvanvig (1986) 87; Leftow (1991) 160; Zagzebski (1991) 38–39. Sorabji, however, followed by Zagzebski, makes it clear that Boethius the author did not himself explicitly think that he was tackling ANA. For a fuller discussion of why this approach to the argument of *Consolation* V should be rejected, see Marenbon (Forthcoming-1).

32. See chapter 4.

33. Boethius also makes the same type of distinction in his first commentary (*1inIsag.* 121:20 –124:7 and explains it in the same way: the terminology, though, is slightly different—things that are necessary *simpliciter* or *nulla mentione praesentis temporis facta* are contrasted with things that are necessary merely because they are happening in the present.

34. For a thorough discussion, see Knuuttila (1993). Although some of Knuuttila's views about Aristotle's theory of modality are controversial, the view cited here is widely held.

35. See Knuuttila (1993) 53–54, 61.

36. *2InDI* 241:20–22: 'sed ista cum condicione quae proponitur necessitas non illam simplicem secum trahit'; cf. CV.6.28 [108–109]: 'sed haec condicio minime secum illam simplicem trahit'.

37. Note that, as this way of putting it shows, Boethius (like Philosophy in the *Consolation*) is not thinking of necessity as a property of statements but of things; when something is conditionally necessary, it does not have the property of necessity simply—without qualification—but under a condition, just as (*2InDI* 242:15–18) an Ethiopean is not white simply, but he is white in some part (his eyes).

38. So, I consider, (§29b) should be interpreted (and cf. Gruber, 1978, 413). But some commentators think otherwise. The Latin text reads: 'nulla enim necessitas cogit incedere voluntate gradientem, quamvis eum tum cum graditur incedere necessarium sit.' In my translation, I take *incedo* as a synonym of *gradior*, used merely for the sake of elegant variation. Stewart, Rand, and Tester (1973)

and Sharples (1991), however, translate the passage as if there were an intended semantic difference between *incedo* and *gradior*: that *incedo* means 'move forward', something which is entailed by walking but not equivalent to it. Sharples (p. 230) interprets the passage as making a contrast between the fact that necessarily walking involves moving forward ('If you walk, necessarily you move forward') and the point that whether a person moves forward is not in itself necessary but a matter of choice. Sharples's interpretation should be rejected because (1) Philosophy does not say '*If* you walk, necessarily you move forward' but '*at the moment when you* walk' (. . . *tum cum* . . .'); (2) at CV.6.34 [128–29], Philosophy refers back to the example of a man walking (*gradiens*) making it clear that what she has in mind is the necessity of the present; (3) the line of thought fails to connect with the next section, where God's present knowledge of things is discussed, unless this section is taken as dealing with the necessity of the present.

39. CV.6.32 [120–24], discussed in n. 2 above.

40. Ammonius (1897) 153:10–154:20 makes a distinction between two types of necessities, absolute and with qualification, when discussing the same passage in *On Interpretation* (19a23ff.) about which Boethius first uses his distinction in *2InDI*. Yet Ammonius's distinction is really rather different from Boethius's. Ammonius's idea is that a sentence is necessary just in case it is always true, whenever it is said. A sentence that fulfils this criterion without any extra qualification being needed—e.g. 'the sun moves'—is absolutely necessary as is what it describes. Sentences that do not fulfil this criterion—e.g., 'I am sitting'—can be made to fulfil it by adding a qualification (in the example: 'so long as I am sitting') and they, along with the events they describe, are necessary with qualification.

41. See Huber (1976) 20–58; Lloyd (1990) 154–59; and Sharples (1991) 26–27 on Boethius's originality in combining his arguments. Courcelle (1967) 214–21, (1969) 308–311 argues that Boethius is heavily dependent on Ammonius, but it is (a) on balance more likely than not that Boethius did not know Ammonius directly (see above) and (b) Courcelle clearly underestimates his originality, as Huber has shown. The reading of the argument V.3–6 which I advance here strongly supports the claim for Boethius's originality.

CHAPTER 8

1. I, m.1, the opening poem, which sets the scene;

I, m. 2, which is introduced as Philosophy's lament over the disturbance of Boethius's mind (I.1.14 [51–52]);

I, m. 3, Boethius's retrospective reflection on the beginnings of his cure (and so, uniquely among the poems, the voice of Boethius the narrator looking *back*, as opposed to Boethius the character);

I, m. 5, Boethius's complaint that human acts have been left out of the divine order, which he prefaces with the comment 'So I want to cry out' (CI.4. 46 [174]);

III, m. 2, which (uniquely in the work) brings up for the first time the idea that is developed in the next prose;

III, m. 9, which is announced as a prayer;

III, m. 11, because it brings up the name of Plato which is then mentioned as if it were already under discussion at the beginning of III.12;

IV, m. 1, Philosophy's promise to give wings to Boethius's mind;

IV, m. 6, which Philosophy says she will sing to refresh Boethius's mind, tired by the long argument;

V, m. 3, which continues from the character Boethius's posing of the problem of prescience to Philosophy and reports his attitude to the apparently insoluble difficulty he is facing; and also

II, m. 8, III, m. 12, and probably I, m. 7 and IV, m.7—that is to say the poem that ends each of the first four books (Book V ends with prose).

In the case of II, m. 8 and III, m. 12, the next book begins with an explicit reference to the song finishing; in the other two cases, the next book begins with a comment that probably refers back to the poem just finished but could be taken as referring back to the prose section before it (CIII.1.1 [1] *Iam cantum illa finiverat*; CIV.1.1 [1–2] *Haec cum Philosophia . . . leniter suaviterque cecinisset*; CII.1.1 [1] *Post haec paulisper obticuit . . .*; CV.1.1 [1] *Dixerat . . .*).

2. II, m. 2 is, however, a somewhat complicated case, because in the prose section before it, Philosophy has been taking the part of Fortune and saying what Fortune would say, and so the poem might plausibly be attributed to Fortune as impersonated by Philosophy: see Gruber (1978) 180 and (against such a view) Scheible (1972) 52.

3. O'Daly (1991, 104–177) studies in detail the use of natural imagery.

4. Cf. Dronke (1994) 42–43.

5. On the links between Stoic moral thought and the rejection of fear, hope, pain, and sorrow in these poems, see Scheible (1972) 33, 44–45; O'Daly (1991) 100–102, 135–38.

6. On *anamnēsis*, see also the discussion below of V, m. 3.

7. O'Daly (1991) 190–207 and Lerer (1986) 153–64 look in detail at this poem, including its relation to poems by Ovid, Virgil, and Seneca on the story of Orpheus.

8. Compare III m.12. 55–59: 'For the person who, defeated, turns his eyes to the cave of Tartarus loses whatever excellent he is bringing when he looks at

those below' with IV, m.1.27–30: 'Now, if you care to look at the world's night that you have left, you will recognize that the fierce tyrants, whom wretched peoples fear, are exiles.'

9. On IV, m. 3 see Scheible (1972) 137–40, Crabbe (1981), Lerer (1985) 180–90, O'Daly (1991) 207–20; on IV, m. 7, see Scheible (1972) 152–56, Lerer (1985) 190–201.

10. The fullest and finest study of these four linked poems is by John Magee (forthcoming-1).

11. As shown well in Magee (Forthcoming-1). Traiana (1981) also provides some detailed commentary on 1, m.5.

12. See Lerer (1985) 220–25 and Magee (Forthcoming-1) 696.

13. Cf. the analysis (with a different conclusion) in Scheible (1972) 163–65.

14. Cf. O'Daly (1991) 40–41, 175–76.

15. See Klingner (1921) 38–67.

16. Klingner believes that Boethius's main source is Proclus's commentary on the *Timaeus* and gives parallels. Courcelle (1967, 163–64; 1969, 301–302) accepts his account, but Scheible (1972, 101–112) disagrees, arguing that Boethius the author knew Proclus's views and deliberately departed from them.

17. See below.

18. Relihan (1990) develops an unusual view about Philosophy's appearance, arguing that it suggests that she is returning from the land of the dead. See also the introductory material (and the phrasing chosen for the translation) in Relihan (2001).

19. See Gruber (1969) for a detailed study.

20. On the Neoplatonic exegesis of this passage, see Schmidt-Kohl (1965) 1–3.

21. Cf. Courcelle (1967) 21 [my translation]: 'We expect strange visions, unheard-of revelations, like those of Poimandres . . . Well, what does Philosophy offer? Technical arguments, syllogisms, exempla—that is to say, the usual apparatus of anyone who engages in reasoning or demonstration.'

22. Whether she is the leader of this army is uncertain: she refers in the third person (CI.3.13 [44]) to 'our leader' (*nostra dux*): the feminine suggests that the reference may be to herself—Gruber (1978, 108) certainly takes it in this way—but perhaps she has in mind *sapientia* (cf. Tester's translation) or *veritas*.

23. E.g., CI.3.6 [18]—Plato; CV.1.11 [35–36])—Aristotle. Even Lucan, a philosophically minded poet, is described as 'one of her family' (CIV.6.33 [130–31).

24. Cf. CI.3.8 [27–30]; cf. CIII.2.12 [48–51] against Epicurus, and V, m. 4 against the Stoics.

25. I am here following Courcelle (1967) 21–22; cf. Shanzer (1984) 359 and Magee (Forthcoming-2).

26. CIV.6.53–54 [196–99]. Plato writes (*Timaeus* 28c): 'And it is difficult to find him—he who is as it were the father of the universe—and when you have found him it is not right to show him to the crowd.' This parallel is noted by Courcelle (1967) 21–22.

27. For the attribution to the *Corpus Hermeticum*, see Shanzer (1983).

28. Consider, e.g., CV.5.11–12 [46–56]—mentioned by Courcelle (1967) 22, and CV.6.25 [94–100]—cited by Magee (Forthcoming-2).

29. See chapter 9.

30. A piece by Cassiodorus was discovered by the German scholar, Holder-Egger, in which the author of the *Consolation* was clearly identified with the writer of the *opuscula sacra*. The piece was named the *Anecdoton Holderi*, after its discoverer: cf. Usener, 1877.

31. A good list is given in Fortescue (1925) 204–206. It contains 25 parallels but only three (including the one at CIII.12.22 [63–64]) that are close.

32. See Mohrmann (1976).

33. See above, discussion of III, m. 9.

34. CIII.12.22 [63–64]: 'Est igitur summum, inquit, bonum, quod regit cuncta fortiter suaviterque disponit'; *Sap*. viii, 1: 'adtingit enim a fine usque ad finem fortiter et disponit omnia suaviter.'

35. Mohrmann (1976, 60) speculates that the source here might be the Book of Wisdom directly, or perhaps the citation comes via Augustine or from the liturgy. But, as she recognizes, given Boethius's comment, the words must have been intended as either Biblical or liturgical or both. Rand's view (1904, 25 fn.) that the parallel 'seems purely accidental' fails to take account of this comment by Boethius.

36. Cf. Courcelle (1967) 226–31, 340 and cf. above, Chapter 7, n. 20. Courcelle also mentions the use of the words '*fortuna*' and '*fatum*' proscribed by Augustine. But Philosophy's view that both are, ultimately, aspects of divine providence is fully consistent with Christian doctrine.

37. Klingner (1921) 117.

38. There have been some perhaps rather exaggerated attempts to show the closeness of the *Consolation* to Augustine's writings: see Carton (1931) and Silk (1939).

39. Chadwick (1981) 249. For a much earlier, and less qualified, version of the Augustinist position, see Fortescue (1925) xxviii–lxviii.

40. Almost certainly, Courcelle exaggerates the closeness of the link between Boethius and the Alexandrian writers; see especially chapter 7 above.

41. Courcelle (1967) 337–44; (1969) 318–22.

42. See Mohrmann (1976) 55–59.

43. Boethius the character does accept Plato's doctrine of recollection (CIII.12.1 [1–4]; CVm.3.28–31) and so the preexistence of souls before their

incarnation. But this view had been considered an acceptable one by Augustine and became unacceptable only in the Middle Ages. Boethius the character certainly does not commit himself to any doctrine of reincarnation.

44. CI.V.10 [36–37]: '. . . uti quae caelum terras quoque pax regeret' refers back to ll.47–48 of I, m. 5, where Boethius says: '. . . quo caelum regis immensum/ firma stabiles foedere terra!' and parallels Matthew vi, 10, 'fiat voluntas tua sicut in caelo et in terra' (part of the Lord's Prayer); cf. Magee (Forthcoming—2). On the language of the passage at the end of the work (CV.6.46 [170–72]) where Philosophy is responding to Boethius's questions at CV.3.33–34 [97–107], see Mohrmann 1976, 309.

45. I am grateful to Brad Inwood for suggesting this possibility.

46. Klingner (1921) 115.

47. Gruber (1981).

48. The link with Martianus was made by one of Boethius's very early readers, who wrote a brief prologue to the *Consolation* in which he remarks '. . . in prison [Boethius] wrote these books in the form of a satire (*per satyram*), in imitation of Martianus Felix Capella, who first had written the books on the marriage of Mercury and Philology in the same way with poems' (printed in Peiper, 1871, xxx–xxxi and Fortescue, 1925, 178 = *Testimonia* §8). There are a number of almost certain borrowings of phrases from Martianus in the *Consolation*. On Boethius and the *Paraenesis*, see Gruber (1978) 18.

49. Relihan (1993, 164–75) makes the case for regarding the *Paraenesis* as a parody. Relihan also discusses (152–63) the late fifth-century *Mythologies* of Fulgentius—a work known to Boethius—as a comic prosimetrum.

50. Relihan (1993, 137–51) advances the extreme view that Martianus designed his work to be self-undermining. Balanced views of the mixture of comedy and seriousness in Martianus are presented by Shanzer (1986) and Dronke (1994) 28–30, 34–38.

51. Dronke (1994) 30–31, 38–46. Dronke is referring to a definition of the Menippean genre by Mikhail Bakhtin, which he discusses on pp. 4–5.

52. Relihan (1993) 193. The whole discussion of the *Consolation* is on pp. 187–94.

53. Dronke (1994) 43–45; Magee (Forthcoming-1) 697.

CHAPTER 9

1. See White (1981); there is also useful information in Gibson and Smith (1996), especially pp. 26–28.

2. For general studies, see Lewry (1981), Isaac (1953 [*On Interpretation* only]), and Marenbon (2000b [the gloss and commentary tradition and its relation to Boethius]).

3. Full details of the manuscripts of Boethius's translations of Aristotle and Porphyry are found in the *Aristoteles Latinus* edition.

4. The version of Boethius's translation most widely used up to the twelfth century was not Boethius's genuine text but a composite version, based on Boethius's genuine text and another version, perhaps an earlier draft by Boethius: on this, and the pseudo-Augustinian paraphrase, see Minio-Paluello (1962) and cf. above, Chapter 3, n. 7.

5. See Lewry (1981) 103–104 and (on *On Interpretation*) Isaac (1953) 35–44.

6. See Lewry (1981) 108–113 and cf. Marenbon (2000b) 78, n. 4.

7. Dod (1982) 50.

8. See Marenbon (2000b) 99.

9. See Marenbon (2000b) 82–83, 100–101 and Marenbon (1997) 29–30.

10. See Anonymous (1995) for an edition and discussion.

11. For this paragraph, see especially Marenbon (2000b).

12. The commentaries by Abelard on the *Isagoge*, *Categories*, and *On Interpretation* are edited in Abelard (1919–1931). For a fuller discussion of the matters raised here, see Marenbon (1997) 101–116, 174–201 and Marenbon (Forthcoming-3).

13. See Isaac (1953) 62–85; Lewry (1981) 118–119.

14. See Lewry (1981) 103–104.

15. See Isaac (1953) 98–105.

16. Lewry (1981) 119–20.

17. Abbo of Fleury knew both (Lewry, 1981, 96–97), but SC was the more usually studied of the two monographs.

18. On the textual tradition of the group, see Magee (1994) and (1998) lviii–lv.

19. See Gibson and Smith (1996) 5.

20. Richer (1877) 101.

21. Abbo of Fleury (1966) and, replacing it for the treatise on hypothetical syllogisms, Abbo of Fleury (1997).

22. Van de Vyver (1929) 443–46.

23. Green-Pedersen provides a catalogue of commentaries on TD (1984, 418–31), and Iwakuma (Forthcoming) lists twelfth-century commentaries to the other logical treatises. I am contributing a section on the commentaries on Boethius's logical treatises for the Boethius volume of the *Catalogus Translationum et Commentariorum* (ed. L. Nauta; publication expected ca. 2005).

24. Lohr (1982) 50.

25. Marenbon (2000b) 87–88.

26. On the whole, complex question of the 12th- and 13th-century interpretations of TD, see Green-Pedersen (1984) 163–264.

27. Green-Pedersen (1984) 139–43.

28. See Abbo of Fleury (1997) especially VIII–X, XXVI–XXX, XLV–L.

29. Abelard's work in this area has been first properly understood by Christopher Martin (see Martin, 1987, and Martin, Forthcoming), and I outline his ideas in this paragraph. I am very grateful to Dr. Martin for allowing me to see some of his unpublished notes and drafts on this subject.

30. Cf. Marenbon, 1997, 202-208.

31. See Martin (1991).

32. But cf. Schupp (1988).

33. The best general study is Gibson (1981).

34. See Marenbon (1981) 46, 56, 65, and Gibson (1981) 216.

35. On Gottschalk and Hincmar, see Gibson (1981) 217–19; on Ratramnus, see Marenbon (1981) 68–69.

36. D'Onofrio (1980).

37. The glosses are published, misattributed to Eriugena, in Rand (1906). See Cappuyns (1931) (but his conclusions are suspect); for MSS up to s. xii, see Troncarelli (1988) 15–19, and Jeudy (1991) 474-75.

38. See Abelard (1987) 83–201 for the text. There is an extended discussion in Jolivet (1997).

39. Gilbert of Poitiers (1966) and, for analysis, see Nielsen (1982), and Jacobi (1995) and (1998).

40. On Gilbert as an exegete and theologian, see Marenbon (1983) and the qualifications in Marenbon (1998) 167–68.

41. They are published as Thierry's work in Thierry of Chartres (1971).

42. Edited in Häring (1965).

43. See Gibson (1981) 227.

44. Schrimpf (1966) 147-49.

45. Thomas Aquinas (1992).

46. McInerny (1990) argues against the generally accepted view that Aquinas is putting forward ideas that Boethius would not at all have recognized as his own.

47. Courcelle (1967) remains the fundamental guide, but it needs modification in many places (as given by the literature cited below), and especially in its account of the ninth- and tenth-century commentaries: cf. Troncarelli (1973). Beaumont (1981) summarizes but also updates Courcelle for the period up to 1200 and questions some of his conclusions. A remarkable study of the use of the *Consolation* up to the twelfth century, based on close study of many manuscripts, is provided in Troncarelli (1987).

48. See Troncarelli (1981).

49. Alcuin (1851) 849–54; cf. Courcelle (1967) 33–47 and Brunhölzl (1965).

50. Peiper (1871) xxv–xxix; cf. Brown (1976).

51. Courcelle (1967) 259–63; cf. Beaumont (1981) 282–83 and Troncarelli (1973). For a list of MSS of this material, see Wittig (1983) 188–89.

52. Edited (with valuable introduction) in Troncarelli (1981) 137–96. Courcelle's account of this commentary (1969, 269–70) turns out to be misleading, but so (Wittig, 1983) is Troncarelli's view that the commentary is related to one composed by Asser and used by Alfred when making his Old English translation of the *Consolation*.

53. There is no full edition, but there are substantial extracts in Stewart (1916) and Silk (1935) 312–43. On the changes and additions, see Bolton (1977) and Beaumont (1981) 288–92; the commentary on III, m. 9, printed in Silvestre (1952), with an unconvincing attribution to Eriugena, is probably a revision of Remigius's.

54. Troncarelli (1981) 64–79.

55. Marenbon (1994) 172–73.

56. The commentary is edited in Huygens (1954) 37–54.

57. Ed. in Huygens (1954) 11–26. Huygens also prints (28–32) another commentary on III, n. 9 which uses the *Timaeus* skilfully (Bovo only had Macrobius's Commentary on the *Dream of Scipio*) to bring out the meaning of the poem.

58. William of Conches (1999). There are a number of other twelfth-century commentaries, some of them related to William's; see Courcelle (1967) 303–15 and Jeauneau (1959); Beaumont (1981) 296 [discusses unedited commentary in Glasgow University Hunterian MS U.5.19 (279)]; Häring (1969); Anonymous (1978).

59. The version is found in 10 manuscripts from the late thirteenth/early fourteenth century; although it has been argued that it was made in the middle or later thirteenth century (Nauta, 1993; William of Conches, 1999, lxxxiii–lxxxv), the earlier idea that it is a revision by William himself has not been convincingly dismissed (cf. Dronke, 2002). There were various other later medieval adaptations of William's commentary: see Minnis and Nauta (1993) 8–9.

60. There are as yet uninvestigated commentaries that may date from this century—e.g., that in MS. Göttingen, Universitätsbibliothek, Philol. 167: cf. William of Conches (1999) xcviii–xcix. The dating of William of Aragon's commentary is disputed. One of its manuscripts explicitly dates it to 1335. Some scholars (Crespo, 1973; followed by Minnis, 1981, 314) have argued that it must antedate Jean de Meun's translation (certainly before 1305) because Jean uses it in his prologue. But it has not been shown that the borrowing is Jean's rather than William's; see Dronke (1994) 125–26, n. 40.

61. The dip in interest is suggested by a decline in the number of manuscripts of the *Consolation* from the thirteenth century (according to a survey of libraries in the UK and Ireland); see Gibson and Smith (1996) 24–25.

62. For a discussion and edition of the first question, see Chappuis (1993); on the second question (briefly), see Chappuis (1997).

63. No published edition exists; there are generous extracts, with translation, from the unpublished edition of E. T. Silk in Minnis (1996) 36–81.

64. Minnis and Nauta (1996) 5.

65. See Nauta (1997).

66. Cf. Minnis and Nauta (1996).

67. See Abelard (2001), Introduction, lxviii–lxxiv.

68. Peter Dronke pertinently (and kindly) pointed out to me that Albert the Great begins his commentary on Book X of Aristotle's *Ethics* by quoting the beginning of III, m. 1, and says that in these lines of poetry the whole matter of Book X is touched on and treated (Albert the Great, 1987, 708). Albert clearly knows Boethius's *Consolation* well, as later references in this discussion indicate. But more investigation would be needed to determine whether Boethius's prosimetrum was of more than peripheral importance to the interpretation Albert provides of Aristotle.

69. Ockham's most important text is his *Tractatus de praedestinatione et de praescientia dei respectu futurorum contingentium* in Ockham (1978) 507–503 [Transl. Ockham ([1983]). For a survey of the various formulations of Ockham's solution discussed recently, see Zagzebski (1991) 66–97.

70. III, sections 96–116; Abelard (1987) 539–47.

71. See chapter 8, and Index: 'propositionality'.

72. See chapter 8.

73. See chapter 8.

74. See *Commentary on Sentences*, I, d. 38, q. 1, a. 5, ad 4; *On Truth* q. 2, a. 12, ad 7; *Summa Theologiae* I, 14, a. 13 ad 2. This paragraph draws on ideas I developed at much greater length at a conference in St. Andrews in 1999; I intend at some stage to develop them in a detailed article.

75. See Patch (1927) and (for the early Middle Ages) Frakes (1988).

76. For an account of how Boethius, and other ancient Menippean Satires, influenced medieval prosimetra, see Dronke (1994). Modern editions and translations of these prosimetra are: Hildebert of Lavardin (2000), Adelard of Bath (1903); Bernardus Silvestris (1978), trans. Bernardus Silvestris (1974); Alan of Lille (1978), trans. Alan of Lille (1980).

77. Edited Sedgefield (1899); cf. Otten (1964), Wittig (1983).

78. Edited Tax (1986–).

79. The Old Provençal *Boeci* (Schwarze, 1963) is more of a (hagiographical) account of Boethius's death than a translation of the *Consolation*.

80. For details of the French translations, see Thomas and Roques (1938); Dwyer (1976) 8–17; Cropp (1987), (1997).

81. See Ricklin (1997).

82. See Keightley (1987).
83. See Goris and Wissink (1997).
84. See Gibson and Smith (1996) 19–20.
85. Edited Science (1927); cf. Johnson (1987).
86. Edited Megas (1996) and Siena (1967) respectively.
87. See Dwyer (1976).
88. See the articles on this subject in Minnis (1987) and (1993).
89. Ricklin (1997) 271–72.
90. See Hoenen (1997).
91. The lineation can vary from edition to edition: I give that of Guillaume de Lorris (1974).
92. For Chaucer's texts, I use Chaucer (1987). Among the important discussions of Chaucer's use of Boethius are Jefferson (1917), Patch (1927), Robertson (1962) [an extreme view, according to which the *Consolation* provides the orthodox Christian point of reference to which Chaucer wishes to remain firmly attached], Minnis (1982), Payne (1981).

BIBLIOGRAPHY

Abbo of Fleury (1966) *Abbonis Floriacensis opera inedita*. 1 *Syllogismarum categoricarum et hypotheticarum enodatio*, ed. A. Van de Vyver (Bruges; De Tempel).

Abbo of Fleury (1997) *De syllogismis hypotheticis*, ed. F. Schupp (Leiden/New York/Cologne; Brill) (Studien und Texte zur Geistegeschichte des Mittelalters 56).

Abelard (1919–31) *Peter Abaelards philosophische Schriften* (Münster; Aschendorff) (Beiträge zur Geschichte der Philosophie und Theologie des Mittelalters 21).

Abelard (1987) *Petri Abaelardi opera theologica* III, ed. E. M. Buytaert and C. J. Mews (Turnhout; Brepols) (Corpus Christianorum, Continuatio Mediaeualis 13).

Adelard of Bath (1903) *De eodem et diverso*, ed. H. Willner (Münster; Aschendorff) (Beiträge zur Geschichte der Philosophie und Theologie des Mittelalters 4, 1).

Alan of Lille (1978) *De planctu Naturae*, ed. N. M. Häring, *Studi medievali*, ser. 3, 19, 797–879.

Alan of Lille (1980) *The Plaint of Nature*, trans. J. J. Sheridan (Toronto; Pontifical Institute of Mediaeval Studies) (Mediaeval Sources in Translation 26).

Albert the Great (1987) *Super Ethica, Commentum et quaestiones*, VI–X, ed. W. Kübel (Münster; Aschendorff) (Alberti Magni opera omnia 14,2).

Alcuin (1851) *Opera omnia* II (Paris; Migne) (*Patrologia Latina* 101).

Alexander of Aphrodisias (1883) *In Aristotelis analyticorum priorum libros II commentarium*, ed. M. Wallies (Berlin; Reimer) (Commentaria in Aristotelem Graeca 2,1).

Alexander of Aphrodisias (1892) *Scriptora minora*, ed. I. Bruns (Berlin; Reimer) (Supplementum Aristotelicum 2.2).

Alexander of Aphrodisias (1991) *On Aristotle Prior Analytics 1.1–7*, trans. J. Barnes, S. Bobzien, K. Flannery, and K. Ierodiakonou (London; Duckworth).

Alexander of Aphrodisias (1992) *Quaestiones 1.1–2.15*, trans. R. W. Sharples (London; Duckworth).

Ammonius (1891) *In Porphyrii Isagogen sive V voces*, ed. A. Busse (Berlin; Reimer) (Commentaria in Aristotelem Graeca 4.3).

Ammonius (1895) *In Aristotelis Categorias commentarius*, ed. A. Busse (Berlin; Reimer) (Commentaria in Aristotelem Graeca 4.4).

Ammonius (1897) *In Aristotelis de Interpretatione commentarius*, ed. A. Busse (Berlin; Reimer) (Commentaria in Aristotelem Graeca 4.5).

Ammonius (1991) *Ammonius 'On Aristotle Categories'*, trans. S. M. Cohen and G. B. Matthews (London; Duckworth).

Ammonius (1996) *On Aristotle 'On Interpretation' 1–8*, trans. D. Blank (London; Duckworth).

Ammonius and Boethius (1998) *On Aristotle 'On Interpretation' 9*, trans. D. Blank and N. Kretzmann (London; Duckworth).

Amory, P. (1997) *People and Identity in Ostrogothic Italy, 489–554* (Cambridge; Cambridge University Press).

Anonymous (1978) *Scientia et virtus. Un commentaire anonyme de la consolation de Boèce*, ed. S. Durzsa (Budapest; Hungarian Academy of Sciences) (Publicationes Bibliothecae Academiae Scientiarum Hungaricarum 5(80).

Anonymous (1995) *Excerpta Isagogarum et Categoriarum*, ed. G. D'Onofrio (Turnhout; Brepols) (Corpus Christianorum, Continuatio Mediaeualis 120).

Aristotle (1989) *Aristotle: Prior Analytics*, trans. R. Smith (Inadianapolis/Cambridge, Mass.; Hackett).

Aristoteles Latinus (1961–) [Latin translations of Aristotle's works], ed. L. Minio-Paluello and others, (Bruges/Paris; Desclée de Brouwer, later Leiden; Brill).

Asztalos, M. (1993) 'Boethius as a Transmitter of Greek Logic to the Latin West: The *Categories*', *Harvard Studies in Classical Philology* 95, 367–407.

Bark, W. (1946) 'Boethius's Fourth Tractate, the so-called *De fide catholica*', *Harvard Theological Review* 39, 55–69 (reprinted in Fuhrmann and Gruber, 1984, 232–246).

Barnes, J. (1981) 'Boethius and the Study of Logic' in Gibson (1981), 73–89.

Beaumont, J. (1981) 'The Latin Tradition of the *De Consolatione Philosophiae*' in Gibson (1981) 278–305.

Beierwaltes, W. (1967) *Plotin: Über Ewigkeit und Zeit. Enneade III 7* (Frankfurt; Klostermann) (Quellen der Philosophie, Texte und Probleme 3).

Bernardus Silvestris (1973) *Cosmographia*, trans. W. Wetherbee (New York; Columbia University Press).

Bernardus Silvestris (1978) *Cosmographia*, ed. P. Dronke (Leiden; Brill).

Bieler (1957) *Boethius. 'De Consolatione Philosophiae'* (Turnhout; Brepols) (Corpus Christianorum, Series Latina) (revised ed. 1984).

Blumenthal, H. J. (1990) 'Neoplatonic Elements in the *De anima* Commentaries' in Sorabji (1990), 305–324.

Bolton, D. K. (1977) 'The Study of the *Consolation of Philosophy* in Anglo-Saxon England', *Archives d'histoire doctrinale et littéraire* 44, 33–78.

Bower, C. (1978) 'Boethius and Nicomachus: An Essay Concerning the Sources of *De Institutione Musicae*', *Vivarium* 16, 1–45.

Bower, C. M., and Palisca, C. V. (trans. and ed.) (1989) *Boethius: Foundations of Music* (New Haven/London; York University Press).

Brandt (1906) *Anicii Manlii Severini Boethii in Isagogen Porphyrii Commenta* (Vienna/Leipzig; Tempsky/Freitag) (Corpus Scriptorum Ecclesiasticorum Latinorum 38).

Brosch, H. J. (1931) *Der Seinsbegriff bei Boethius, mit besonderer Berücksichtung der Beziehung von Sosein und Dasein* (Innsbruck; Rauch Verlag) (Philosophie und Grenzwissenschaften IV.1).

Brower, J., and Guilfoyle, C. (forthcoming) *The Cambridge Companion to Abelard* (Cambridge/New York; Cambridge University Press).

Brown, V. (1976) 'Lupus of Ferrières on the metres of Boethius' in Nauman and O'Meara (1976), 63–79.

Brunhölzl, F. (1965) 'Der Bildungsauftrag der Hofschule' in *Karl der Grosse: Lebenswerk und Nachleben*, II (Düsseldorf: Schwann), 28–41.

Caldwell, J. (1981) 'The *De Institutione Arithmetica* and the *De Institutione Musica*' in Gibson (1981) 135–154.

Cappuyns, M. (1931) 'Le plus ancien commentaire des "Opuscula sacra" et son origine', *Recherches de théologie ancienne et médiévale* 3 (1931) 237–272.

Carton, R. (1930) 'Le christianisme et l'augustinisme de Boèce', *Revue de philologie* 1, 573–659.

Cassiodorus (1937) *Cassiodori Senatoris Institutiones*, ed. R. A. B. Mynors (Oxford; Oxford University Press).

Cassiodorus (1973) *Magni Aurelii Cassiodori Variarum Libri XII*, ed. A. J. Fridh (with his *De anima*) (Turnhout; Brepols) (Corpus Christianorum, Series Latina 96).

Chadwick, H. (1980) 'The Authenticity of Boethius's Fourth Tractate *De fide catholica*', *Journal of Theological Studies* n.s. 31, 551–556.

Chadwick, H. (1981) *Boethius. The Consolations of Music, Logic, Theology, and Philosophy* (Oxford; Oxford University Press).

Chappuis, M. (1993) *Le traité de Pierre d'Ailly sur la 'Consolation' de Boèce, Qu. 1* (Amsterdam/Philadelphia; Gruner) (Bochumer Studien zur Philosophie 20).

Chappuis, M. (1997) 'Le traité de Pierre d'Ailly sur la *Consolation* de Boèce, Question 2. Étude préliminaire' in Hoenen and Nauta (1997), 69–86.

Chaucer, G. (1987) *The Riverside Chaucer*, ed. L. D. Benson (Boston; Houghton Mifflin).

Cicero (1833) *Opera omnia* V.1, ed. J. C. Orelli (Turin; Orelli, Fuesslini & Co.).

Corcoran, J. (1974) 'Aristotle's Natural Deduction System' in J. Corcoran (ed.), *Ancient Logic and Its Modern Interpretations* (Dordrecht/Boston; Reidel) (Synthese Historical Library 9), 85–131.

Courcelle, P. (1967) *La Consolation de Philosophie dans la tradition littéraire* (Paris; Études Augustiniennes).

Courcelle, P. (1969) *Late Latin Writers and Their Greek Sources* (Cambridge, Mass.; Harvard University Press).

Crabbe, A. (1981) 'Literary Design in the *De Consolatione Philosophiae*' in Gibson (1981), 237–274.

Crespo, R. (1973) 'Il prologo alla traduzione della 'Consolatio Philosophiae' di Jean de Meun e il commento di Guglielmo d'Aragona' in *Romanitas et Christianitas. Studia Iano Henrico Waszink* . . . , ed. W. den Boer et al. (Amsterdam and London; North Holland), 55–70.

Cropp, G. M. (1987) 'Le Livre de Boece de Consolacion: From Translation to Glossed Text' in Minnis (1987), 63–88.

Cropp, G. M. (1997) 'The Medieval French Tradition' in Hoenen and Nauta (1997), 243–265.

Daley, B. E. (1984) 'Boethius's Theological Tracts and early Byzantine Scholasticism', *Mediaeval Studies* 46, 158–191.

Damascius (1999) *The Philosophical History. Text with Translation and Notes*, ed. P. Athanassiadi (Athens; Apameia).

David (1904) *Davidis prolegomena et in Porphyrii Isagoge commentarium*, ed. A. Busse (Berlin; Reimer) (Commentaria in Aristotelem Graeca 18.2).

De Libera, A. (1996) *La querelle des universaux de Platon à la fin du Moyen Age* (Paris; Seuil).

De Libera, A. (1999) *L'Art des généralités. Théories de l'abstraction* (Paris; Aubier).

De Rijk, L. M. (1964) 'On the Chronology of Boethius's Works on Logic', *Vivarium* 2, 1–49, 122–162.

De Rijk, L. M. (1981) 'Boèce logicien et philosophe: ses positions sémantiques et sa métaphysique de l'être' in Obertello (1981), 141–156.

De Rijk, L. M. (1988) 'On Boethius's Notion of Being. A Chapter of Boethian Semantics' in N. Kretzmann (ed.), *Meaning and Inference in Medieval Philosophy* (Dordrecht/Boston/London; Kluwer) (Synthese Historical Library 32).

Dexippus (1888) *In Aristotelis Categorias dubitationes et solutiones*, ed. A. Busse (Berlin; Reimer) (Commentaria in Aristotelem Graeca 4.2).

Dexippus (1989) *On Aristotle 'Categories'*, trans. J. Dillon (London/ Ithaca, N.Y.; Duckworth).

Dod, B. (1982) 'Aristoteles Latinus' in *The Cambridge History of Later Medieval Philosophy. From the Rediscovery of Aristotle to the Disintegration of Scholasticism*, ed. N. Kretzmann, A. Kenny, and J. Pinborg (Cambridge; Cambridge University Press), 45–79.

D'Onofrio, G. (1980) 'Giovanni Scoto e Boezio: tracce degli "Opuscula sacra" e della "Consolatio" nell'opera eriugeniana', *Studi medievali* 21,2, 707–752.

Dronke, P. (1969) Review of Courcelle (1967) in *Speculum* 44 (1969) 123–28 (reprinted in Fuhrmann and Gruber, 1984, 436–443).

Dronke, P. (1994) *Verse with Prose from Petronius to Dante. The Art and Scope of the Mixed Form* (Cambridge, Mass./London; Harvard University Press).

Dronke, P. (2002) 'William of Conches and the "New Aristotle,"' *Studi medievali*, 3a serie, 43, 157–163.

Düring, I. (1961) *Aristotle's Protrepticus. An Attempt at Reconstruction* (Studia Graeca et Latina Gothoburgensia 12) (Stockholm/Göteborg/Uppsala; Almqvist & Wiksell).

Dürr, K. (1951) *The Propositional Logic of Boethius* (Amsterdam; North Holland).

Dwyer, R. A. (1976) *Boethian Fictions. Narratives in Medieval French Versions of the Consolatio Philosophiae* (Cambridge, Mass.; Mediaeval Academy of America) (The Mediaeval Academy of America, Publication 83).

Ebbesen, S. (1981) *Commentators and Commentaries on Aristotle's Sophistici Elenchi* I (Leiden; Brill) (Corpus Latinum Commentariorum in Aristotelem Graecorum 7,1); pp. 133–70 are reprinted in Sorabji (1990), 141–171.

Ebbesen, S. (1990) 'Boethius as an Aristotelian Commentator' in Sorabji (1990), 373–391.

Elias (1900) *In Porphyrii Isagogen et Aristotelis Categorias commentaria*, ed. A. Busse (Berlin; Reimer) (Commentaria in Aristotelem Graeca 18.1).

Elsässer, M. (1988) *A.M.S. Boethius. Die Theologischen Traktate (Lateinisch-deutsch)* (Hamburg; Meiner) (Philosophische Bibliothek 397).

Folkerts, M. (1970) *Boethius's Geometrie II. Ein mathematisches Lehrbuch des Mittelalters* (Wiesbaden; Franz Steiner) (Boethius. Texte und Abhandlungen zur Geschichte der exacten Wissenschaften 9).

Fortescue, A. (1925) *Anici Manli Severini Boethi de Consolatione Philosphiae libri quinque* (London; Burns, Oates and Washbourne).

Frakes, J. C. (1988) *The Fate of Fortune in the Early Middle Ages. The Boethian Tradition* (Leiden, New York, Copenhagen and Cologne; Brill) (Studien und Texte zur Geistesgeschichte des Mittelalters 23).

Friedlein, G. (1867) *Anicii Manlii Torquati Severini Boetii De institutione arithmetica libri duo; De institutione musica libri quinque* (Leipzig; Teubner).
Fuhrmann, M., and Gruber, J. (1984) *Boethius* (Darmstadt; Wissenschafliche Buchgesellschaft) (Wege der Forschung 683).
Gale, R. M. (1991) *On the Existence and Nature of God* (Oxford; Oxford University Press).
Gersh, S. (1986) *Middle Platonism and Neoplatonism: The Latin Tradition* (Notre Dame, Indiana; University of Notre Dame Press).
Gibson, M. (1981a) *Boethius. His Life, Thought and Influence* (Oxford; Blackwell).
Gibson, M. (1981b) 'The *Opuscula Sacra* in the Middle Ages' in Gibson (1981a) 214–34.
Gibson, M., and Smith, L. (1996) *Codices Boethiani. A Conspectus of the Manuscripts of the Works of Boethius* I. Great Britain and the Republic of Ireland (London; Warburg Institute) (Warburg Institute. Surveys and Texts 25).
Gilbert of Poitiers (1966), *Commentaries on Boethius*, ed. N. Häring (Toronto; Pontifical Institute of Mediaeval Studies) (PIMS Studies and Texts 13).
Goris and Wissink (1997) 'The Medieval Dutch Tradition of Boethius's *Consolatio Philosophiae*' in Hoenen and Nauta (1997), 121–165.
Green-Pedersen, N. J. (1984) *The Tradition of the Topics in the Middle Ages: The Commentaries on Aristotle's and Boethius's Topics* (Munich; Philosophia Verlag).
Gruber, J. (1969) 'Die Erscheinung der Philosophie in der Consolatio Philosophiae des Boethius', *Rheinisches Museum* 112, 166–186.
Gruber, J. (1978) *Kommentar zu Boethius De Consolatione Philosophiae* (Berlin/New York; De Gruyter) (Texte und Kommentare—eine altertumswissenschaftliche Reihe 9).
Guillaume de Lorris (1974) *Guillaume de Lorris et Jean de Meun. Le Roman de la Rose*, ed. D. Poirion (Paris; Garnier-Flammarion).
Guillaumin, J. Y. (1995) *Boethius: De institutione arithmetica* (Paris; Belles Lettres).
Hadot, P. (1959) 'Un fragment du commentaire perdu de Boèce sur les Catégories d'Aristote dans le *Codex Bernensis 363*', *Archives d'histoire doctrinale et littéraire du Moyen Age* 26, 11–27.
Hadot, P. (1963) 'La distinction de l'être et de l'étant dans le 'De Hebdomadibus' de Boèce', *Miscellanea Mediaevalia*, ed. P. Wilpert (Berlin; De Gruyter) II, 147–153.
Hadot, P. (1970) 'Forma essendi: interprétation philologique et interprétation philosophique d'une formule de Boèce', *Les Études Classiques* 38, 143–56.
Hadot, P. (1971) *Marius Victorinus. Recherches sur sa vie et ses oeuvres* (Paris; Études Augustinienes).
Hadot, P. (1973) 'De Tertullien à Boèce. Le développement de la notion de la

personne dans les controverses théologiques' in I. Meyerson (ed.) *Problèmes de la personne* (Paris/The Hague; Mouton) (École Pratique des Hautes Études, VIè section, Congrès et Colloques 13).

Hadot, P. (1997) *Plotin ou la simplicité du regard* (Paris; Gallimard).

Häring, N. M.(1965) *Life and Works of Clarembald of Arras, a Twelfth-Century Master of the School of Chartres* (Toronto; Pontifical Institute of Mediaeval Studies) (PIMS Studies and Texts 10).

Häring, N. M. (1969) 'Four Commentaries on the *De Consolatione Philosophiae* in MS Heiligenkreuz 130', *Mediaeval Studies* 31, 287–316.

Heather, P. (1996) *The Goths* (Oxford; Blackwell).

Henry, D. (1967) *The Logic of St Anselm* (Oxford; Oxford University Press).

Hildebert of Lavardin (2000) *Hildeberts Prosimetrum De Querimonia und die Gedichte eines Anonymus*, ed. P. Orth (Vienna; Verlag der Österreichischen Akademie der Wissenschaften).

Hoenen, M. F. M. (1997) 'The Transmission of Academic Knowledge. Scholasticim in the Ghent Boethius (1485) and other commentaries on the *Consolatio*' in Hoenen and Nauta (1997), 167–214.

Hoenen, M. F. M., and Nauta, L. (eds.) (1997) *Boethius in the Middle Ages. Latin and Vernacular Tradition of the 'Consolatio Philosophiae'* (Leiden/New York/Cologne; Brill) (Studien und Texte zur Geistesgeschichte des Mittelalters 58).

Hoffmann, P. (1992–93) 'Résumé' in *Annuaire. Résumé des conférences et travaux, École pratique des hautes etudes, Vè section*, 101, 241–245.

Huber, P. (1976) *Die Vereinbarkeit von göttlicher Vorsehung und menschlicher Freiheit in der Consolatio Philosophiae des Boethius* (Zurich; Juris).

Hudry, F. (1997) 'L' "hebdomade" et les règles. Survivances du débat scolaire alexandrin', *Documenti e studi sulla tradizione filosofica medievale* 8, 319–337.

Huygens, R. B. C. (1954) 'Mittelalterliche Kommentare zum *O qui perpetua* . . .', *Sacris Erudiri* 6, 373–427.

Ibn al-Tayyib (1979) *Ibn al-Tayyib's Commentary on Porphyry's Eisagoge*, trans. K. Gyekye (Albany; State University of New York Press).

Isaac, J. (1953) *Le 'Peri Hermeneias' en occident de Boèce à Saint Thomas. Histoire littéraire d'un traité d'Aristote* (Paris; Vrin) (Bibliothèque Thomiste 29).

Iwakuma, Y. (forthcoming) 'Prologues of Commentaries on the *Logica Vetus* Literature in the Twelfth Century', *Didascalia* 3.

Jacobi, K. (1995) 'Natürliches Sprechen—Theoriesprache—Theologische Rede. Die Wissenschaftslehre des Gilbert von Poitiers', *Zeitschrift für philosophische Forschung* 49, 511–528.

Jacobi, K. (1998) 'Gilbert of Poitiers' in *Routledge Encyclopaedia of Philosophy*, ed. E. Craig, (London/New York; Routledge), IV, 68–72.

Jeauneau, E. (1959) 'Un commentaire inédit sur le chant 'O qui perpetua' de Boèce', *Rivista critica di storia della filosofia* 14, 65–81 [reprinted in

E. Jeauneau, *'Lectio Philosophorum'. Recherches sur l'École de Chartres* (Amsterdam; Hakkert, 1973) 309–31].

Jefferson, B. L. (1917) *Chaucer and the 'Consolation of Philosophy'* (Princeton; Princeton University Press).

Jeudy, C. (1991) 'Remigii autissiodorensis opera (*Clavis*)' in *L'École carolingienne d'Auxerre de Muretach à Remi, 830–908*, ed. D. Iogna-Prat, C. Jeudy, and G. Lobrichon (Paris; Beauchesne), 457–500.

Johnson, I. R. (1987) 'Walton's Sapient Orpheus' in Minnis (1987), 139–168.

Jolivet, J. (1997) *La Théologie d'Abélard* (Paris; Éditions du Cerf).

Jolivet, J., and De Libera, A. (1987) *Gilbert de Poitiers et ses contemporains* (Naples; Bibliopolis) (History of Logic 5).

Kaylor, N. H., Jr. (1992) *The Medieval Consolation of Philosophy. An Annotated Bibliography* (London and New York; Garland, 1992) (Garland Medieval Bibliographies 7).

Keightley, R. G. 'Boethius in Spain: a Classified Checklist of Early Translations' in Minnis (1987), 169–187.

Kenny, A. (1976) 'Divine Foreknowledge and Human Freedom' in A. Kenny (ed.), *Aquinas: A Collection of Critical Essays* (Notre Dame, Ind.; University of Notre Dame Press) [first published 1979], 255–270.

Kenny, A. (ed.) (1994) *Oxford Illustrated History of Western Philosophy* (Oxford; Oxford University Press).

Kirwan, C. (1989) *Augustine* (London/New York; Routledge).

Klingner, F. (1921) *De Boethii Consolatione Philosophiae* (Philologische Unterschungen 27) (reprint 1966: Zurich/Dublin; Weidmann).

Knuuttila, S. (1993) *Modalities in MedievalPhilosophy* (London/New York; Routledge).

Kretzmann, N. (1967) 'Semantics, History of' in *The Encyclopaedia of Philosophy* VII, ed. P. Edwards (New York/London; Macmillan and the Free Press/Collier-Macmillan), 359–406.

Kretzmann, N. (1985) '*Nos Ipsi Principia Sumus*: Boethius and the Basis of Contingency' in *Divine Omnipotence in Medieval Philosophy: Islamic, Jewish and Christian Perspectives* (Dordrecht; Reidel), 23–50.

Kretzmann, N. (1998) 'Boethius and the Truth about Tomorrow's Sea Battle' in Ammonius (1998), 24–52.

Kvanvig, J. (1986) *The Possibility of an All-Knowing God* (Basingstoke; Macmillan).

Leftow, B. (1991) *Time and Eternity* (Ithaca/London; Cornell University Press).

Lerer, S. (1985) *Boethius and Dialogue. Literary Method in* The Consolation of Philosophy (Princeton; Princeton University Press).

Lewry, O. (1981) 'Boethian Logic in the Medieval West' in Gibson (1981), 90–134.

Lloyd, A. C. (1990) *The Anatomy of Neoplatonism* (Oxford; Oxford University Press).

Lohr, C. H. (1982) 'Aristoteles Latinus' in *The Cambridge History of Later Medieval Philosophy*, ed. N. Kretzmann, A. Kenny, and J. Pinborg (Cambridge; Cambridge University Press, 1982), 45–79.

MacDonald, S. (1988) 'Boethius's Claim that all Substances are Good', *Archiv für Geschichte der Philosophie* 70, 245–279.

McInerny, R. (1990) *Boethius and Aquinas* (Washington, D.C.; Catholic University of America Press).

Magee, J. (1989) *Boethius on Signification and Mind* (London/New York/Copenhagen/Cologne; Brill) (Philosophia Antiqua 52).

Magee, J. (1994) 'The Text of Boethius's *De divisione*', *Vivarium* 32 (1994), 1–50.

Magee, J. (Forthcoming) 'Anicius Manlius Severinus Boethius' in *The Blackwell Companion to Medieval Philosophy*, ed. J. Gracia and T. Noone (Oxford/Malden, Mass.; Blackwell).

Magee, J. (ed.) (1998) *Anicii Manlii Severini Boethii 'De divisione liber'* (Leiden/Boston/Cologne; Brill) (Philosophia Antiqua 77).

Maioli, B. (1978) *Teoria dell'essere e dell'esistente e classificazione delle scienze in M.S. Boezio. Una delucidazione* (Rome; Bulzoni) (Università degli studi di Siena, Facoltà di Magistero: sede di Arezzo—Quaderni dell'Istituto di scienze filosofiche 4).

Marenbon, J. (1981) *From the Circle of Alcuin to the School of Auxerre* (Cambridge; Cambridge University Press).

Marenbon, J. (1983) 'Gilbert of Poitiers' in *A History of Twelfth-Century Western Philosophy*, ed. P. Dronke (Cambridge; Cambridge University Press) 328–52 = Marenbon (2000a) Item XIV.

Marenbon, J. (1984) 'Carolingian Thought' in *Carolingian Culture: Emulation and Innovation*, ed. R. McKitterick (Cambridge; Cambridge University Press), 171–192 = Marenbon (2000a) Item III.

Marenbon, J. (1997) 'Glosses and Commentaries on the *Categories* and *De interpretatione* before Abelard' in *Dialektik und Rhetorik im früheren und hohen Mittelalter*, ed. J. Fried (Munich; Historisches Kolleg) (Schriften des historischen Kollegs, Kolloquien 27), 21–49 = Marenbon (2000a), Item IX.

Marenbon, J. (1998) 'The Twelfth Century' in *The Routledge History of Philosophy*, III (The Middle Ages) (London; Routledge), 150–187.

Marenbon, J. (2000a) *Aristotelian Logic, Platonism and the Context of Early Medieval Philosophy in the West* (Aldershot/Burlington/Singapore/Sydney; Ashgate (Variorum Collected Studies Series 696).

Marenbon, J. (2000b) 'Medieval Latin Commentaries and Glosses on Aristotelian Logical texts, Before ca. 1150 A.D.' (= *Glosses and Commentaries on Aristotelian Logical Texts: The Syriac, Arabic and Medieval Latin Traditions*, ed. C. Burnett (London; Warburg Institute, 1993) (Warburg Institute Surveys and Texts 23, 77–127) and 'Supplement to the Working Catalogue and Supplementary Bibliography' in Marenbon (2000a), item II.

Marenbon, J. (Forthcoming-1) 'Le temps, la prescience et le déterminisme dans la *Consolation de Philosophie*' in 'Boèce et la chaîne des savoirs', ed. A. Galonnier.

Marenbon , J. (Forthcoming-2) 'Interpreting Boethius: Rationality and Happiness in *De consolatione Philosophiae*' in *Rationality and Happiness: From the Ancients to the Early Medievals*, ed. J. Gracia and J. Yu (Rochester; University of Rochester Press).

Marenbon, J. (Forthcoming-3) 'Life, Milieu and Intellectual Contexts' in Brower and Guilfoyle (forthcoming).

Marenbon, J. (Forthcoming-4) 'Boethius's Intellectual Aims and His Work as a Commentator on Aristotelian Logic' in *Philosophy, Science and Exegesis in Greek, Arabic and Latin Commentaries*, ed. P. Adamson, H. Baltussen, and M. Stone (London; Institute of Classical Studies).

Marenbon, J. (Forthcoming-5) 'Eternity' in *The Cambridge Companion to Medieval Philosophy*, ed. S. McGrade (Cambridge; Cambridge University Press).

Martin, C. J. (1987) 'Embarrassing Arguments and Surprising Conclusions in the Development of Theories of the Conditional in the Twelfth Century' in Jolivet and De Libera (1987), 377–400.

Martin, C. J. (1991) 'The Logic of Negation in Boethius', *Phronesis* 36 (1991), 277–304.

Martin, C. J. (1999) 'Non-Reductive Arguments from Impossible Hypotheses in Boethius and Philoponus', *Oxford Studies in Ancient Philosophy* 17, 279–302.

Martin, C. J. (Forthcoming) 'Logic' in Brower and Guilfoyle (forthcoming).

Masi, M. (1983) *Boethian Number Theory: A Translation of the 'De institutione arithmetica'* (Amsterdam; Rodopi).

Matthews, J. (1981) 'Anicius Manlius Severinus Boethius' in Gibson (1981), 15–43.

Megas, A. (1996) *Voēthiou Paramythias tēs philosophias metaphrasē Maximos Planoudes* (Thessalonika; University Studi Press).

Meiser, C. (1877) *Anicii Manlii Severini Boetii commentarii in librum Aristotelis Peri Hermeneias pars prior* (Leipzig; Teubner).

Meiser, C. (1880) *Anicii Manlii Severini Boetii commentarii in librum Aristotelis Peri Hermeneias pars posterior* (Leipzig; Teubner).

Merlan, P. (1968) *From Platonism to Neoplatonism* (The Hague; Martinus Nijhoff) (3d edition).

Merle, H. (ed. and trans.) (1991) *Boèce. Courts traités de théologie. Opuscula sacra* (Paris; éditions du Cerf).

Migne, J.-P. (1847) *Manlii Severini Boetii opera omnia* (Paris; Migne) (*Patrologia Latina* 64).

Mignucci, M. (1985) 'Logic and Omniscience: Alexander of Aphrodisias and Proclus', *Oxford Studies in Ancient Philosophy* 3, 219–246.

Minio-Paluello, L. (1962) 'Note sull'Aristotele latino medievale: XV. Dalle *Categoriae* decem pseudo-agostiniane (temistiane) al testo vulgato aristotelico boeziano', *Rivista di filosofia neoscolastica* 54 (1962), 137–47 = Minio-Paluello (1972), 448–458.

Minio-Paluello, L. (1972) *Opuscula: the Latin Aristotle* (Amsterdam; Hakkert).

Minnis, A. (1981) 'Aspects of the Medieval French and English Traditions of the *De consolatione* philosophiae' in Gibson (1981), 312–361.

Minnis, A. J. (1982) *Chaucer and Pagan Antiquity* (Woodbridge and Totowa, N.J.; Boydell and Brewer, and Rowan and Littlefield) (Chaucer Studies 8).

Minnis, A. J. (ed.) (1987) *The Medieval Boethius. Studies in the Vernacular Translations of 'De Consolatione Philosophiae'* (Cambridge; Brewer).

Minnis, A. J. (ed.) (1993) *Chaucer's Boece and the Mediaeval Tradition of Boethius* (Cambridge; Brewer) (Chaucer Studies 18).

Minnis, A. J., and Nauta, L. (1993) '*More Platonico loquitur*. What Nicholas Trevet Really Did to William of Conches' in Minnis (1993), 1–34.

Mohrmann, C. (1976) 'Some Remarks on the Language of Boethius, "Consolatio Philosophiae"' in Naumann and O'Meara (1976), 54–61 (reprinted in Fuhmann and Gruber, 1984, 302–310).

Moorhead, J. (1992) *Theoderic in Italy* (Oxford; Oxford University Press).

Moreschini, C. (2000) *Boethius: de consolatione Philosophiae; Opuscula theologica* (Munich/Leipzig; K.G. Saur).

Morton, C. (1982) 'Marinus of Avenches, the "Excerpta Valesiana", and the Death of Boethius', *Traditio* 38 (1982), 107–36.

Nash-Marshall, S. (2000) *Participation and the Good. A Study in Boethian Metaphysics* (New York; Crossroad).

Nauman, B., and O'Meara, J. J. (eds.) (1976) *Latin Script and Letters A.D. 400–900. Festschrift presented to L. Bieler*.

Nauta, L. (1993) 'The Thirteenth-Century Revision of William of Conches's Commentary on Boethius' in Minnis (1993), 189–191.

Nauta, L. (1997) 'The Scholastic Context of the Boethius Commentary by Nicholas Trevet' in Hoenen and Nauta (1997), 41–67.

Nielsen, L. O. (1982) *Theology and Philosophy in the Twelfth Century* (Leiden; Brill) (Acta theologica danica 15).

Nikitas, D. Z. (1990) *Boethius, De topicis differentiis kai hoi buzantines metafraseis tōn Manouēl Holobōlou kai Prochorou Kudōnē* (Athens/Paris/Brussels; Academy of Athens/Vrin/Ousia) (Corpus Philosophorum Medii Aevi. Philosophi Byzantini 5).

Notker Labeo (1986–) *Boethius 'De Consolatione Philosophiae'*, ed. P. W. Tax (Tübingen; Niemeyer) (Altdeutsche Textbibliothek 94, 100, 101).

Obertello, L. (1969) *A. M. Severino Boezio: 'De hypotheticis syllogismis'* (Brescia; Paideia) (Istituto di Filosofia dell'Università di Parma, Logicalia 1).

Obertello, L. (1974) *Severino Boezio* (Genoa; Academia Ligure di Scienze e Lettere).

Obertello, L. (1979) *Severino Boezio. La Consolazione della Filosofia. Gli opuscoli teologi* (Milan; Rusconi).

Obertello, L. (1981) *Congresso Internazionale di Studi Boeziani. Atti* (Rome; Herder).

Ockham, W. (1978) *Opera philosophica* II, ed. E. A. Moody, G. Gál, A. Gambatese, S. Brown, and P. Boehner (St. Bonaventure, N.Y; Franciscan Institute, St. Bonaventure University).

Ockham, W. (1983) *Predestination, God's Foreknowledge and Future Contingents*, ed. and trans. M. M. Adams and N. Kretzmann (Indianapolis, Ind.; Hackett) (2d ed.).

O'Daly, G. (1991) *The Poetry of Boethius* (London; Duckworth).

O'Meara, D. (1993) *Plotinus. An Introduction to the 'Enneads'* (Oxford; Oxford University Press).

Otten, K. (1964) *König Alfeds Boethius* (Tübingen; Niemeyer) (Studien zur englischen Philologie, n.f. 3).

Patch, H. R. (1927) *The Goddess Fortuna in Mediaeval Literature* (Cambridge, Mass.; Harvard University Press).

Patch, H. R. (1929) 'Fate in Boethius and the Neoplatonists', *Speculum* 4, 66–72.

Patzig, G. (1968) *Aristotle's Theory of the Syllogism*, trans. J. Barnes (Dordrecht; Reidel).

Payne, F. A. (1981) *Chaucer and Menippean Satire* (Madison, Wisconsin/London; University of Wisconsin Press).

Peiper, L. R. S. (1871) *Boethius, Philosophiae Consolationis libri quinque* (Leipzig; Teubner).

Peter Abelard (1919–31) *Peter Abaelards Philosophische Schriften*, ed. B. Geyer (Münster; Aschendorff) (Beiträge zur Geschichte der Theologie und Philosophie des Mittelalters 21).

Peter Abelard (1987) *Opera Theologica* III, ed. E. M. Buytaert and C. Mews (Turnhout; Brepols). (Continuatio Mediaevalis 13).

Peter Abelard (2001) *Collationes*, ed. and trans. J. Marenbon and G. Orlandi (Oxford; Oxford University Press).

Pike, N. (1970) *God and Timelessness* (London; Routledge and Kegan Paul).

Pingree, D. (1981) 'Boethius's Geometry and Astronomy' in Gibson (1981), 155–161.

Pizzani, U. (1965) 'Studi sulla fonte del "De Institutione Musica" di Boezio', *Sacris Erudiri* 16, 5–164.

Plato (1979), *Gorgias*, trans. T. Irwin (Oxford; Oxford University Press).

Porphyry (1887) *Porphyrii Isagoge et in Aristotelis Categorias commentarium*, ed. A. Busse (Berlin; Reimer) (CAG 4.1).

Porphyry (1992) *On Aristotle's Categories*, trans. S. K. Strange (London; Duckworth).

Porphyry (1998) *Isagoge*, ed. A. de Libera (Paris; Vrin).

Prior, A. (1953) 'The Logic of Negative Terms in Boethius', *Franciscan Studies*, 13, 1–6.

Prior, A. (1967) *Past, Present and Future* (Oxford; Oxford University Press).

Proclus (1864) *Commentarius in Platonis Parmenidem* (Paris) (Procli opera inedita 3) (reprinted photomechanically: Hildesheim, Georg Olms, 1961).

Proclus (1903) *In Platonis Timaeum Commentarii* I (Leipzig; Teubner).

Proclus (1963) *The Elements of Theology*, ed. and trans. E. R, Dodds, 2d ed. (Oxford; Oxford University Press).

Proclus (1966–68) *Commentaire sur le Timée*, trans. A. J. Festugière (Paris; Vrin).

Proclus (1977, 9) *Trois études sur la providence*: tom. I *Dix problèmes concernant la providence*, tom. II *Providence, fatalité, liberté*, ed. D. Isaac (Paris; Les Belles Lettres).

Proclus (1987) *Commentary on the Parmenides*, trans. G. R. Morrow and J. M. Dillon (Princeton, N.J.; Princeton University Press).

Pseudo-Elias (1967) *Pseudo-Elias (Pseudo-David): 'Lectures on Porphyry's* Isagoge', ed. L. G. Westerink (Amsterdam; North Holland).

Rand, E. K. (1904) 'On the Composition of Boethius's Consolatio Philosophiae', *Harvard Studies in Classical Philology* 15, 1–28 [reprinted in Fuhrmann and Gruber (1984), 249–77].

Rand, E. K. (1906) *Johannes Scottus* (Munich) (Quellen und Untersuchungen zur lateinischen Philologie des Mittelalters I, 2) (unaltered reprint: Frankfurt; Minerva, 1966).

Reichenberger, K. (1954) *Untersuchungen zur literarischen Stellung der Consolatio Philosophiae* (Cologne; Romanisches Seminar der Universität Köln) (Kölner Romanistische Arbeiten, n.f. 3).

Relihan, J. C. (1990) 'Old Comedy, Menippean Satire, and Philosophy's Tattered Robes in Boethius's *Consolation*', *Illinois Classical Studies* 15, 183–194.

Relihan, J. C. (1993) *Ancient Menippean Satire* (Baltimore and London; John Hopkins University Press).

Relihan, J. C. (2001) *Boethius, 'Consolation of Philosophy'* (Hackett; Indianapolis, 2001).

Richer (1877) *Richeri historiarum libri IV*, ed. G. Waitz (Hanover; Hahn).

Ricklin, T. (1997) '. . . *Quello non conosciuto da molti libro di Boezio*. Hinweise zur *Consolatio Philosophiae* in Norditalien' in Hoenen and Nauta (1997), 267–286.

Robertson, D. W. (1962) *A Preface to Chaucer. Studies in Medieval Perspectives* (Princeton, N.J.; Princeton University Press).

Scheible, H. (1972) *Die Gedichte in der Consolatio Philosophiae* (Heidelberg; Winter, 1972).

Schlapkohl, C. (1999) *Persona est naturae rationabilis individua substantia. Boethius und die Debatte über der Personbegriff* (Marburg; Elwert) (Marburger Theologische Studien).

Schmidt-Kohl, V. (1965) *Die neuplatonische Seelenlehre in der Consolatio Philosophiae des Boethius* (Meisenheim am Glan; Hain).

Schrimpf, G. (1966) *Die Axiomenschrift des Boethius (De Hebdomadibus) als philosophisches Lehrbuch des Mittelalters* (Leiden; Brill) (Studien zur Problemgeschichte der antiken und mittelalterlichen Philosophie 2).

Schupp, F. (1988) *Logical Problems of the Medieval Theory of Consequences* (Naples; Bibliopolos) (History of Logic 6).

Schurr, V. (1935) *Die Trinitätslehre des Boethius im Lichte der 'Skythischen Kontroversen'* (Paderborn; Schöningh) (Forschungen zur christlichen Literatur und Dogmengeschichte 18,1).

Schwarze, C. (1963) *Das altprovenzalische 'Boeci'* (Münster; Aschendorff) (Forschungen z. romanischen Philologie 12).

Science, M. (1927) *Boethius: De Consolatione Philosophiae Translated by John Walton Canon of Oseney* (London; Oxford Universit Press) (Early English Texts Society OS170).

Sedgfield, W. J. (ed.) (1899) *King Alfred's Old English Version of Boethius* (Oxford; Oxford University Press).

Shanzer, D. (1983) ' "Me quoque excellentior": Boethius, *De Consolatione* 4.6.38', *Classical Quarterly* 33, 277–83.

Shanzer, D. (1984) 'The Death of Boethius and the "Consolation of Philosophy"', *Hermes* 112, 352–366.

Shanzer, D. (1986) *A Philological and Literary Commentary on Martianus Capella 'De Nuptiis Philologiae et Mercurii' Book I* (Berkeley/Los Angeles/London; University of California Press) (University of California Publications: Classical Studies 32).

Sharples, R. W. (ed. and trans.) (1991) *Cicero: On Fate and Boethius: The Consolation of Philosophy, IV, 5–V,6* (Warminster; Aris and Phillips).

Shiel, J. 'Boethius's Commentaries on Aristotle' in Sorabji (1990), 349–372.

Siena, S. J. (1967) *Boezio: De consolatione Philosopiae, traduzione ebraica di 'Azaria ben r. Joseph ibn Abba Mari, detto Bonafoux Bonfil Astruc, 5183–1423* (Turin/ Jerusalem; Istituto di studi ebraici/ Scuola rabbinica S. H. Margulies-Disegni).

Silk, E. T. (1935) *Saeculi noni auctoris in Boetii consolationem Philosophiae commentarius* (Rome; American Academy in Rome) (Papers and Monographs of the American Academy in Rome 9).

Silk, E. T. (1939) 'Boethius's *Consolatio Philosophiae* as a Sequel to Augustine's *Dialogues* and *Soliloquia*', *Harvard Theological Review* 32, 19–39.

Silvestre, H. (1952) 'Le commentaire inédit de Jean Scot Érigène au mètre IX du livre III du 'De consolatione philosophiae' de Boèce', *Revue d'histoire ecclésiastique* 47, 44–122.

Simplicius (1907) *In Aristotelis Categorias commentarium*, ed. K. Kalbfleisch (Berlin; Reimer) (CAG 8).

Simplicius (1990–) *Commentaire sur les Catégories. Traduction commentée*, under the direction of I. Hadot (Leiden; Brill).

Siorvanes, L. (1996) *Proclus: Neo-Platonic Philosophy and Science* (Edinburgh; Edinburgh University Press).

Smiley, T. (1973) 'What Is a Syllogism?', *Journal of Philosophical Logic* 2, 136–154.

Sorabji, R. (1980) *Necessity, Cause, and Blame. Perspectives on Aristotle's Theory* (London; Duckworth).

Sorabji, R. (1983) *Time, Creation and the Continuum* (London; Duckworth).

Sorabji, R. (ed.) (1990) *Aristotle Transformed. The Ancient Commentators and their Influence* (London; Duckworth).

Spade, P. V. (1994) *Five Texts on the Mediaeval Problem of Universals: Porphyry, Boethius, Abelard, Duns Scotus, Ockham* (Indianapolis, Ind./Cambridge, Mass.; Hackett).

Spade, P. V. (1996) 'Boethius against Universals: the Arguments in the Second Commentary on Porphyry', Internet publication on http//www.phil.indiana.edu/~spade/

Speca, A. N. (2001) *Hypothetical Syllogistic and Stoic Logic* (Leiden; Brill) (Philosophia Antiqua 87).

Stewart, H. F. (1916) 'A commentary by Remigius Autissiodorensis on the *De consolatione Philosophiae* of Boethius's, *Journal of Theological Studies* 17, 22–42.

Stewart, H. F., Rand, E. K., and Tester, S. J. (1973) *Boethius: The Theological Tractates; The Consolation of Philosophy* (Cambridge, Mass./ London; Harvard University Press).

Strange, S. K. (1987) 'Plotinus, Porphyry and the Neoplatonic Interpretation of the *Categories*', in *Aufstieg und Niedergang der römischen Welt*, II 36,2, ed. W. Haase and H. Temporini, 955–974.

Striker (1973) 'Zur Frage nach der Quellen von Boethius's *de hypotheticis syllogismis*', *Archiv für Geschichte der Philosophie* 55, 70–75.

Stump, E. (1974) 'Boethius's Works on the Topics', *Vivarium* 12, 77–93.

Stump. E. (1978) *Boethius's 'De topicis differentiis'* (Ithaca/London; Cornell University Press).

Stump, E. (1988) *Boethius's 'In Ciceronis Topica'* (Ithaca/London; Cornell University Press).

Stump, E., and Kretzmann, N. (1981) 'Eternity', *Journal of Philosophy* 78, 429–58 (reprinted in *The Concept of God*, ed. T. V. Morris (Oxford; Oxford University Press, 1987, 219–252).

Thierry of Chartres (1971) [attributed] *Commentaries on Boethius by Thierry of Chartres and His School* (Toronto; Pontifical Institute of Mediaeval Studies) (PIMS Studies and Texts 20).

Thomas Aquinas (1992) *Opera omnia* L (Rome/Paris; Commissio Leonina/ Vrin).

Thomas, A., and Roques, M. (1938) 'Traductions français de la *Consolatio philosophiae* de Boèce', *Histoire littéraire de la France* 37, 423–432.

Traiana, A.(1981) 'Per l'esegesi di una lirica Boeziana (*cons.* 1, *m.* 5)' in A. Traini, *Poeti latini (e neolatini). Noti e saggi filologici* II (Bologna; Pàtron).

Troncarelli, F. (1973) 'Per una ricerca sui commenti altomedievali al 'De Consolatione' di Boezio' in *Miscellanea in memoria di Georgio Cencetti* (Turin; Bottega d'Erasmo), 363–380.

Troncarelli, F. (1981) *Tradizioni perdute. La 'Consolazione Philosophiae' nell'alto medioevo* (Padua; Antenor) (Medioevo e umanesimo 42).

Troncarelli, F. (1987) *Boethiana aetas. Modelli grafci e fortuna manoscritta della 'Consolatio Philosophiae' tra IX e XII secolo* (Alessandria; edizioni dell'Orso) (Biblioteca di scrittura e civiltà 2).

Troncarelli, F. (1988) 'Aristoteles Piscatorius. Note sulle opere teologiche di Boezio e sulla loro fortuna', *Scriptorium* 42, 3–19.

Tweedale, M. M. (1976) *Abailard on Universals* (Amsterdam; North Holland).

Usener, H. (1877) *Anecdoton Holderi. Ein Beitrag zur Geschichte Roms in Ostgotischer Zeit* (Leipzig; Teubner).

Van de Vyver, A. (1929) 'Les étapes du développement philosophique du haut moyen âge', *Revue belge de philologie et d'histoire* 8, 425–52.

Walsh, P. G. (1999) *Boethius: 'The Consolation of Philosophy'* (Oxford; Oxford University Press).

Watts, V. (1999) *Boethius: 'The Consolation of Philosophy'* (Harmondsworth; Penguin; revised ed.).

Weidemann, H. (1998) 'Die Unterscheidung zwischen einfacher und bedingter Notwendigkeit in der *Philosophiae Consolatio* des Boethius', dans *Philosophiegeschichte und logische Analyse. Logical Analysis and History of Philosophy. Philosophiegeschichte im Überblick. History of Philosophy in General*, ed. A. Newen and U. Meixner (Paderborn/Munich/Vienne/Zurich; Schöningh), 195–207.

Westerink, L. G. (1990) 'The Alexandrian Commentators and the Introductions to their Commentaries' in Sorabji (1990), 325–348.

White, A. (1981) 'Boethius in the Medieval Quadrivium' in Gibson (1981), 162–205.

William of Conches (1999) *Glosae super Boetium*, ed. L. Nauta (Turnhout; Brepols) (Corpus Christianorum, Continuatio Mediaeualis 158: Guillelmi de Conchis opera omnia II).

Wittig, J. S. (1983) 'King Alfred and Its Latin Sources: A Reconsideration', *Anglo-Saxon England* 11, 157–198.

Zagzebski, L. T. (1991) *The Dilemma of Freedom and Foreknowledge* (New York/ Oxford; Oxford University Press).

INDEX LOCORUM

The references given are either to standard section divisions or numberings, or to the section or page (and line) numbers of the edition given in the Bibliography here. The references to Boethius's *Consolation* are to the section numbering used in Moreschini (2000) and Bieler (1957), and to his *Opuscula sacra* to the section and line numbering in Moreschini (2000). For *On Division* and *On Topical Differentiae* and the Commentary on Cicero's *Topics*, I give the column numbers and letters of *Patrologia Latina* 64; although this is not the edition used in my text, it is the most commonly available, and I give references to it there as well as to the critical editions.

GENERAL INDEX

An asterisk denotes an author for whom there are also entries in the *Index Locorum*.